Computer Science Workbench

Editor: Tosiyasu L. Kunii

H. Kitagawa T.L. Kunii

The Unnormalized Relational Data Model

For Office Form Processor Design

With 78 Figures

Springer-Verlag Tokyo Berlin Heidelberg New York
London Paris Hong Kong

HIROYUKI KITAGAWA
Assistant Professor
Institute of Information Sciences
and Electronics
University of Tsukuba
1-1-1 Tennodai, Tsukuba
Ibaraki, 305 Japan

TOSIYASU L. KUNII
Professor and Chairman
Department of Information Science
Faculty of Science
The University of Tokyo
7-3-1 Hongo, Bunkyo-ku
Tokyo, 113 Japan

Series Editor:
TOSIYASU L. KUNII
Professor and Chairman
Department of Information Science
Faculty of Science
The University of Tokyo
7-3-1 Hongo, Bunkyo-ku
Tokyo, 113 Japan

Library of Congress Cataloging-in-Publication Data

Kitagawa, H. (Hiroyuki), 1955– The unnormalized relational data model: for office form processor design/H. Kitagawa, T.L. Kunii. p. cm.— (Computer science workbench) Includes bibliographical references.
ISBN-13: 978-4-431-68101-4   e-ISBN-13: 978-4-431-68099-4
DOI: 10.1007/ 978-4-431-68099-4
(U.S.): 1. Data base design. 2. Relational data bases. I. Kunii, Tosiyasu. II. Title. III. Series. QA76.9.D26K58   1989 005.75'6—dc20

© Springer-Verlag Tokyo 1989
Softcover reprint of the hardcover 1st edition 1989

The use of registered names, trademarks, etc. in this publication does not imply, even in the absence of a specific statement, that such names are exempt from the relevant protective laws and regulations and therefore free for general use.

Typesetting: Macmillan India Ltd., Bangalore

Series Preface

Computer Science Workbench is a monograph series which will provide you with an in-depth working knowledge of current developments in computer technology. Every volume in this series will deal with a topic of importance in computer science and elaborate on how you yourself can build systems related to the main theme. You will be able to develop a variety of systems, including computer software tools, computer graphics, computer animation, database management systems, and computer-aided design and manufacturing systems. Computer Science Workbench represents an important new contribution in the field of practical computer technology.

TOSIYASU L. KUNII

Preface

The evolution of database systems research is itself a story. Long after the emergence of systems derived from practical applications, Codd's relational data model has gradually occupied the theoretical domain of database systems and is moving into the realms of practical use. Certainly, the theoretical foundation makes database design, validation, and testing easier. However, Codd's model allows only flat tables to be handled, while most business and engineering data in practice are in nested table forms. Thus, a recent major obstacle in database systems development is the large gap between the theory and the practice.

This book aims at filling the gap by giving a rigorous foundation for handling practical data in the nested table forms which are also called "unnormalized relations." In fact, we can even develop a form translator based on the method explained in this book. Otherwise-identical business and engineering data which differ in format from one enterprise to another can be easily compiled into one another by the form translator.

In this book, the nested table data model is presented to provide a theoretical basis for modeling practical data. Then, its applications are discussed through the design and implementation of a database work-bench featuring the interactive manipulation of form-based documents. The use of nested tables is developed further in the context of application system generation.

The book does not assume a reader's familiarity with database systems, and can be used by practitioners, researchers, and students, for self-study or as a textbook for a one semester course on the topic of database systems.

HIROYUKI KITAGAWA
TOSIYASU L. KUNII

Acknowledgments

This book grew out of many years of our research on the use of unnormalized relations to handle business and engineering forms in a practical manner. Formalization of and theoretical study on the nested table data model and its application were initiated at the Kunii Laboratory of the University of Tokyo. We would like to thank all members of the Kunii Laboratory, Department of Information Science, the University of Tokyo for their help to us.

We are grateful to Dr. Yukio Mizuno, Dr. Kiichi Fujino, and Mr. Sohei Misaki of NEC Corporation and to Professor Motoei Azuma of Waseda University for their encouragement to our work. Further research on nested tables and also the development of the FORMDOQ prototype were done when Kitagawa was with the NEC Software Product Engineering Laboratory. Thanks are also due to many members of the laboratory who were involved in the development of the FORMDOQ prototype.

We would like to thank Professor Shi Bing Yao of the University of Maryland for his discussions and encouragement to our early work.

Finally, we wish to thank Michiko Kitagawa for her help in preparing the manuscript of the book.

Table of Contents

1 Introduction

In the last few years, there has been an increasing demand for computer systems to support directly both routine and casual office information-handling activities. Under the theme of office automation (OA), considerable research work has been done [141, 143], and both OA equipment and software packages are emerging as commercial products.

Although office data processing has been gradually automated, especially in routine business applications, using the currently available office information systems and equipment, it is still heavily dependent on office workers' manual handling of office forms. Moreover, form handling in the current systems is implemented in a rather ad hoc manner. For example, most business application systems treat forms just as formatting information for online data entries and report outputs. In word-processing environments, forms are usually just combinations of character strings embedded in text data to represent visually formatting lines and boxes. For further automation of office information processing, we have to establish structured form handling based on an appropriate form data model. Needless to say, most users of office information systems are office workers. They are experts in their fields, but are end-users having little computer background, if any. What they want to do is to manipulate office data as if they were handling conventional form-based slips and documents. Therefore, the technique to be implemented must represent a compromise between the requirement for user-friendliness and the need for formality and uniformity.

This book discusses the theory and practice of manipulation of forms based on the unnormalized relational data model. A data model is a logical representation scheme of data associated with a set of operators for manipulating the target data. Extensive research has been done on data models relating to research on database design and data semantics. Among them, the *relational data model* proposed in 1970 by E. F. Codd [23] is the most popular one and widely accepted by researchers and practitioners. In the relational data model, data objects are modeled as flat tables under the *first normal form (1NF) constraint*. This constraint excludes nests of columns and/or rows from the relational data model. Although the 1NF constraint is the key to maintaining simplicity of the model, modeling of complex objects such as forms, text and graphics data sometimes becomes difficult. For this reason, extensions of the original relational data model discarding the 1NF constraint have been proposed by researchers, ourselves included. They are generically referred to as *unnormalized relational data models* or *Non-First-Normal-Form* (NF^2) *relational data models.*[1]

The model discussed intensively here was named the *nested table data model* (*NTD*) in 1979 [69]. In NTD, data are modeled as a collection of tables, named *nested tables* (*NTs*), which may have nested repeating groups. Under NTD, a variety of form-based slips and documents can be formally and uniformly handled as NTs within computer systems. Features for user-friendly manipulation of form-based documents can be developed on top of NTD.

In this book, we discuss the unnormalized relational data model as an approach to form manipulation, focusing on the following three topics:

1. Definition and theoretical study of the unnormalized relational data model.
2. Application of the unnormalized relational data model to form-based document manipulation.
3. Application of the unnormalized relational data model to the specification of form-based interactive application systems.

Through the above discussion, manipulation of forms based on the unnormalized relational data model is both theoretically and experimentally investigated. For our study, NTD is used as a typical and well-defined instance of the unnormalized relational data model.

This book consists of six chapters. This chapter, Chap. 1, is an introduction to the main topics.

Chapter 2 briefly surveys important research activities relating to the three main topics in this book. Firstly, research trends relevant to the unnormalized relational data model are surveyed. Secondly, efforts to develop form-based document manipulation systems are introduced. Thirdly, research and development efforts on form-based application development are reviewed. Chapter 2 not only introduces the history of the research in this field, but also clarifies the academic contribution of the discussion presented in this book. Chapter 2 covers the significant research results up to the present but does not represent a complete survey. Therefore, Chap. 2 includes many references for further reading.

In Chap. 3, we focus our discussion on the definition and theoretical study of NTD, a typical instance of the unnormalized relational data model. Data objects named NTs and a number of related concepts are formally defined. Two separate sets of operators are also defined to specify data manipulation in NTD. One set contains operators named *nested table handles* (*NT handles*) and is intended to model "static" data manipulation. The other contains operators named *nested table operations* (*NT operations*), which are intended to model more "dynamic" algebraic manipulation of NTs. Concepts such as dependencies and normalization in NTD are also discussed by analogy with the relational data model. Based on such definitions, the formal properties and data manipulation capability of NT operations are studied in the remaining part of Chap. 3.

In Chap. 4, we discuss the application of the unnormalized relational data model to a form-based document manipulation system. The design and implementation of a *form document workbench* named *FORMDOQ* are discussed. FORMDOQ provides a number of interactive facilities for developing and managing form-based

---

[1] Unnormalized relations considered in our study are generically referred to as *nested relations*, too. In this book, "unnormalized relations" and "nested relations" are interchangeable when they are used as generic terms.

electronic documents (abbreviated here as *form documents*) which may include text and graphics data. FORMDOQ uses NTD as a canonical model of form documents. Although a number of form systems have been developed previously, management of form data according to the unnormalized relational data model is a unique feature of FORMDOQ. The form-handling scheme in FORMDOQ and its logical architecture are intensively discussed. The major implementation issues are also discussed. A prototype FORMDOQ has been implemented under the UNIX[2] operating system. Graphics-based interactive session examples and experimental evaluation results are presented to complete the discussion.

In Chap. 5, we discuss another use of NTD: specification of form-based interactive application systems. Office data handling is usually classified into two types: one is predetermined routine processing, and the other is ad hoc data handling [101]. Traditionally, the former has often been automated by application programs coded by staff for application development. However, some research efforts have been made to replace time-consuming coding with more high level specification of applications under the theme of *application generation*. One of current trends in office application generation is the use of forms as building blocks to facilitate application development by office users. An application system usually involves transactions consisting of file handling, form-based interactive sessions, and report generation. Therefore, the scheme for modeling application data and procedures involved in these transactions is a key of application generation technology. In Chap. 5, we propose an architecture for application generation, named *FORMAG*. The FORMAG application system model features the use of NTD as a uniform data model for file handling, interactive screen-based sessions, and report generation. An application system model and application development environments under FORMAG are discussed in Chap. 5. There, an application procedure specification language, named *NTPL*, is proposed based on the NT handles defined in Chap. 3.

The last chapter, Chap. 6, is the conclusion. Chapters 3 through 5 have overview and summary sections which enable readers to get the essence of the chapters quickly.

---

[2] UNIX is a trademark of AT & T Bell Laboratories.

2 Historical Background

One of the most important issues in current office automation research is computer-based manipulation of *office forms*. Here, we interpret the terms *office* and *form* in a wide sense. The term *office* includes not only the conventional clerical office but also the engineering design office, sales expert's office, business consultant's office, clinical business office, and any other office where paper work is done. Thus we interpret the term *form* as any sheet of paper which has predetermined purposes of documentation. Traditionally, a variety of forms have been devised and utilized in office data handling. The main reasons for such widespread use of forms are summarized as follows:

1. Forms provide office workers with powerful guidelines for data specification and recognition. Thoughtful arrangement of data in a form visually reinforces the meanings of specific entries of data items. Preprinted horizontal and vertical lines and labeled rows and columns also facilitate office workers' data entry and understanding. Time required for paper work can also be greatly reduced, since routine documentation procedures are omitted with the use of preprinted formats.

2. Forms contribute to standardization of office data presentation, specification, and manipulation. Predetermined formats in forms prescribe the presentation and specification of office data. In addition, it is usually the case that the design of forms is tightly related to that of procedures involved in daily office data manipulation. In many business and engineering fields, such standardization brought about by the use of forms has had a positive impact on productivity of office activities [7, 27, 83].

3. In both business and engineering applications, office work is usually performed from a number of viewpoints. For example, an order-processing application is composed of a number of more primitive tasks such as customer information management, order taking, shipping, and payment. As another example, the specification of software system design is done from viewpoints concerning system functions, data flow, control flow, and so on. Normally, in both cases, the attention of a worker can be focused on only one facet of an entire application or system at a time. Forms are often used purposely to limit the scope of office workers and engineers. In other words, forms can be seen as windows through which workers can look at the target of current interest. In this way, forms pack a set of relevant data from certain viewpoints. Therefore, they greatly facilitate modular manipulation of a very large amount of office data.

4. In offices today, it is a basic requirement to manipulate office data combining diagrams, text, images, and so on, as well as alphanumeric data. Forms, being very general frameworks for data packing, can be used in combination with such complex data.

A variety of forms have been used because of their usefulness, and form manipulation is a key to automation of office information-processing activities. This book is devoted to a systematic study of form manipulation based on the unnormalized relational data model. As mentioned in Chap. 1, our discussion is focused on the following three topics:
1. Definition and theoretical study of NTD as a basis of the form data model.
2. Design and implementation of a form document manipulation system based on NTD.
3. Use of NTD for the specification of interactive application systems.

Forms have been viewed mainly from the standpoint of external data presentation formats and the man-machine interface, but such a systematic study on forms is strongly required today. Needless to say, there are a number of works on each of the above three aspects of form handling which relate to our study. In this chapter, other researchers' efforts and relevant results are surveyed from viewpoints corresponding to the above three topics.

2.1 Form Data Model

Extensive work has been done on development and analysis of data models, especially in the field of database management [146]. Among the many data models which have been proposed, three major ones are widely implemented and commercially available. They are the *relational, hierarchical*, and *network data models* [30, 131, 145, 148].

The relational data model, in essence, allows only flat tables (referred to as *relations* or the *first normal form (1NF) relations*) for data structures and features logical simplicity [6, 19, 23, 65]. Two types of scheme are defined for specifying data manipulations in the relational data model. One is the *relational algebra* defining algebraic operations on relations. The other is the *relational calculus* defining a non-procedural logic-based expression scheme for relational data manipulation. Their expressive power is proved to be equivalent under the concept of *relational completeness* [25]. There have been some approaches to employ the relational data model as an underlying data model for form manipulation [85, 142]. Dynamic restructuring of data can be modeled within the framework of the relational data model as algebraic manipulation of relations. It is a unique property of the relational data model and is appropriate for modeling form editing and restructuring operations. However, conventional forms usually have hierarchical data structures, e.g., nests of data items, or tabular organizations of data, and the relational data model is too simple to handle directly such form data structures.

In contrast to the relational data model, the hierarchical data model [144] and the network data model [138] can handle more sophisticated data structures. Both can straightforwardly model hierarchical form data structures. However, they were heuristically developed from hierarchical EDP (electronic data processing) file

systems and owe their popularity to various commercial implementations. Therefore, relevant concepts and terminology are theoretically not well-defined, and
cannot provide a sound basis for systematic study and analysis of form manipulation. In addition, the hierarchical and network data models are static in nature.
That is, operations provided in the data models are mainly dedicated to retrieval
and update of records in files, and are unsatisfactory for data restructuring. Data
restructuring is assumed to be performed only on very special occasions under the
name of database reorganization. However, in the world of form manipulation, data
restructuring is frequently required. For example, editing existing forms to generate
report forms would require selection of data items and reorganization of data
structures. NTD, the data model which we define in this book, can directly handle
hierarchical form data structures, using the concept of the NT, yet still provides
formal operations named NT operations to model dynamic form manipulation.

Operations which model dynamic manipulations of hierarchical data structures
were first studied by Shu et al. in the context of hierarchical database reorganization
in 1975 and 1977 [128, 129]. The term *form* was used, in their context, to stand for
the file structure in the hierarchical database. They proposed a language named
CONVERT to express database reorganization procedures and also a database
reorganization system EXPRESS. CONVERT was later applied to query specification for the hierarchical data model [56]. CONVERT includes a number of
constructs for dynamically handling hierarchical data structures, for example, to
apply to report generation. NT operations defined in Chap. 3 are also intended to
model hierarchical data manipulation. NT operations resulted from our efforts to
provide a sound and formal basis for form manipulation, while CONVERT was
proposed as a high-level language. Therefore, NT operations are more primitive
and well-defined, when compared with the CONVERT operations.

To our best knowledge, a basic model for form processing, using hierarchical NT
data structures and dynamic data manipulation operations, was first proposed in
1979 by the authors [69] and further elaborated in a series of papers [67, 70, 71,
73–75]. The initial design of NTD was presented, and OFP (a language for Office
Form Processing) was also proposed as an example-oriented query formulation for
form data, resembling QBE (Query By Example)[1] [161–163, 166]. More sophisticated form-processing languages based on hierarchical data structures and QBE-
like specifications were also proposed by Luo and Yao in 1981 [89] and by Shu et
al. in 1982 [87, 130]. They were named FOBE (Form Operation By Example) and
FORMAL (Forms Oriented Manipulation Language), respectively.

As mentioned previously, NTD is an instance of the unnormalized relational data
model, removing the first normal form constraint from the original relational data
model. Since the late 1970s, a number of works have contributed to research on
unnormalized extensions of the relational data model, mainly from a theoretical
viewpoint. Recently, the unnormalized relational data model, under the name of
nested relations, has become one of the most active research topics, as the demand
for complex object manipulation grows for database systems. In 1987, the first
international workshop dedicated to this topic was held in Darmstadt, West

---

[1] QBE is a language developed by International Business Machines Corporation.

Germany [123]. The September 1988 issue of *IEEE Data Engineering* was a special issue on nested relations [98]. Here, we survey the major research trends on the topic, but it is not a complete survey. References to the workshop material and other papers are recommended for further review of the state of the art.

The first study in this direction was done in 1977 by Makinouchi on data structures in the unnormalized relational data model [90]. He proposed extensions of functional and multivalued dependencies in the relational data model [24, 38], and defined a "normal" form for unnormalized relations. In Chap. 3, we discuss dependencies and a normal form in NTD. Here, we define two types of dependencies, local dependency and global dependency. Dependencies as discussed by Makinouchi are equivalent to local ones by our definition.

Theoretical study on the basic properties of extended relational algebra was done by the authors in 1980 in the context of a preliminary version of NTD [70, 71]. There, two NT operations, NEST and FLAT, essential for handling hierarchical data structures, were defined and their commutativity and reversibility properties were studied. Necessary dependency concepts based on Makinouchi's definition were also introduced. A similar study on extended relational algebra was also presented in 1982 by Jaeschke and Schek [60]. They considered interaction of NEST and JOIN as well as NEST and FLAT. In addition, they defined a new type of dependency named "weak multivalued dependency" to specify the necessary condition for commutativity of two NEST operations. However, their extension to the relational data structure was very restrictive in that they allowed only set data occurrences in relations, namely one-level nesting in nested relations. Manipulation of unnormalized relations was also studied by Arisawa and others in 1983 [5] and later in [93, 94]. Their work was done along the line presented by Jaeschke and Schek, and the discussion was based on the same restricted version of the extended relational data structure.

Fischer and Thomas [41, 140] formally defined a full set of operations for extended relational algebra in 1983. They studied properties of their operations more extensively based on the work of Jaeschke and Schek. Their extended relational data structure was more general than that of Jaeschke and Schek. They permitted multiple levels of hierarchies as NTD does. However, their operations were still more restrictive than NT operations in that they were applicable only at the outermost level of hierarchical data structures. In Sect. 3.6, we clarify basic properties of NT operations. Some of the properties were similarly studied by Fischer and Thomas for their extended relational algebra. However, our results are more general, since NT operations are applicable at any hierarchical level.

Abiteboul and Bidoit [1] proposed an extended relational model named the *Verso model* in 1984. The Verso model treated multiple levels of hierarchies. When we see the hierarchical relation instance as a tree of records, two sibling records must have different values for at least one field in the Verso model. In other words, every sibling subtree structure had to be identifiable by its root record. This *keying assumption* is reasonable for most stable data structures. However, it is rather restrictive in modeling transient data structures such as intermediate results of algebraic operations. Unnormalized relations essentially equivalent to the Verso relations were studied by Roth, et al. under the name of *partitioned normal form (PNF)* in 1984 and 1988 [114, 115]. In NTD, the Verso relational structures are referred to as *Well-classified NTs*. In the Verso relational algebra, nests of selection primitives were introduced to formulate complicated selections.

Jaeschke and Schek later presented their continuing research results. In their revised model, multiple levels of hierarchies were permitted in data structures called NF^2 (*Non-First-Normal-Form*) *relations*. The early version of NF^2 relational model was presented in 1982 [119]. Schek and others presented a set of algebraic operations for NF^2 relations in 1985 and 1986 [118, 120]. Basically, their NF^2 relational operations are still applicable only at the outermost level of hierarchical data structures. In their formulation, nests of operational primitives are permitted in more general form than in the Verso model. Owing to the extension, algebraic operations are, in fact, applicable to nodes at any hierarchical level. Jaeschke proposed two different types of NF^2 relational algebra in 1985 [58, 59]. One is called *nonrecursive algebra* in the sense that nests of operational primitives are not considered. Nonrecursive algebra operations are defined to simulate the effects of the original relational operations as precisely as possible, with help of implicit NEST and FLAT operations. They are applicable to inner nodes in the hierarchy. The other algebra proposed by Jaeschke is called *recursive algebra*. It allows nests of algebraic operational primitives in very general form.

NTD is based on the pioneering study by the authors in 1979 [69]. Table 2.1 compares NTD with the above-mentioned extended relational models[2]: the Fischer and Thomas model, the Verso model, and the NF^2 relational model comprising three sets of algebraic operations. With respect to data structures, they all permit multiple levels of hierarchies. The Verso model is more restrictive, forcing the keying assumption mentioned previously. The third and fourth rows show properties of algebraic operations in the models. Operations in the Fischer and Thomas model and the Schek model are applicable only at the outermost level, while operations in the other models including NTD are applicable at any level of the hierarchy.

The Verso model introduced a nest of selection primitives, while Schek's algebra and Jaeschke's recursive algebra permit more general forms of operational primitive nesting. The other models including NTD do not allow such nesting. Although nestings of operational primitives facilitate the specification of operations, validation of given expressions and their interpretation sometimes become complicated. Our intent in developing NTD is not to define the most powerful data model but to provide a sound basis for form manipulation. For this reason, possibly complicated nesting is not considered, to maintain the simplicity of the model.

Some models in Table 2.1 seem too closely oriented to the original relational data model. For example, as mentioned before, Jaeschke's nonrecursive algebra operations are defined to "simulate" the original relational operations as precisely as possible in the NF^2 relational model. Therefore, they are well-defined in a pure theoretical sense but sometimes complicated and/or awkward to model practical data handling. For instance, the results of extended join operations could be

---

[2] Since this area is an active one and each model is supposed to be still under refinement, this comparison cannot be a final one. The authors' intent is just to give a concise summary of the discussion for readers.

Table 2.1. Extended Relational Model

	Fischer and Thomas	Verso model	NF² relational model				
			Schek	Jaeschke (Nonrecursive algebra)	Jaeschke (Recursive algebra)	NTD	
Data structure							
Hierarchy levels	Multiple levels	Multiple levels	Multiple levels	Multiple levels	Multiple levels	Multiple levels	
Keying assumption	No	Yes	No	No	No	No	
Algebraic operation							
Operation node level	Outermost level	Any level	Outermost level	Any level	Any level	Any level	
Nests of operational							
primitives	No	In selection	Yes	No	Yes	No	
Static operation	?	?	(Extension of SQL)			NT Handles	

NTD, Nested table data model

difficult to understand. Also, extended selection operations basically allow comparison of two attributes only when they belong to the same group. In the design of NTD, we did not stick to purism.

When we define some operations, it is important to consider their capability. Chapter 3 of this book includes a discussion on the data manipulation capability of NT operations. Although Abiteboul and Bidoit [1] referred to relational completeness property [25] of their operations in 1984, the capability of the extended relational algebra operations was at first not well-investigated. In 1984 and 1988, Roth and others formulated a calculus for unnormalized relations [114, 115] and showed that its expressiveness was equivalent to the algebra of Fischer and Thomas [41]. Later in 1987, Van Gucht studied the expressiveness of the algebra of Fischer and Thomas from the viewpoint of *BP-completeness* [149]. BP-completeness is a language-independent measure for expressiveness, and the relational algebra and calculus were proved to be BP-complete [11, 102]. Gyssens and Van Gucht proposed *powerset algebra* for unnormalized relations based on their investigation on the expressiveness in 1988 [48, 49]. Manipulation of flat relations by the extended relational algebra was studied in 1988 by Paredaens and Van Gucht [103]. In Chap. 3, we consider the data manipulation capability of NT operations from another viewpoint. We study it in the light of data manipulation capability provided by the original relational algebra plus NEST and FLAT operations. Our study identifies some conditions under which NT operations are expressible as sequences of FLAT, relational algebra, and NEST operations. Commutativity and reversibility of NT operations are also investigated from this viewpoint.

In the study on the data manipulation capability of the NT operations, mapping between first normal form relations (flat NTs) and unnormalized relations (NTs) is considered. Similar studies have been presented independently by Kitagawa and Kunii in 1979, 1980, and 1982 [69–71], by Arisawa et al. in 1983 [5], and by Schek and others in 1985, 1986, and 1987 [118, 121, 122, 124]. In the approaches by Arisawa et al. and by Schek and others, unnormalized relations are assumed to be internal representations of first normal form relations, reducing data redundancy. The approach here assumes the converse situation. Since the manipulation of first normal form relations is well established within the framework of the relational data model, its role with respect to NT handling is considered in our approach.

In the approach by Arisawa et al. and in ours, "canonical" structures are defined as those obtained by applying NEST operations to flat data structures. However, as mentioned before, data structures considered by Arisawa et al. allow only set data occurrences, namely one level nesting. The *Canonical NTs* considered in this book may include multiple level hierarchies. Therefore, "canonicality" can be determined only by data occurrence structures in the definition by Arisawa et al., while our "canonicality" concerns schemas associated with data occurrences. Fischer and Van Gucht investigated some subclasses of unnormalized relations in 1985 and 1986. *Nested relations*[3] equivalent to our Canonical NTs were also identified by

---

[3] Today, "nested relation" is often used as a general term to designate an unnormalized relation, as mentioned in Chap. 1. Fischer and Van Gucht originally used this term to name a particular subclass of unnormalized relations.

them. They identified other subclasses such as *permutable nested relations* and *normalization-lossless structures*, and investigated polynomial-time algorithms to tell whether a given structure belonged to any subclass [40, 150].

In addition to NT operations, NTD provides a set of operations, named NT handles, for more static data manipulation such as navigation in NTs and data occurrence update. For NF^2 relations, the SQL^4-type [20, 31] language HDBL (Heidelberg Database Language) is designed to cover such static data manipulation [106].

Dependencies in unnormalized relations were also discussed by some of the above-mentioned researchers in studies of their operations' properties [5, 40–43, 60, 122]. Some include extensions of Makinouchi's definition other than ours. Studies on design criteria of unnormalized relations based on dependencies were presented by Kambayashi et al. [62–64] and by Ozsoyoglu and Yuan [99, 100]. Kambayashi et al. extensively discussed the design of unnormalized relations from a user interface point of view. Ozsoyoglu and Yuan studied a nested normal form decomposition of the universal relation based on multivalued and functional dependencies. Design issues on unnormalized relations were also studied by Roth and Korth [113].

A thorough formalization integrating the relational, hierarchical, and network data models was presented by Jacob in 1982 [57]. His formalization is named *Database Logic*. Some of the notation used in Chap. 3 is inspired by his formalization of hierarchical data structures.

Formal study on several aspects of the relational data model without assuming the first normal form constraint was reported in a series of papers by Kobayashi [79–81]. Transformations concerning unnormalized relations and the extended relational calculus were discussed there.

As discussed below, NTD is used for an underlying model for the form system FORMDOQ. Efforts to develop a DBMS (Database Management System) prototype supporting the NF^2 relational model by researchers in the IBM Heidelberg Scientific Center and the Technical University of Darmstadt are reported in [29, 88, 104, 121]. The concept of database kernel and the physical file structures for NF^2 relations are discussed in these reports. Implementation of unnormalized relational databases is also reported in [34]. There are some other research efforts on the unnormalized relational data model (e.g., [55, 155]). The workshop material [123] and the special issue of *IEEE Data Engineering* [98], both mentioned previously, include research overview reports. In particular, an excellent survey of research activities in Japan is given by Kambayashi [61].

2.2 Form System

Since computer-based form manipulation is one of the most important issues in the recent research on office automation, a lot of work has been done on form systems. At first, a number of languages based on forms were proposed. QBE was originally

---

[4] SQL is an ISO standard database language.

proposed as a data definition and manipulation language for the relational database in 1975 [161, 163]. Later, its basic idea was also applied to specification of queries to the hierarchical database in 1976 [162], and further extended to manipulation of office objects including form-based documents and slips in 1981 [164, 165]. As mentioned before, QBE-like example-oriented specification was incorporated into languages designed for hierarchical form data handling, such as OFP in 1980 [74], FOBE in 1981 [89], and FORMAL in 1982 [87, 130]. OFP and FOBE were proposed as data manipulation languages for an information repository consisting of form documents, while FORMAL was designed as a language for specifying office application procedures involving forms.

Research on forms from the viewpoint of OFP and FOBE led to the design and implementation of form systems which handle form documents as data objects. APAD (Application Adaptable Database System) proposed in 1979 by the authors was based on an underlying relational database and supports form data structures under the NT concept as user views [67, 69, 75]. OFS (Office Form System) reported in 1982 by Tsichritzis implemented form manipulation also based on the relational data structures [142]. However, their form data structures were restricted to those coinciding with underlying relational data structures to avoid troublesome view-update problems [18, 26, 32, 97]. Therefore, only simple forms containing no hierarchical data structures could be handled in OFS.

The capability to manipulate forms in sophisticated graphics-based interactive workstation environments was implemented in Xerox STAR[5] as a record-processing feature in 1983 [107, 126, 132]. In the STAR environments, form documents with user-friendly presentation forms can be developed using combined graphics and text-editing facilities. However, each form document is actually an external presentation of a record in a file, and the actual unit for data management is not a form document but a file. In addition, only one-level nesting is allowed in STAR record files, and restructuring of data structures is severely restricted in STAR. OFFICEAID developed in 1984 by Lochovsky and co-workers has an graphics-based interactive interface inspired by STAR [85]. Like OFS, OFFI-CEAID is also based on an underlying relational database. Therefore, hierarchical form data structures are only allowed in virtual documents, which cannot be updated. The development of form systems is also reported in [3, 66, 147].

FORMDOQ, presented in Chap. 4, resulted from our research on form data structures in 1984 [68, 72, 76]. It is the implementation of a form system that systematically utilizes a hierarchical form data model instantiated by NTD. Since considerable emphasis is placed on graphics-based interactive facilities for developing and managing form documents, we call FORMDOQ a "form document workbench" rather than just a form system. Although STAR partially allows such hierarchies for form manipulation, its forms are just views to conventional record files, as mentioned above. Since FORMDOQ directly supports hierarchical form data structures in terms of NTs, FORMDOQ features dynamic manipulation of form documents based on the NT operations.

In the systems mentioned above, forms are manipulated as data objects. There is another direction of research on forms, in which forms are used as building blocks

---

[5] The official name is the 8010 Information System.

for specifying office application procedures. The specifications are usually interpreted or translated into executable codes, so that the application development can be done quickly. Therefore, the research work reviewed here is also tightly related to specification of application systems, the third topic of the book. In 1975, deJong and Zloof proposed a visual programming language SBA (System for Business Automation) combining QBE and forms [33, 166]. Concepts in SBA were later developed into OBE in 1981 [164, 165]. Programming based on forms was also investigated by Hammer et al. [50], Embley et al. [28, 37], Fong [44], Shirota et al. [127] and Shu et al. [87, 130]. Shu et al. proposed a system named OPAS based on FORMAL in 1982. Expressions proposed in those approaches are generally applicable to specification of triggered actions and semantic constraints involved in form manipulation. A formalization of triggers was given in 1982 by Tsichritzis [142], and a form-based language for specifying semantic data manipulation constraints was proposed by Ferrans also in 1982 [39]. The use of forms as abstractions of interactive commands was proposed by Hayes in 1984 [53].

An environment for application specification based on forms was developed in 1982 by Rowe and Shoens [117] under UNIX. The system is named FADS (Form Application Development System). FADS is designed to facilitate application development on the relational database management system INGRES [137]. It uses an extended version of the data manipulation language QUEL for specification of database manipulation, and includes a set of tools such as editors and a debugger for developing query and data update procedures. ADE (Application Development Environments) provides more general environments for application development, extending FADS [116]. An application development facility combining the relational database and forms was also proposed by Yao et al. in 1984 [159]. In their approach, a database language named XQL is used instead of QUEL [86]. The relationship between these form-based approaches to application development and the approach presented in Chap. 5 is explained later in more detail.

Analysis of form flow is another interesting topic in the research on forms. A formalization for form flow analysis was proposed in 1982 by Tsichritzis [142]. Nutt and others designed a Petri-Net-like [105] model, named ICN (Information Control Net), for form flow specification [36, 96]. Ellis and others developed a prototype form-based office information system OFFICETALK-D in 1982 in a distributed system environment based on ICN [35].

2.3 Form-based Application Specification

Cost-effective development of reliable software systems and programs has been extensively studied as the central issue of software engineering. A considerable number of engineering disciplines have been explored and some of them have proved effective in practical software projects. They include software development methodologies (e.g., phased approach, top-down design, object-oriented modeling), specification techniques and tools (e.g., specification languages and schemes, validation techniques, structured programming), development environments (e.g., programming environments, computer-aided software engineering tools), and management and control disciplines (e.g., configuration control, software metrics, cost estimation) (for instance, [4, 7–10, 12, 15, 16, 27, 45, 51, 52, 77, 82, 84, 95, 108, 109, 111, 112, 134–136, 139, 152–154, 156]).

Nevertheless, problems in software development, in particular in the development of application systems, are not completely resolved. Many enterprises still encounter difficulties such as programs that do not meet the initial requirements, poor handling of changes of requirements, and backlogs of undeveloped applications. The recent widespread use of microprocessor-based small computers in business makes the situation even worse [110]. It has brought about a tremendous number of computer application requirements, and made it inevitable for non-professional programmers to develop application systems.

Recently, attention has been focused on a new approach for application system development using *application generators* [14, 17, 21, 46, 47, 54, 92, 151]. Application generators usually guide application system development by providing high level primitives and tools for specifying input/output formats, data validation logic, triggered actions, and so on [91]. The specification languages used in the application generators are sometimes referred to as *4GL* (the *fourth generation language*) [92, 151]. Today, most application generators are developed around particular database management systems for integrated data management. Data communication facilities for interactive man-machine dialog, query languages, and report writers are usually provided as principal tools for application development. Currently available application generators are practical integrations of those application development tools.

As far as office applications are concerned, many researchers' efforts, which we have already surveyed, have identified forms as natural abstractions of office data. A number of form systems were mainly intended to facilitate application system development in offices. OBE was defined as an extension of QBE for office application development [164, 165]. OBE has a relational database system in its core, and QBE expressions embedded in formatted screens are used for specifying application data processing. Text-editing and mailing functions are also provided to implement applications combining document handling and forwarding common in offices. OPAS, proposed by Shu et al. in 1982, is an office application development system based on forms [87, 130]. OPAS uses hierarchical data structures similar to those in NTD as an underlying data model. A language, FORMAL, is used for QBE-like example-oriented specifications of application procedures. FADS, developed in 1982 by Rowe and Shoens, can also be classified into a form-based application development system [117]. FADS uses the relational database system INGRES for data management as mentioned before. FORMAN-AGER/XDB,[6] developed in 1984 by Yao et al., is another application development system based on a relational database system [158, 159].

In Chap. 5, we propose an architecture for application generation, named FORMAG, on the basis of NTD. This approach views screen-based interactive sessions and file manipulation (including report generation) as the principal elements in most business applications. A structured application system model is defined, in which both the interactive session and file manipulation are modeled

---

[6] XDB is a trademark of XDB Systems Incorporated.

using NT data structures. The work described in Chap. 5 is an extension of the previous research of Yao and Kitagawa in 1985 [158], which was done in the context of XDB. The uniqueness of that approach was that application generation was based on a structured application system model. However, in that approach, file manipulation was modeled in the relational data model, while an informal model was used for specifying interactive sessions. In the approach presented in Chap. 5, both are uniformaly modeled on the basis of NTs. As mentioned above, OPAS utilizes a hierarchical data structure similar to NTs for modeling application data processing. OPAS is focussed on the specification of distributed office application procedures, while FORMAG is oriented toward a small application system. The OPAS system is unique in that every transaction is abstracted into a combination of form procedures, each of which takes one or more input forms and produces one output form. However, this approach is too heavily oriented to abstraction of data manipulation procedures, and as a consequence, the actual application system structures are blurred in their specifications. For example, file handling, the interactive screen-based session, and report generation are abstracted into form procedures and not distinguishable. In contrast, FORMAG uses NTD as an underlying data model for application specification, but important application system elements are explicitly visible in the specification. Attention is paid not to obscure data-processing practices by too much abstraction. Therefore, the application specifications in FORMAG provide a basis for the systematic generation of executable application systems.

3 Nested Table Data Model (NTD)

3.1 Overview

In this chapter, a new data model named the *nested table data model* (*NTD*) is proposed as a canonical model for data definition and manipulation of forms and form-based documents (here termed *form documents*) in computer environments. In NTD, *nested tables* (*NTs*) are used as canonical data representations. Briefly, an NT is a table with nests of columns and rows. An example of an NT PROG_SPEC is shown in Fig. 3.1. NTs are abstract representations of data in form documents such as those printed and written on paper and displayed on screen. For example, data in a sample form document shown in Fig. 3.2 are directly representable as a row in NT PROG_SPEC shown in Fig. 3.1. Fig. 3.3 illustrates the mapping between real external form documents and NTs. Generally, data in a form document can be mapped down into an NT having only one row. Thus, it would seem that we need not consider NTs having multiple rows. However, we offen have to handle a bunch of form documents based on the same form. In addition, NTs having more than one row are useful in modeling NT data handling. For these reasons, we allow NTs to have multiple rows, which makes NTD useful as an underlying data model.

NTD provides primitives for modeling data manipulation for form documents as well as data representation. In these sense, NTD also serves as a canonical model of

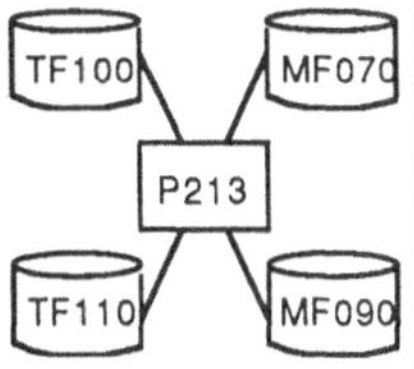

Fig. 3.1. Nested table

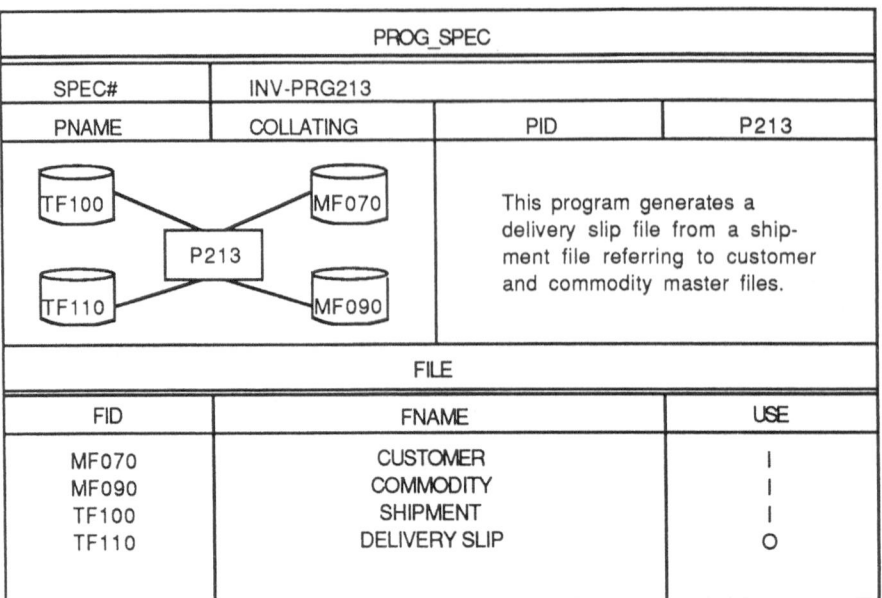

PROG_SPEC

SPEC#	INV-PRG213		
PNAME	COLLATING	PID	P213

TF100   MF070   P213   TF110   MF090

This program generates a delivery slip file from a shipment file referring to customer and commodity master files.

FILE		
FID	FNAME	USE
MF070	CUSTOMER	I
MF090	COMMODITY	I
TF100	SHIPMENT	I
TF110	DELIVERY SLIP	O

Fig. 3.2. Sample form document

form document manipulation in the computer world. Usually, in a real world, form documents are handled in a variety of ways involving cross-referencing and reformatting. To achieve general machine processing of form documents, we have to establish a computer world model for both definition and manipulation of form documents. NTD resulted from our research efforts toward this goal.

This chapter defines NTD and its related concepts. A discussion of the formal model properties follows the definition. Sections 3.2 through 3.4 are devoted to the definition of the model, and Sects. 3.5 and 3.6 present an analysis of the model. In Sect. 3.2, the definition of NT and relevant terminology are given. In Sect. 3.3, a set of primitives for accessing and updating data occurrences in NTs is defined. The primitives are called *NT handles*. They form a basis for modeling "static" data manipulation, as normally expressed in data manipulation languages in the database world. In Sect. 3.4, a set of operations for algebric NT manipulation is defined. These are called *NT operations* and are used to express more "dynamic" manipulation of NTs than that specified by NT handles. In Sect. 3.5, dependency concepts and normalization in NT environments are considered. In Sect. 3.6, formal properties of data manipulation by NT operations are intensively studied. First, basic properties of the major NT operations are clarified. The commutability and reversibility of operations are investigated. Then, the data maniuplation capability of NT operations is studied on the basis of the investigation results. Sect. 3.7 summarizes the discussion in Chap. 3. Appendix A gives a quick summary which correlates basic terms and notions of NTD with those of the NF^2 relational data model.

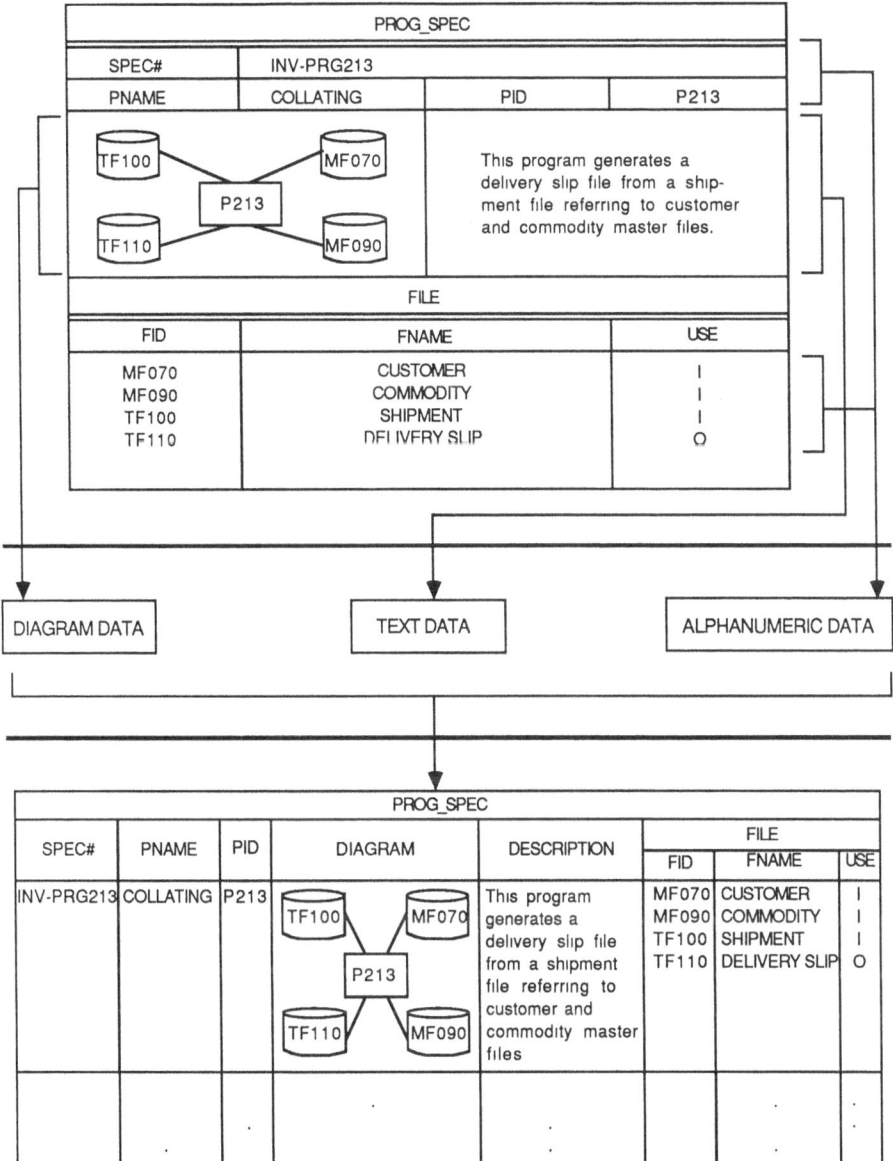

Fig. 3.3. Mapping between form documents and NTs

3.2 Nested Table

Intuitively, NTs are tables with nests of columns and rows. Now, we define an NT more formally. A *nested table (NT) T* is defined as the followint triple:

$$T=(NN, NS, NO),$$

where NN is an *NT name*, NS is an *NT schema*, and NO is an *NT occurrence*. An NT scheme NS is a set of *group schemas* which meet the *tree condition* given later. A group scheme GS_i $(1 \leq i \leq m)$ in NS is an expression of the following form:

$$G_i \langle C_1^i, \ldots, C_{n_i}^i \rangle \ (n_i \geq 1),$$

where G_i is a name designating the *group*, and C_j^i $(1 \leq j \leq n_i)$ is a name designating a *component* of G_i. Here, group names G_i $(1 \leq i \leq m)$ are different from each other within an NT schema NS, and so are $C_1^i, \ldots, C_{n_i}^i$ within a group schema GS_i.

If a component C_j^i appears as a group name G_k in another group schema GS_k $(k \neq i)$, then the component designated by C_j^i is the group G_k. In such a case, G_k is called a *child* of G_i, and G_i is called a *parent* of G_k. The set of child groups of G_i is denoted by $cg(G_i)$. Components that do not appear as group names are called *fields*. The set of fields of group G_i is denoted by $cf(G_i)$. Group G_i is referred to as an *entry group* of fields in $cf(G_i)$. The set $cf(G_i) \cup cg(G_i)$ is denoted by $cc(G_i)$. For two distinct groups G_k and G_i $(1 \leq i, k \leq m)$, if there exist groups $G_{j_1}, \ldots, G_{j_h}$ $(h \geq 0)$ such that $G_k \in cg(G_{j_1})$, $G_{j_h} \in cg(G_i)$, and $G_{j_g} \in cg(G_{j_{g+1}})$ for every $1 \leq g < h$, G_k is called a *descendant* of G_i, and G_i is called an *ancestor* of G_k. The sets of descendant groups and ancestor groups of G_i are denoted by $dg(G_i)$ and $ag(G_i)$, respectively. The sets $dg(G_i) \cup \{G_i\}$ and $ag(G_i) \cup \{G_i\}$ are denoted by $dg+(G_i)$ and $ag+(G_i)$, respectively.

Group schemas in NS must satisfy the following *tree condition*:

a) There exists one group called the *root*, which has no parent.
b) Every group other than the root has just one parent and is a descendant of the root.

The following subset $NSS_{G_i} \subseteq NS$,

$$NSS_{G_i} = \{GS_j \mid GS_j \in NS \wedge G_j \in dg+(G_i)\}$$

is called an *NT subschema* for G_i. Since a group G_i is always accompanied by a group schema $G_i \langle C_1^i, \ldots, C_{n_i}^i \rangle$, the terms *group* and *group schema* are used interchangeably when precise distinction of their meanings is not required.

Every field and group E has a *domain* of data *occurrences* denoted by $dom(E)$. The domain $dom(E)$ is defined as follows:

1. If E is a field, the domain $dom(E)$ is defined as a set of atomic data items. In the application of NTD described in Chap. 4, we consider integer, float, character string, text and graphics domains. Integer, float, and character string domains are called *basic domains*, and text and graphics domains are called *extended domains*. We could also consider image domains, voice domains, and so on as extended domains.

2. If E is a group with group schema $G_k \langle C_1^k, \ldots, C_{n_k}^k \rangle$, the domain $dom(E) = dom(G_k)$ is defined as follows:

$$dom(E) = dom(G_k) = 2^{dom(C_1^k) \times \ldots \times dom(C_{n_k}^k)}$$

Elements in $dom(C_1^k) \times \ldots \times dom(C_{n_k}^k)$ is called *clusters*, and $dom(C_1^k) \times \ldots \times dom(C_{n_k}^k)$ is called the *cluster domain* of G_k and denoted by $cdom(G_k)$. In other words, an occurrence of G_k is a set of clusters in $cdom(G_k)$. The clusters are called G_k *clusters* to specify explicitly that they can appear in occurrences of G_k.

An NT occurrence NO is an occurrence of the root group G_R, namely,

$$NO \in 2^{dom(C_1^R) \times \ldots \times dom(C_{n_R}^R)}$$

or

$$NO \subseteq dom(C_1{}^R) \times \ldots \times dom(C_{n_R}{}^R).$$

If an NT schema is composed of only one group schema, the NT is called a *flat NT*. Flat NTs are obviously equivalent to relations in the relational data model.

Given group $G_i \langle C_1{}^i, \ldots, C_{n_i}{}^i \rangle$ and a G_i cluster t, the data occurrence for component $C_j{}^i$ in t is denoted by $t[C_j{}^i]$. This notation is also used for a subset of components $C \subseteq \{C_1{}^i, \ldots, C_{n_i}{}^i\}$, and $t[C]$ means a cluster consisting of t's data occurrences for components in C. In other words, $t[C][C_j{}^i] = t[C_j{}^i]$ for every $C_j{}^i \in C$. When another group $G_j \langle C_1{}^j, \ldots, C_{n_j}{}^j \rangle$ and a G_j cluster u are given, a cluster in $dom(C_1{}^i) \times \ldots \times dom(C_{n_i}{}^i) \times dom(C_1{}^j) \times \ldots \times dom(C_{n_j}{}^j)$ concatenating t and u is denoted by (t, u). This notation is also used in combination with the above notation, for example, $(t[C], u)$.

NTs defined above can be represented in tabular formats. An example has been shown in Fig. 3.1. Its NT schema is composed of the following two group schemas:

PROG_SPEC⟨SPEC#, PNAME, PID, DIAGRAM, DESCRIPTION, FILE⟩
FILE⟨FID, FNAME, USE⟩.

In this NT schema, PROG_SPEC and FILE are groups, the former being the root. The root group PROG_SPEC has fields SPEC#, PNAME, PID, DIAGRAM, DESCRIPTION, and a child group FILE. The group FILE has fields FID, FNAME, and USE. In Fig. 3.1, the NT occurrence corresponds to the table contents. The hierarchical data structure complying with the NT schema is represented by nested rows. In Fig. 3.1, the NT schema is visually represented in the table header tagged with the table. It can also be represented as a tree, as shown in Fig. 3.4.

So far, we have treated components $C_1{}^i, \ldots, C_{n_i}{}^i$ in a group schema $G_i \langle C_1{}^i, \ldots, C_{n_i}{}^i \rangle$ as an ordered sequence. However, each component is identifiable by its name following the naming convention that their names are unique within the group

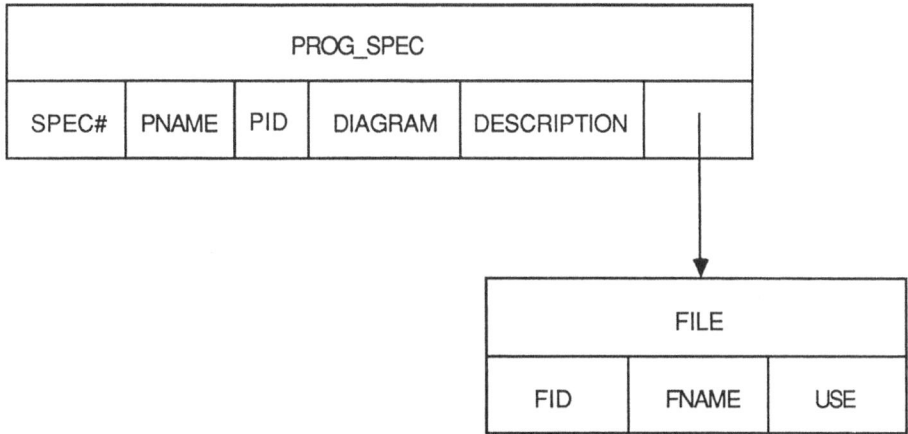

Fig. 3.4. NT schema tree

schema. Therefore, in principle, we can ignore the ordering of components without obscuring the meaning. However, in some cases, for example, for tabular representation of NTs as shown in Fig. 3.1, we have to decide the ordering of components.

NT data structures thus defined give a number of advantages. Mainly from the viewpoint of form data modeling, NT structures have the following characteristics:

1. Conventional form documents usually have hierarchical data structures (e.g., nests of data items, tabular clustering of data, repeating groups). In this regard, data structures in form documents and NT data structures have much in common. Therefore, data in form documents can be directly represented in NT canonical structures. An example of such mapping has been shown in Fig. 3.3.
2. One-to-one, one-to-many, or many-to-many relationship can be modeled in NT data structures. This capability is also often required to handle data such as complex data appearing in form documents. As surveyed in Chap. 2, many researchers employed two-dimensional flat tables for logical simplicity to model form data within the framework of the relational data model. However, flat tables are sometimes too primitive for the purpose.
3. Although tables with nests of columns and rows have more complex structures than flat tables, the basic concept is not too complicated for the office user to capture. Therefore, the user can readily manipulate data specified in form documents considering them as a collection of NTs without burdensome training and education. Reorganization of form documents by means of NT operations exemplifies this advantage, as discussed in Chap. 4.
4. NTs are natural extensions of flat tables in the relational data model. Therefore, the theory for NTD can be constructed on the basis of existing research on the relational data model. In fact, basic theory on relational algebra and dependency in the relational data model is used as a starting basis for our investigation of NTs, as explained in the following sections.
5. Data in extended domains (e.g., text and graphics) can be induced in NTs as raw data items. This feature has a pragmatic significance in the use of NTs as a basis for development of practical form systems.

3.3 Nested Table Handle

We cannot complete the definition of a data model without specifying its data manipulation primitives. Sects. 3.3 and 3.4 are devoted to the formalization of data manipulation primitives in NTD. In this section, basic data access and update primitives named *nested table handles* (*NT handles*) are introduced. They are used for retrieval, deletion, insertion, and modification of data occurrences in NTs. NT handles are "static" data manipulation primitives in the sense that they do not change NT schemas. Operations performed by NT handles have an effect only on NT occurrences. In contrast to NT handles, NT operations introduced in Sect. 3.4 achieve "dynamic" NT handling, such as algebraic manipulations of NTs.

NT handles provide a basic interface for accessing and updating data in the NT occurrence of a given NT. To define NT handles, we have to determine a scheme used to address each data item in an NT occurrence.

3.3.1 Addressing Scheme

Given an NT, a group is designated by its name, and a field is designated by a concentration of the entry group name and the field name. Given an occurrence O_i of a group G_i, each G_i cluster t in O_i is identified by a unique internal sequence number. The sequence number is called the *cluster number* and the cluster number assigned to a cluster t is denoted by $cn(t)$. The cluster number is assumed to be assigned automatically by the NT data management utility. The cluster number assigned to a cluster may not be altered during the lifetime of the cluster, or may have to be reassigned, for example, if another cluster is inserted to or deleted from O_i. It depends on the implementation of the NT data management utility. In examples given in the following part of this section, the cluster number is assumed to designate the relative position of the cluster in the tabular representation.

The cluster number is local to each occurrence of G_i. The *cluster address* $ca(t)$, which globally identifies a cluster t in an NT occurrence, is defined as follows:

$$ca(t) = \begin{cases} cn(t) & \text{if } G_i \text{ is the root} \\ ca(u).cn(t) & \text{otherwise,} \end{cases}$$

where u is a G_j cluster such that $G_i \in cg(G_j)$ and $t \in u[G_i]$. In other words, the cluster address is a concatenation of cluster numbers of nested clusters along the hierarchical path from the root to G_i.

Each G_i cluster t in a given NT is addressed by

$$\langle\text{group}\rangle\text{'}@\text{'}\langle\text{cluster\_address}\rangle,$$

where $\langle\text{group}\rangle$ is a group name of G_i and $\langle\text{cluster\_address}\rangle$ is the cluster address of t. For example, the third FILE cluster (TF100, SHIPMENT, I) in the NT PROG_SPEC shown in Fig. 3.1 is addressed by FILE@1.3. Occurrences of a field and a group in t are also addressable by

$$\langle\text{group}\rangle\text{'}@\text{'}\langle\text{cluster\_address}\rangle\text{'}[\text{'}\langle\text{field}\rangle\text{'}]\text{'},$$

and

$$\langle\text{group}\rangle\text{'}@\text{'}\langle\text{cluster\_address}\rangle\text{'}[\text{'}\langle\text{group}\rangle\text{'}]\text{'},$$

respectively. In the latter case, the first $\langle\text{group}\rangle$ can be omitted, since the group name is unique within an NT and there is no ambiguity if it is omitted. These expressions are naturally extended to cases where a set of cluster addresses is given in place of $\langle\text{cluster\_address}\rangle$.

3.3.2 Primitive NT Handle

NT handles are defined based on the above addressing scheme. They include the following five *primitive NT handles*.

SEARCH: *search G_i in N where SC_i*

Here, N is an NT name, G_i is a group of N, and SC_i is a selection condition. SEARCH is used to get a set of cluster addresses of G_i clusters which meet the selection condition SC_i.

The syntax for the selection condition SC_i is given by the following BNF (Backus Naur Form) expression:[1]

$\langle$selection_condition$\rangle$::$=$|$\langle$selection$\rangle$| '('$\langle$selection_condition$\rangle$')'
       |'NOT' $\langle$selection_condition$\rangle$
       |$\langle$selection_condition$\rangle$ 'AND' $\langle$selection_condition$\rangle$
       |$\langle$selection_condition$\rangle$ 'OR' $\langle$selection_condition$\rangle$
$\langle$selection$\rangle$::$=\langle$primitive_selection$\rangle$|$\langle$set_selection$\rangle$
$\langle$primitive_selection$\rangle$::$=\langle$p_left$\rangle\langle$p_comp$\rangle\langle$p_right$\rangle$
$\langle$set_selection$\rangle$::$=\langle$s_left$\rangle\langle$s_comp$\rangle\langle$s_right$\rangle$
$\langle$p_left$\rangle$::$=\langle$p_term$\rangle$
$\langle$p_right$\rangle$::$=\langle$p_term$\rangle$|$\langle$p_constant$\rangle$
$\langle$p_comp$\rangle$::$=$ '$=$'|'$\neq$'|'$<$'|'$>$'|'$\leq$'|'$\geq$'
$\langle$p_term$\rangle$::$=\langle$p_reference$\rangle$|$\langle$aggregate$\rangle$ '(' $\langle$s_reference$\rangle$')'
$\langle$p_reference$\rangle$::$=\langle$group1$\rangle$ '['$\langle$field1$\rangle$']'|'['$\langle$field1$\rangle$']'
$\langle$aggregate$\rangle$::$=$'SOME'|'ANY'|'AVG'|'CNT'|'SUM'|'MAX'|'MIN'
$\langle$s_reference$\rangle$::$=\langle$group2$\rangle$ '['$\langle$field2$\rangle$']'
$\langle$p_constant$\rangle$::$=\langle$value$\rangle$
$\langle$s_left$\rangle$::$=\langle$s_term$\rangle$
$\langle$s_right$\rangle$::$=\langle$s_term$\rangle$ | $\langle$s_constant$\rangle$
$\langle$s_comp$\rangle$::$=$'$=$' |'$\neq$'| '$\subset$'| '$\not\subset$' |'$\subseteq$'| '$\not\subseteq$'|'$\supset$'|'$\not\supset$'|'$\supseteq$'|'$\not\supseteq$'|
       'INTERSECT' | 'NOT_INTERSECT'
$\langle$s_term$\rangle$::$=\langle$s_reference$\rangle$
$\langle$s_constant$\rangle$::$=$'{'$\langle$value_set$\rangle$'}'
$\langle$value_set$\rangle$::$=\langle$value$\rangle$|$\langle$value$\rangle$ ',' $\langle$value_set$\rangle$.

Here, $\langle$group1$\rangle$ is the name of a group G_1 such that $G_1 \in ag+(G_i)$, and $\langle$group2$\rangle$ is the name of a group which does not meet this condition. Components $\langle$field1$\rangle$ and $\langle$field2$\rangle$ are fields of groups designated by $\langle$group1$\rangle$ and $\langle$group2$\rangle$, respectively. If $\langle$group1$\rangle$ is G_1, [$\langle$field1$\rangle$] can be used as an abbreviation for $\langle$group1$\rangle$ [$\langle$field1$\rangle$].

To specify the evaluation rule for the selection condition, we must define some notation. Given two groups G_j and G_k in an NT, the *leaf common ancestor group* denoted by $lca(G_j, G_k)$ is defined as a group such that
a) $lca(G_j, G_k) \in ag+(G_j)$.
b) $lca(G_j, G_k) \in ag+(G_k)$.
c) There is no descendant group of $lca(G_j, G_k)$ that meets the above two conditions. For each G_j cluster t, the $lca(G_j, G_k)$ cluster which directly or indirectly includes t is denoted by $lca(t, G_j, G_k)$.

The selection condition SC_i is evaluated for each G_i cluster t to decide whether t meets the condition or not. Evaluation of $\langle$p_reference$\rangle$ and $\langle$s_reference$\rangle$ is done according to the followine rule:

---

[1] Primitive comparison operators, set comparison operators, and aggregates are defined here as a minimal set for specifying selection conditions on data items in basic domains. More domain-specific operators and aggregates can be added within the framework of the above definition.

a) Evaluation of ⟨p_reference⟩: $G_j[F_k]$
   Evaluation_of $(G_j[F_k]) = lca(t, G_i, G_j)[F_k]$.
b) Evaluation of ⟨s_reference⟩: $G_j[F_k]$
   Evaluation_of $(G_j[F_k]) = \{u[F_k]\,|\,u$ is a G_j cluster directly or indirectly included in $lca(t, G_i, G_j)\}$.

Note that ⟨p_reference⟩ designates an atomic data item in the evaluation, and that ⟨s_reference⟩ designates a set of atomic data items. Other constructs in the selection condition are evaluated in a usual way. The primitive SEARCH finally returns

$$\{ca(t)\,|\,t \text{ is a } G_i \text{ cluster in } N \text{ which meets } SC_i\}.$$

For example, if

search FILE *in* PROG_SPEC *where* FILE[USE] = 'I'

is applied to PROG_SPEC shown in Fig. 3.1, the set of cluster addresses {1.1, 1.2, 1.3, ...} is returned as the result. The same form of the selection condition is used in the NT operation SELECT as explained in Sect. 3.4. More elaborated examples of selection conditions are given there.

GET: *get* G_i @ $CA_i[F_j, \ldots]$ *in* N
       get G_i@$CA_i[G_j][F_k, \ldots]$ *in* N

Here, N is an NT name, G_i is a group of N, $G_j \in dg(G_i)$, and CA_i is a set of cluster addresses for G_i clusters. $F_j, \ldots$ are fields of G_i, and $F_k, \ldots$ are fields of G_j. This handle is used to get field occurrences in G_i clusters addressed by CA_i. The first GET listed above returns a set of field occurrences

$$\{t[F_j, \ldots]\,|\,t \text{ is a } G_i \text{ cluster and } ca(t) \in CA_i\},$$

and the second one returns a set of field occurrences

$$\{u[F_k, \ldots]\,|\,u \text{ is a } G_j \text{ cluster and } u \text{ is directly or indirectly included in a } G_i \text{ cluster } t \text{ such that } ca(t) \in CA_i\}.$$

When $[F_j, \ldots]$ (or $[F_k, \ldots]$) is omitted, it is assumed that all fields of G_i (or G_j) are specified.
   For example, if

get FILE @ {1.1, 1.2} [FID] *in* PROG_SPEC

is applied to PROG_SPEC shown in Fig. 3.1, the set of data items {'MF070', 'MF090'} is returned as the result.

DELETE: *delete* G_i @ CA_i *in* N

Here, N is an NT name, G_i is a group of N, and CA_i is a set of cluster addresses for G_i clusters. This handle is used to delete the following G_i clusters:

$$\{t\,|\,t \text{ is a } G_i \text{ cluster and } ca(t) \in CA_i\}.$$

INSERT: *insert* G_i @ $CA_j[⟨value\_list⟩]$ *in* N

Here, N is an NT name, G_i is a group of N, and CA_j is a set of cluster addresses for G_j

clusters, where $G_i \in cg(G_j)$. If G_i is the root of N, '$@CA_j$' is omitted. This handle inserts a G_i cluster whose component occurrences are given by $\langle$value_list$\rangle$ into G_j clusters addressed by CA_j. G_j clusters addressed by CA_j must exist in N. Even if G_i has child groups, values for group occurrences are not specified in $\langle$value_list$\rangle$, and NULL values are assigned as their initial values. Insertion of clusters for the descendent groups is done by nested application of INSERT. INSERT returns the set of cluster addresses assigned to the inserted clusters.

MODIFY: *modify $G_i @ CA_i[F_j: \langle$value$_j\rangle, \dots]$ in N*

Here, N is an NT name, G_i is a group of N, and CA_i is a set of cluster addresses for G_i clusters. This handle is used to replace the following occurrences of field F_j

$$\{t[F_j] \mid t \text{ is a } G_i \text{ cluster and } ca(t) \in CA_i\}$$

with $\langle$value$_j\rangle$.

3.3.3 Composite NT Handle

Combining the first SEARCH handle with the other four handles, we can define the following four *composite NT handles* for conditional NT accesses and updates. The meanings of symbols are the same as above, unless otherwise specified:

Conditional Get: CGET

> *cget $G_i[F_j, \dots]$ in N where SC_i*
>
> $= get\ G_i @ (search\ G_i\ in\ N\ where\ SC_i)[F_j, \dots]\ in\ N.$
>
> *cget $G_i[G_j][F_k, \dots]$ in N where SC_i*
>
> $= get\ G_i @ (search\ G_i\ in\ N\ where\ SC_i)[G_j][F_k, \dots]\ in\ N.$

Conditional Delete: CDELETE

> *cdelete G_i in N where SC_i*
>
> $= delete\ G_i @ (search\ G_i\ in\ N\ where\ SC_i)\ in\ N.$

Conditional insert: CINSERT

> *cinsert $G_i[\langle$value_list$\rangle]$ in N where SC_j*
>
> $= insert\ G_i @ (search\ G_j\ in\ N\ where\ SC_j)\ [\langle$value_list$\rangle]\ in\ N.$

Here, G_j is the parent of G_i and note that the selection condition SC_j is specified for G_j.

Conditional Modify: CMODIFY

> *cmodify $G_i[F_j: \langle$value$_j\rangle, \dots]$ in N where SC_i*
>
> $= modify\ G_i @ (search\ G_i\ in\ N\ where\ SC_i)[F_j: \langle$value$_j\rangle, \dots]\ in\ N.$

The NT handles defined here and in Sect. 3.3.2 are abstractions of primitives necessary for accomplishing basic accesses and updates to NT data occurrences.

Therefore, they may be applied to practical data manipulation requirements in different ways. For example, they provide a basis for formulating data access and update routines for application programs to manipulate data files physically representing NTs. NT handles also provide a basic framework for a high-level data manipulation language. Their application in this direction is elaborated upon in Chap. 5.

3.4 Nested Table Operation[2]

We complete the definition of NTD by introducing operations for the dynamic manipulation of NTs. They are called *nested table operations* (*NT operations*). NT operations algebraically manipulate NTs by deriving new NTs from existing ones. As mentioned in Sect. 3.2, NTs include relations in the relational data model as their special cases. Some of the NT operations are natural extensions of *relational algebra* operations originally introduced by Codd [23, 25]. We first define seven *primitive NT operations*. Then, we define some *composite NT operations* which are shorthand for combined uses of primitive NT operations.

3.4.1 Primitive NT Operation

Primitive NT operations are further divided into two groups, namely, *NF operations* and *XR operations*.

3.4.1.1 NF Operation

NF operations are essential for handling hierarchical data structures in NTs. They include the unary operations NEST and FLAT, defined as follows:

NEST: $N[G_i, G_j\langle C_j\rangle]$

Here, G_i is a group, $C_i = cc(G_i)$, $C_j \subseteq C_i$, $C_j \neq \varnothing$, and $G_j\langle C_j\rangle$ is a new group schema. This operation creates as a child of G_i a new group G_j consisting of components C_j. An example of the NEST operation is shown in Fig. 3.5.

Formally, let $T' = N[G_i, G_j\langle C_j\rangle](T)$, $T = (NN, NS, NO)$, and $T' = (NN', NS', NO')$. Then,

$$NN' = NN^3$$

$$NS' = (NS - \{G_i\langle C_i\rangle\}) \cup \{G_i\langle(C_i - C_j)G_j\rangle, G_j\langle C_j\rangle\}^{4,5}$$

---

[2] In the remainder of this chapter, we do not consider the NULL value (including the empty set) as a data occurrence in NT for simplicity of the discussion.

[3] In this chapter, we assume that the NT generated by an NT operation inherits the NT name of the (first) operand NT. The discussion here does not lose generality with this assumption.

[4] $(C_i - C_j)G_j$ means the set $(C_i - C_j) \cup \{G_j\}$. Similar abbreviations are used when there is no possibility of confusion.

[5] We assume that groups and fields are named so that the designated modification of NT schemas does not voilate the naming convention for NT.

and

$$NO' = REP(NO, O, G_i, O'),$$

where

$$O' = \{(t[C_i - C_j], FN(t)) \mid t \in O\}$$

$$FN(t) = \{u[C_j] \mid u \in O \wedge u[C_i - C_j] = t[C_i - C_j]\}.$$

Here, $REP(NO, O, G_i, O')$ means NO with every occurrence O of group G_i replaced by O', and $(t[C_i - C_j], FN(t))$ means a cluster concatenating $t[C_i - C_j]$ and $FN(t)$.

FLAT: $F[G_i]$

Here, G_i is a group other than the root. Let $C_i = cc(G_i)$, and let $G_j\langle C_j\rangle$ be the group schema of G'_is parent. This operation removes group G_i, and components C_i are incorporated into components of G_j. An example of the FLAT operation is shown in Fig. 3.6.

Formally, let $T' = F[G_i](T)$, $T = (NN, NS, NO)$, and $T' = (NN', NS', NO')$. Then,

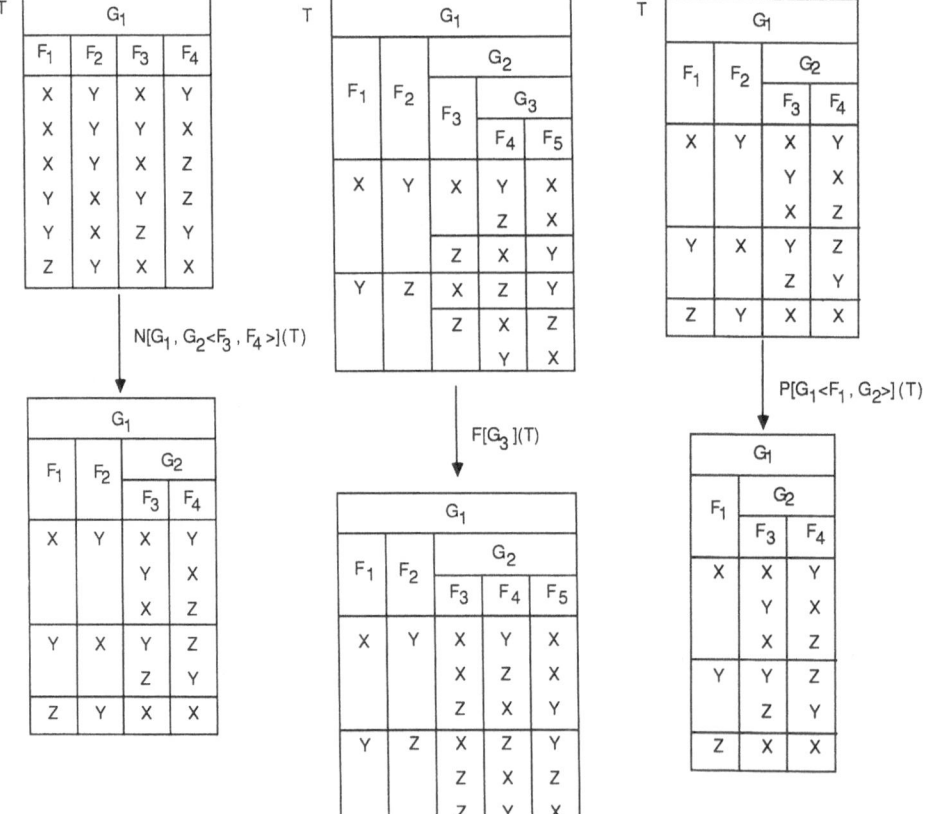

Fig. 3.5. NEST   Fig. 3.6. FLAT   Fig. 3.7. PROJECTION

$$NN' = NN$$

$$NS' = (NS - \{G_i\langle C_i\rangle, G_j\langle C_j\rangle\}) \cup \{G_j\langle(C_j - G_i)C_i\rangle\}$$

and

$$NO' = REP(NO, O, G_j, O'),$$

where

$$O' = \{(t[C_j - G_i], u) \mid t \in O \wedge u \in t[G_i]\}.$$

3.4.1.2 XR Operation

XR operations include two unary operations, PROJECTION and SELECTION, and three binary operations, PRODUCT, UNION, and DIFFERENCE. They are defined such that, when they are applied to flat NTs, their effect is essentially equivalent to that of corresponding relational algebra operations. Therefore, XR operations can be regarded as natural extensions of primitive relational algebra operations.

PROJECTION: $P[G_i\langle C_j\rangle]$

Here, G_i is a group, $C_i = cc(G_i)$, $C_j \subseteq C_i$, and $C_j \neq \emptyset$. This operation prunes away those components of G_i not included in C_j, and also descendants of those. An example of the PROJECTION operation is shown in Fig. 3.7.

Formally, let $T' = P[G_i\langle C_j\rangle](T)$, $T = (NN, NS, NO)$, and $T' = (NN', NS', NO')$. Then,

$$NN' = NN$$

$$NS' = (NS - \{G_i\langle C_i\rangle\} - FP(G_i, C_j)) \cup \{G_i\langle C_j\rangle\},$$

where

$$FP(G_i, C_j) = \{G_k\langle C_k\rangle \mid G_k\langle C_k\rangle \in NS \wedge G_k \in dg+(G_m) \text{ for some } G_m \in C_i - C_j\},$$

and

$$NO' = REP(NO, O, G_i, O'),$$

where

$$O' = \{t[C_j] \mid t \in O\}.$$

SELECTION: $S[G_i, SC_i]$

Here, G_i is a group and SC_i is a selection condition. This operation select G_i clusters which meet the selection condition SC_i. The syntax and interpretation rules for the selection condition have been given in Sect. 3.3. Examples of SELECTION operations are shown in Fig. 3.8.

Formally, let $T' = S[G_i, SC_i](T)$, $T = (NN, NS, NO)$, and $T' = (NN', NS', NO')$. Then,

$$NN' = NN$$

$$NS' = NS$$

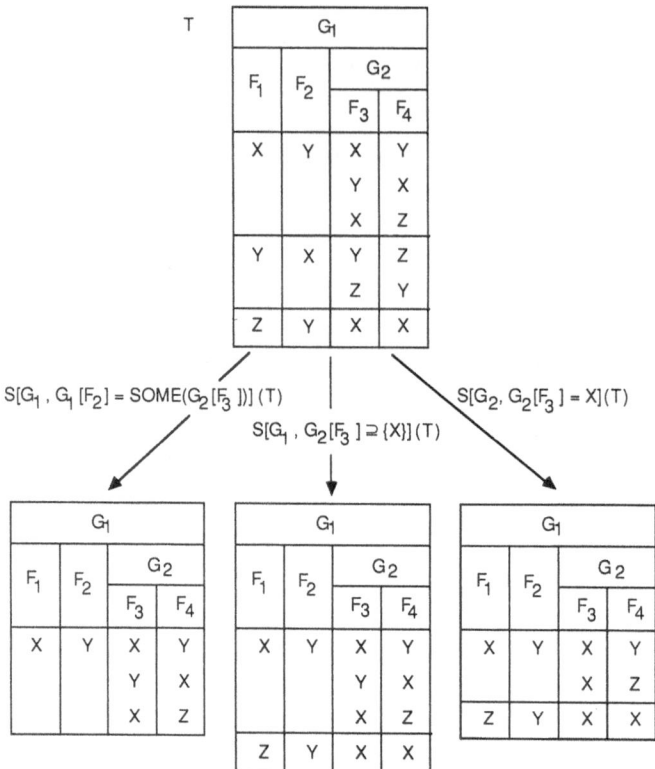

Fig. 3.8. SELECTION

and

$$NO' = REP(NO, O, G_i, O'),$$

where

$$O' = \{t \mid t \text{ is a } G_i \text{ cluster in } O \text{ meeting } SC_i\}.$$

Here, O' might be the empty set. Since we do not consider manipulation of such a NULL value in this context, the meaning of $REP(NO, O, G_i, O')$ is extended to include the following post-processing procedure:

a) If clusters having NULL values (including the empty set) are generated, prune them away.

b) Repeat (a) while applicable.

The extended interpretation holds in the remaining part of this chapter.

PRODUCT: $X[G_i]$

This operation is applied to two NTs T and T'. Here, G_i is a group of T, and let $C_i = cc(G_i)$. This operation combines T and T' concatenating each G_i cluster in T with the set of root clusters in T'. An example of the PRODUCT operation is shown in Fig. 3.9.

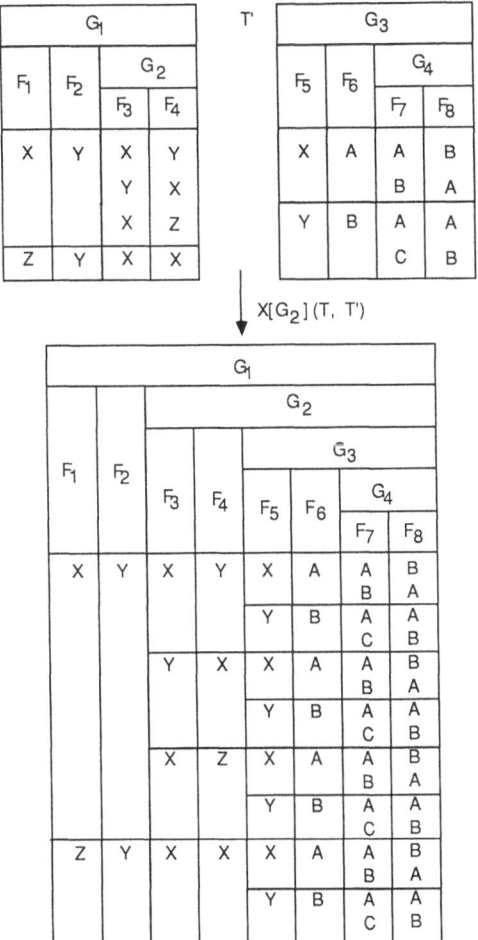

Fig. 3.9. PRODUCT

Formally, let $T'' = X[G_i](T, T')$, $T = (NN, NS, NO)$, $T' = (NN', NS', NO')$, $T'' = (NN'', NS'', NO'')$, and let G'_R be the root of T'. Then,

$$NN'' = NN$$

$$NS'' = (NS - \{G_i\langle C_i\rangle\}) \cup NS' \cup \{G_i\langle C, G'_R\rangle\}$$

and

$$NO'' = REP(NO, O, G_i, O''),$$

where

$$O'' = \{(t, FX) \mid t \in O\}$$

$$FX = \{u \mid u \in NO'\}.$$

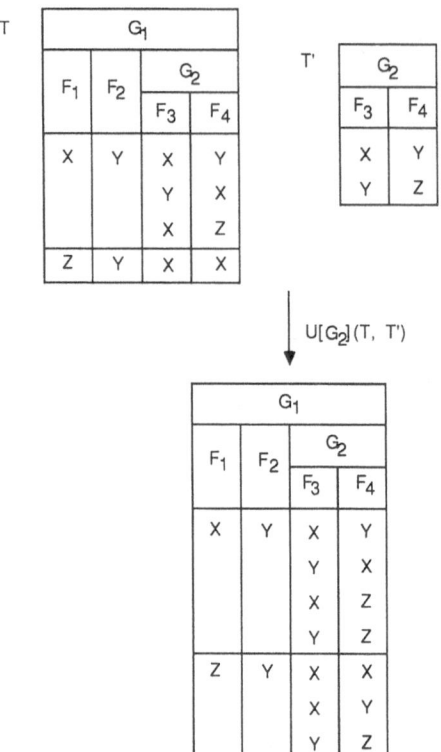

Fig. 3.10. UNION

UNION: $\cup[G_i, MS]$

This operation is applied to two NTs T and T'. Here, G_i is a group of T. This operation generates an NT by appending the root clusters of T' to every occurrence of G_i in T. Here, the NT schema of T' must be isomorphic to the NT subschema for G_i in T, and MS is a mapping specification clarifying the group-to-group and field-to-field isomorphism. If the NT schema of T' and the NT subschema for G_i in T are identical, MS can be omitted. An example of the UNION operation is shown in Fig. 3.10.

Formally, let $T'' = \cup[G_i](T, T')$, $T = (NN, NS, NO)$, $T' = (NN', NS', NO')$, and $T'' = (NN'', NS'', NO'')$. Then,

$$NN'' = NN$$

$$NS'' = NS$$

and

$$NO'' = REP(NO, O, G_i, O''),$$

where

$$O'' = O \cup NO'.$$

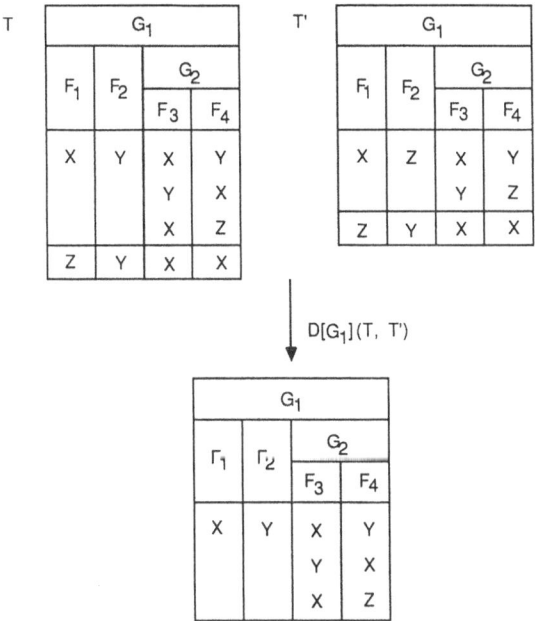

Fig. 3.11. DIFFERENCE

DIFFERENCE: $D[G_i, MS]$

This operation is applied to two NTs T and T'. Here, G_i is a group of T. This operation generates an NT by subtracting the root clusters of T' from every occurrence of G_i in T. Here, the NT schema of T' must be isomorphic to the NT subschema for G_i in T, and MS has the same meaning as in the context of UNION. An example of the DIFFERENCE operation is shown in Fig. 3.11.

Formally, let $T'' = D[G_i](T, T')$, $T = (NN, NS, NO)$, $T' = (NN', NS', NO')$, and $T'' = (NN'', NS'', NO'')$. Then, .

$$NN'' = NN$$

$$NS'' = NS$$

and

$$NO'' = REP(NO, O, G_i, O''),$$

where

$$O'' = O - NO'.$$

3.4.2 Composite NT Operation

Seven composite operations (i.e., INNER_PROJECTION, CARTESIAN_ PRODUCT, EMBED, NATURAL_EMBED, JOIN, NATURAL_JOIN, INTERSECTION) are defined here as convenient shorthand for combinations of primitive NT operations.

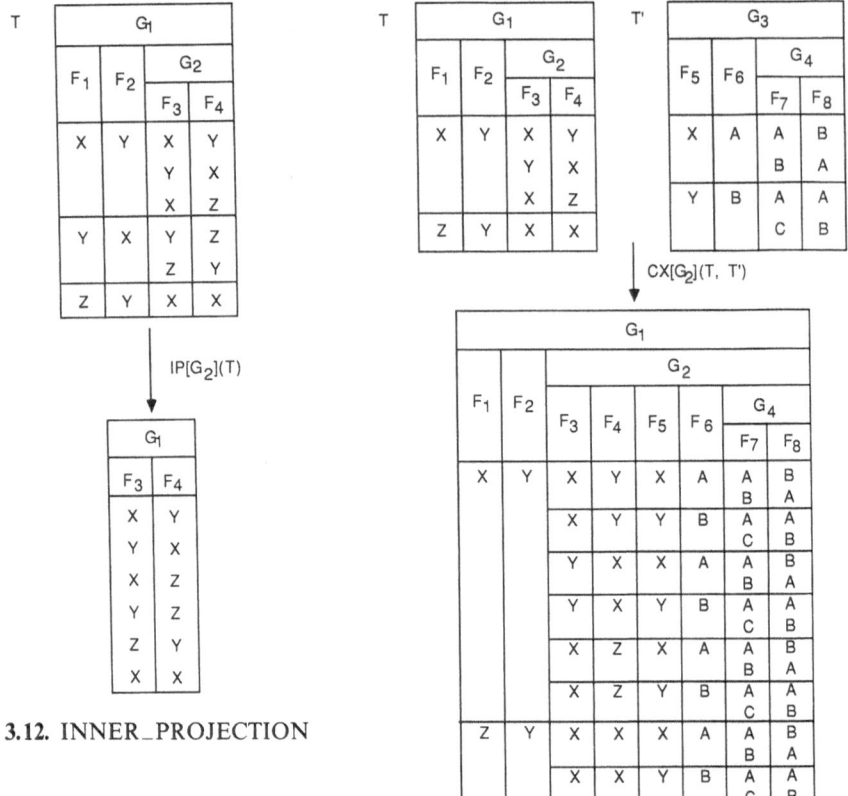

Fig. 3.12. INNER_PROJECTION

Fig. 3.13. CARTESIAN_PRODUCT

INNER_PROJECTION: $IP[G_i]$

This operation is defined as the following sequence of FLAT and PROJECTION operations:

$$IP[G_i](T) = P[G_R\langle C_i\rangle]((\Pi_{G_j\in FIP(G_i)}F[G_j])(T)),^6$$

where G_i is a group of T,

$$FIP(G_i) = \{G_k \mid G_k \text{ is not the root and } G_k \in ag+(G_i) \text{ in } T\},$$

G_R is the root of $(\Pi_{G_j\in FIP(G_i)}F[G_j])(T)$, and C_i are the components of $(\Pi_{G_j\in FIP(G_i)}F[G_j])(T)$ inherited from the components $cc(G_i)$ of T. The INNER_PROJECTION operation extracts group G_i and its descendants. An example of the INNER_PROJECTION operation is shown in Fig. 3.12.

CARTESIAN_PRODUCT: $CX[G_i]$

This operation is defined as the following sequence of PRODUCT and FLAT operations:

---

[6] $\Pi_{G_j\in FIP(G_i)}F[G_j]$ denotes the sequence of FLAT operations. Commutativity of FLAT operations is assured as discussed in Sect. 3.6.

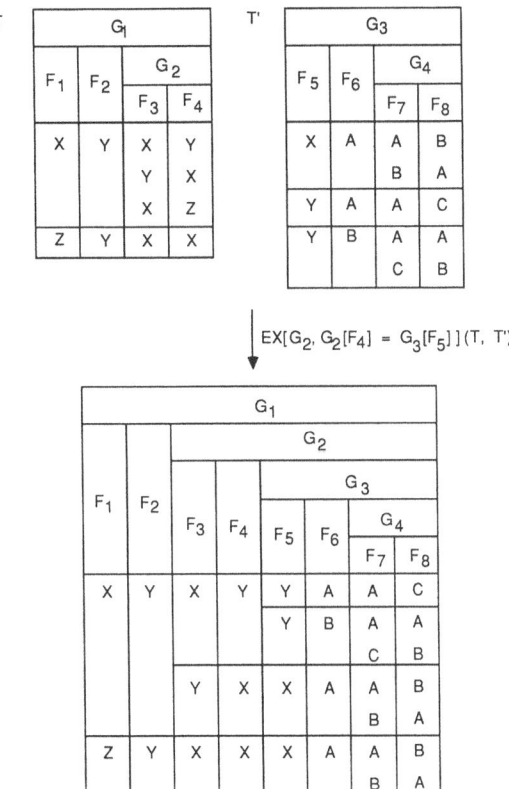

Fig. 3.14. EMBED

$$CX[G_i](T, T') = F[G'_R] X[G_i](T, T'),^7$$

where G_i is a group of T and G'_R is a group of $X[G_i](T, T')$ inherited from the root of T'. An example of the CARTESIAN_PRODUCT operation is shown in Fig. 3.13.

EMBED: $EX[G_i, EC_i]$

This operation is defined as the following sequence of PRODUCT and SELECTION operations:

$$EX[G_i, EC_i](T, T') = S[G'_R, EC_i] X[G_i](T, T'),$$

where G_i is a group of T and G'_R is a group of $X[G_i](T, T')$ inherited from the root of T'. EC_i is a selection condition specifiable in the context of the right-hand side of the above expression. An example of the EMBED operation is shown in Fig. 3.14.

NATURAL_EMBED: $NE[G_i]$

This operation is defined as the following sequence of PRODUCT, SELECTION,

---

[7] $F[G'_R](X[G_i](T, T'))$ is abbreviated as $F[G'_R] X[G_i](T, T')$. Similar abbreviation is used throughout this chapter.

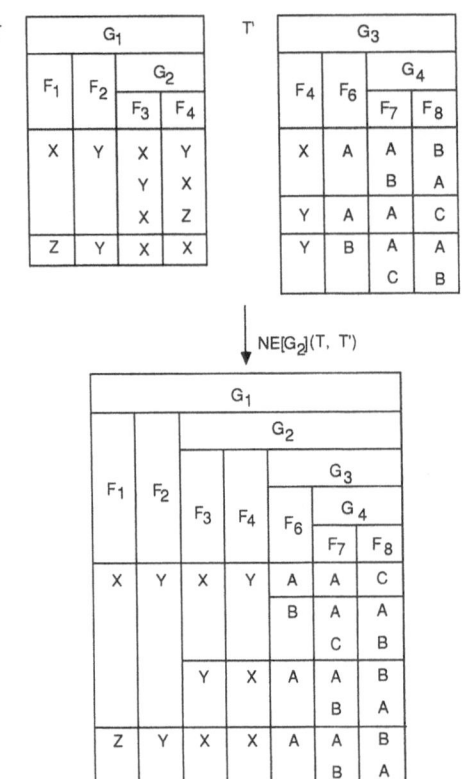

Fig. 3.15. NATURAL_EMBED

and PROJECTION operations:

$$NE[G_i](T, T') = P[G'_R\langle C'_R\rangle]S[G'_R, (\Pi_{(F_j, F'_k)\in FNE(G_i, G'_R)} \text{ AND}$$
$$G_i[F_j] = G'_R[F'_k])]X[G_i](T, T').^8$$

Here, G_i is a group of T, G'_R is a group of $X[G_i](T, T')$ inherited from the root of T'. F_j and F'_k are fields of G_i and G'_R, respectively, and $FNE(G_i, G'_R)$ is the set of field pairs (F_j, F'_k) such that F_j and F'_k have common field name and domain. In addition,

$$C'_R = cc(G'_R) - \{F'_k \mid F'_k \in cc(G'_R) \wedge (F_j, F'_k)\in FNE(G_i, G'_R)\}.$$

An example of the NATURAL_EMBED operation is shown in Fig. 3.15.

JOIN: $JX[G_i, JC_i]$

This operation is defined by replacing PRODUCT with CARTESIAN_PRODUCT in the definition of the EMBED operation. An example of the JOIN operation is shown in Fig. 3.16.

---

[8] $\Pi_{(F_j, F_k)\in FNE(G_i, G'_R)}$ AND $G_i[F_j] = G'_R[F_k]$ denotes the conjunction of the equality conditions.

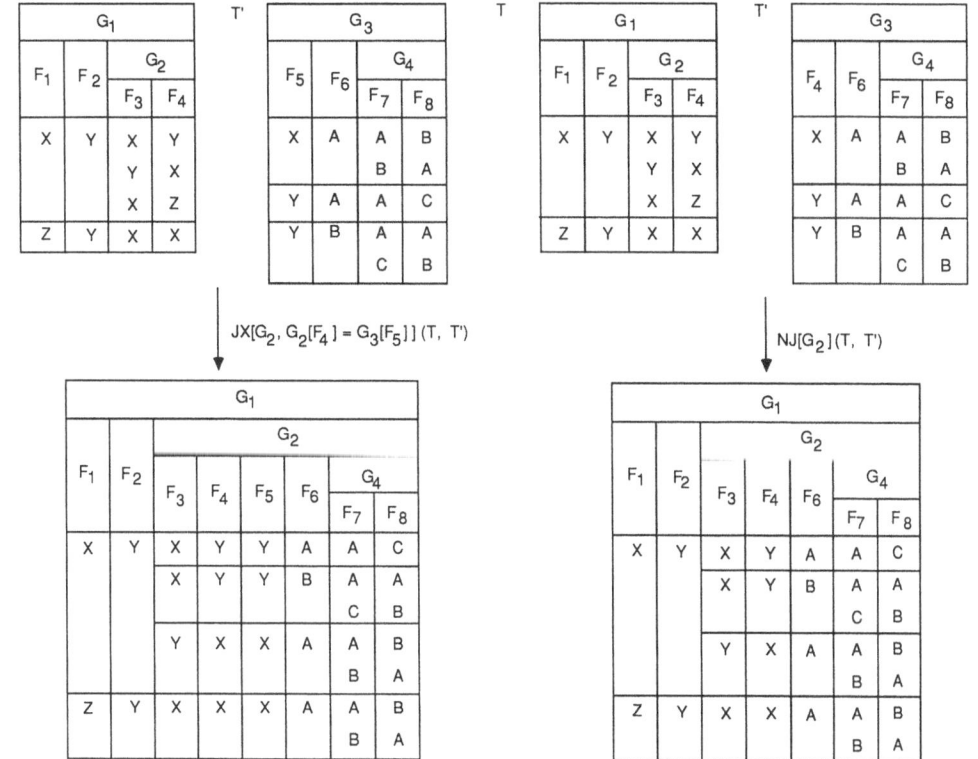

Fig. 3.16. JOIN   **Fig. 3.17.** NATURAL_JOIN

NATURAL_JOIN: $NJ[G_i]$

This operation is defined by replacing PRODUCT with CARTESIAN_PRO-
DUCT in the definition of the NATURAL_EMBED operation. An example of the
NATURAL_JOIN operation is shown in Fig. 3.17.

INTERSECTION: $\cap[G_i, MS]$

This operation is defined as the following sequence of DIFFERENCE and
INNER_PROJECTION operations:

$$\cap[G_i, MS](T, T') = D[G_i, MS'](T, IP[G_i]D[G_i, MS](T, T')),$$

where G_i is a group of T and MS and MS' are mapping specifications for the
DIFFERENCE operations. The above formulation is a counterpart of the following definition of set intersection in terms of set difference:

$$A \cap B = (A - (A - B)).$$

In this context, this equation does not hold straightforwardly, since DIFFER-
ENCE and INTERSECTION can be applied to internal tables. As shown above,

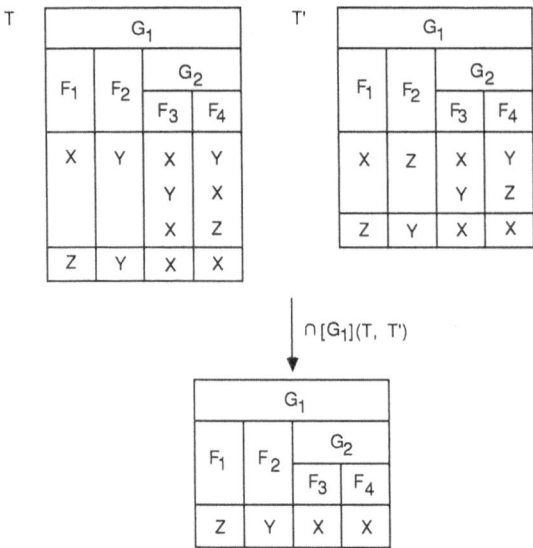

Fig. 3.18. INTERSECTION

INNER_PROJECTION is defined with PROJECTION and FLAT. Therefore, INTERSECTION is actually defined with PROJECTION, FLAT, and DIFFERENCE. An example of the INTERSECTION operation is shown in Fig. 3.18.

3.5 Dependencies and Normalization

In this section, functional dependency and multivalued dependency in NTs are formulated. These concepts were originally proposed for the relational data model [24, 38]. However, the extended counterparts defined in this section serve to express basic properties of NTs. The concepts of functional dependency and multivalued dependency are used to study the basic data-manipulation capability of NT operations in Sect. 3.6. Normalized NT is also defined by analogy to 4NF [38] in the relational data model. This concept will be used to design non-redundant NTs. Historically, as discussed in Chap. 2, the first approach to extend dependencies and normalization to unnormalized relations was presented by Makinouchi [90]. Some of the researchers on unnormalized relations, whose work we have surveyed in Chap. 2, also followed his definition. However, his extension was limited to dependencies which are referred to as "local" in our classification. In this section, we introduce "global" dependencies as well as "local" ones.

In the relational data model, such concepts as dependencies, key, and normalization are usually considered as semantic constraints associated with relational schemas. In contrast, we define them here as properties characterizing NT occurrences, as a result of our efforts to define concepts consistent with their modes of use. However, the concepts are easily modified for use as semantic constraints, as is usual with the relational design theory.

G₁				
F₁	F₂	G₂		
		F₃	F₄	F₅
X	Y	X	Y	X
		Y	Z	X
		Z	Y	Z
Y	Z	X	Y	Y
		Z	Y	Y
X	Z	X	Y	X
		Y	Z	X
		Z	Y	Z

Fig. 3.19. Sample NT

3.5.1 Dependencies

Here, we define dependencies within the framework of NTD and show some of their basic properties.

Definition 3.1. Let G be a group of an NT T, $C = cc(G)$, $X \subseteq C$, and $Y \subseteq C$. Given an occurrence O of G, X *functionally determines* Y in O, if $t[X] = u[X]$ implies $t[Y] = u[Y]$ for every pair of G clusters $t \in O$ and $u \in O$. If X functionally determines Y in every occurrence of G, *local functional dependency (LFD)* (or simply *functional dependency (FD)*) $X \rightarrow Y$ holds in T.

Definition 3.2. Let G be a group of an NT T, $C = cc(G)$, $X \subseteq C$, and $Y \subseteq C$. If $t[X] = u[X]$ implies $t[Y] = u[Y]$ for every pair of G clusters t and u, *global functional dependency (GFD)* $X -(g) \rightarrow Y$ holds in T.

Given an NT (shown in Fig. 3.19), several LFDs and GFDs can be found. LFDs and GFDs holding between two components include:

$$\text{LFD: } F_1 \rightarrow G_2, \ G_2 \rightarrow F_1,$$
$$F_3 \rightarrow F_4, \ F_3 \rightarrow F_5,$$
$$\text{GFD: } F_1 -(g) \rightarrow G_2, \ G_2 -(g) \rightarrow F_1,$$
$$F_3 -(g) \rightarrow F_4.$$

Note that GFD $F_3 -(g) \rightarrow F_5$ does not hold, since, for example, the F_5 values of the first and the fourth G_2 clusters are X and Y, respectively, while their F_3 values are X. Some other LFDs and GFDs can be identified between two sets of components.

It is obvious from the definitions that LFD and GFD are natural extensions of functional dependency in the relational data model. In other words, when a flat NT is considered, both LFD and GFD are equivalent to functional dependency in the relational data model. However, the distinction between LFD and GFD is important in NTs having hierarchical data structures. Regarding the relationship between LFD and GFD, we can derive the following propositions:

Proposition 3.1. Let G be a group of an NT T, $C = cc(G)$, $X \subseteq C$, and $Y \subseteq C$. If GFD $X \dashv(g) \rightarrow Y$ holds in T, LFD $X \rightarrow Y$ also holds in T.

Proof. Let O be an arbitary occurrence of G, $t \in O$, and $u \in O$. Assume $t[X] = u[X]$. Then, $t[Y] = u[Y]$, since t and u are G clusters and GFD $X \dashv(g) \rightarrow Y$ holds in T.
(Q.E.D.)

Proposition 3.2. Let G be the root of an NT T, $C = cc(G)$, $X \subseteq C$, and $Y \subseteq C$. Iff LFD $X \rightarrow Y$ holds in T, GFD $X \dashv(g) \rightarrow Y$ holds in T.

Proof.
[$\rightarrow$] Self-evident, since the root has only one occurrence.
[$\leftarrow$] By Proposition 3.1.   (Q.E.D.)

To define multivalued dependency, we introduce some additional notation here. Let G be a group, $C = cc(G)$, and O be an occurrence of G. The projection of O over $X \subseteq C$ is denoted by $O[X]$, that is

$$O[X] = \{t[X] \mid t \in O\}.$$

The projection of O over $Y \subseteq C$ with an X-value x is denoted by $O_x[Y]$, that is

$$O_x[Y] = \{t[Y] \mid t \in O \wedge t[X] = x\}.$$

Similarly, for an X-value x and a Z-value z ($Z \subseteq C$), $O_{xz}[Y]$ is defined as follows:

$$O_{xz}[Y] = \{t[Y] \mid t \in O \wedge t[X] = x \wedge t[Z] = z\}.$$

Definition 3.3. Let G be a group of an NT T, $C = cc(G)$, $X \subseteq C$, $Y \subseteq C$, and $Z = C - X - Y$. Given an occurrence O of G, X *multidetermines* Y in O, if $O_{xz}[Y] = O_x[Y]$ for every pair of x and z such that $t[X] = x$ and $t[Z] = z$ for some $t \in O$. If X multidetermines Y in every occurrence of G, *local multivalued dependency (LMD)* (or simply *multivalued dependency (MD)*) $X \rightarrow\!\!\!\rightarrow Y$ holds in T.

Definition 3.4. Let G be a group of an NT T, $C = cc(G)$, $X \subseteq C$, $Y \subseteq C$, and $Z = C - X - Y$. If $O_{xz}[Y] = R_x[Y]$ for an arbitrarily selected pair of (not necessarily distinct) occurrences O and R of G, and for every pair of x and z such that $t[X] = u[X] = x$ and $t[Z] = z$ for some $t \in O$ and $u \in R$, *global multivalued dependency (GMD)* $X \dashv(g) \rightarrow\!\!\!\rightarrow Y$ holds in T.

Given an NT (shown in Fig. 3.20), we can find the following LMDs and a GMD in group G_2:

$$\text{LMD: } F_3 \rightarrow\!\!\!\rightarrow F_4, \; F_3 \rightarrow\!\!\!\rightarrow F_5,$$

$$\text{GMD: } F_3 \dashv(g) \rightarrow\!\!\!\rightarrow F_4.$$

As in the case of LFD and GFD, it is obvious from the definitions that LMD and GMD are natural extensions of multivalued dependency in the relational data model. In other words, when a flat NT is considered, both LMD and GMD are equivalent to multivalued dependency in the relational data model. Regarding the relationship between LMD and GMD, we can derive the following propositions:

G₁		G₂		
F₁	F₂	F₃	F₄	F₅
X	Y	X	Y	X
		X	Y	Z
		X	Z	X
		X	Z	Z
		Y	Z	X
X	Y	X	Y	Y
		X	Z	Y
		Y	Z	Y
		Y	Z	Z
		Z	X	X

Fig. 3.20. Sample NT

Proposition 3.3. Let G be a group of an NT T, $C = cc(G)$, $X \subseteq C$, and $Y \subseteq C$. If GMD $X \text{-}(g) \mapsto Y$ holds in T, LMD $X \twoheadrightarrow Y$ also holds in T.

Proof. Let O be an arbitrary occurrence of G, and $Z = C - X - Y$. Then, by the definition of GMD, $O_{xz}[Y] = O_x[Y]$ for every pair of x and z such that $t[X] = x$ and $t[Z] = z$ for some $t \in O$. (Q.E.D.)

Proposition 3.4. Let G be the root of an NT T, $C = cc(G)$, $X \subseteq C$, and $Y \subseteq C$. Iff LMD $X \twoheadrightarrow Y$ holds in T, GMD $X \text{-}(g) \mapsto Y$ holds in T.

Proof.
[→] Self-evident, since the root has only one occurrence.
[←] By Proposition 3.3. (Q.E.D.)

Regarding the relationships between LFD and LMD and between GFD and GMD, the following propositions hold:

Proposition 3.5. Let G be a group of an NT T, $C = cc(G)$, $X \subseteq C$, and $Y \subseteq C$. If LFD $X \to Y$ holds in T, LMD $X \twoheadrightarrow Y$ also holds in T.

Proof. Let O be an arbitrary occurrence of G, and $Z = C - X - Y$. Then, $O_{xz}[Y] = O_x[Y]$ for every pair of x and z such that $t[X] = x$ and $t[Z] = z$ for some $t \in O$, since $O_{xz}[Y] = O_x[Y] = \{t[Y]\}$ by the definition of LFD. (Q.E.D.)

Proposition 3.6. Let G be a group of an NT T, $C = cc(G)$, $X \subseteq C$, and $Y \subseteq C$. If GFD $X \text{-}(g) \to Y$ holds in T, GMD $X \text{-}(g) \mapsto Y$ also holds in T.

Proof. Let O and R be arbitrary occurrences of G, and $Z = C - X - Y$. Then, $O_{xz}[X] = R_x[Y]$ for every pair of x and z such that $t[X] = u[X] = x$ and $t[Z] = z$ for some $t \in O$ and $u \in R$, since $O_{xz}[Y] = \{t[Y]\}$, $R_x[Y] = \{u[Y]\}$, and $t[Y] = u[Y]$ by the definition of GFD. (Q.E.D.)

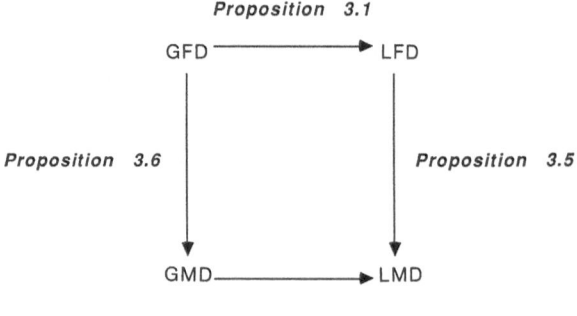

Fig. 3.21. Relationship among LFD, GFD, LMD, and GMD

The relationships among LFD, GFD, LMD, and GMD, as clarified in Propositions 3.1, 3.3, 3.5, and 3.6, are illustrated in Fig. 3.21.

3.5.2 Normalization

Several normal forms (NFs) were proposed based on dependencies in the relational data model. They were formulated in the context of design theories for identifying "well-behaving" relations. They include 1NF (an essential assumption in the relational data model), 2NF, 3NF, Boyce-Codd NF, and 4NF. Following the research approach in the relational data model, we can define *Normalized NT* as a special class of NTs using the dependencies introduced in Sect. 3.5.1. Although discussion on normalization is not the main topic in this chapter, the definition of Normalized NT will indicate another direction for the use of dependency concepts for NTs. As explained below, Normalized NT is defined as a counterpart of 4NF within the framework of NTD. The concept of Normalized NT will be used as a guideline for designing non-redundant NTs.

Definition 3.5. Let G be a group of an NT T, $C = cc(G)$, and $K \subseteq C$. K is a *key* of G in T, if LFD $K \to C$ holds in T and no component in K can be discarded without destroying this property.

Definition 3.6. Let G be a group of an NT T, $C = cc(G)$, $X \subseteq C$, and $Y \subseteq C$. G is a *normalized group* in T, if, whenever LMD $X \twoheadrightarrow Y$ holds in T, where $Y \neq \emptyset$, $Y \nsubseteq X$, and $XY \subset C$, X is a key or a superset of a key of G in T.

Definition 3.7. Given an NT T, T is a *Normalized NT* (*NNT*), when
a) every group is a normalized group, and
b) for every child group G of the root G_R and every key K of G,

F_1	F_2	G_1		
			G_2	
		F_3	F_4	F_5
X	Y	X	Y	Z
		Y	Z	X
		Z	X	Y
Y	Z	X	Z	Y
		Y	X	Z
		Z	Y	X

Fig. 3.22. Sample NNT

b-1) if there exists a key K_R of G_R such that $G \notin K_R$, then T' $= F[G]P[G_R \langle K_R G \rangle](T)$ is a Normalized NT and $K_R K'$ is a key of G_R in T' (K' is the set of components of T' inherited from K of T),

b-2) otherwise, K is equal to $cc(G)$.

Condition (a) in the above definition is a direct extension of the 4NF constraint to NT. Condition (b) is introduced to prune away redundant information repeated in occurrences of internal groups.

It is obvious from the above definition that if a GFD holds in an internal group, the NT is not an NNT. Figure 3.22 shows an example of an NNT. The NTs shown in Figs. 3.19 and 3.20 are not NNTs. In the NT in Fig. 3.19, G_1 is not a normalized group, while G_2 is a normalized group with key F_3. GFD $F_3 \text{–}(g) \rightarrow F_4$ also holds in it. In the NT in Fig. 3.20, G_1 is not a normalized group, and neither is G_2, since, for example, LMD $F_3 \twoheadrightarrow F_5$ holds while $F_3 \rightarrow F_5$ does not hold in it, as explained before.

As mentioned at the beginning of Sect. 3.5, Makinouchi presented a definition of normal form for unnormalized relations. His definition was essentially equivalent to the one formulated above. Design theory for NTs can be further constructed based on the concept of NNT defined. Some published research in this direction was mentioned in Chap. 2.

3.6 Operational Properties of NT Operations

One of the most important features of NTD is dynamic data manipulation by means of NT operations. In Sect. 3.4, primitive NT operations were defined as consisting of NF operations and XR operations. NF operations play an essential role in NTD to handle hierarchical data structures in NTs, while XR operations are defined so that they are extensions of primitive relational algebra operations.

In this section, operational properties of NTD are investigated from the viewpoint of data manipulation by NT operations. Basic properties of NF operations are first clarified in Sect. 3.6.1. Then, these properties are used as the basis for a study of the data manipulation capability of NT operations, presented in Sect. 3.6.2.

3.6.1 Basic Properties

Reversibility and commutativity are important properties relating to data manipulation by NF operations. The initial study on these properties [70] is developed here. The reversibility is considered first, and then commutativity is studied.

The NEST operation is defined to create a new group, whereas the FLAT operation is defined to destroy a group. At first glance, they seem to be inverse operations. However, this is not always the case. We can derive the following propositions regarding such reversibility:

Proposition 3.7. Let G_i be a group of an NT T, $C_i = cc(G_i)$, $C_j \subseteq C_i$, $C_j \neq \emptyset$, $G_j \langle C_j \rangle$ be a new group schema, and $T' = N[G_i, G_j \langle C_j \rangle](T)$. Then, $T = F[G_j](T')$.

Proof. Let $T = (NN, NS, NO)$, $T' = (NN, NS', NO')$ and $T'' = F[G_j](T) = (NN, NS'', NO'')$.[9] Then, by the definitions of the NEST and FLAT operations,

$$NS' = (NS - \{G_i \langle C_i \rangle\}) \cup \{G_i \langle (C_i - C_j) G_j \rangle, G_j \langle C_j \rangle\}$$
$$NS'' = (NS' - \{G_j \langle C_j \rangle, G_i \langle (C_i - C_j) G_j \rangle\}) \cup \{G_i \langle C_i \rangle\}.$$

By substitution, we obtain

$$NS'' = NS.$$

Regarding NT occurrence, by definition,

$$NO' = REP(NO, O, G_i, O')$$
$$O' = \{(t[C_i - C_j], FN(t)) \mid t \in O\}$$
$$FN(t) = \{u[C_j] \mid u \in O \land u[C_i - C_j] = t[C_i - C_j]\}$$
$$NO'' = REP(NO', O', G_i, O'')$$
$$O'' = \{(v[C_i - C_j], w) \mid v \in O' \land w \in v[G_j]\}.$$

Therefore,

$$O'' = \{(t[C_i - C_j], w) \mid t \in O \land w \in FN(t)\}$$
$$= \{(t[C_i - C_j], u[C_j]) \mid t \in O \land u \in O \land u[C_i - C_j] = t[C_i - C_j]\}$$
$$= \{(u[C_i - C_j], u[C_j]) \mid u \in O\}$$
$$= \{u \mid u \in O\}$$
$$= O.$$

Therefore,

$$NO'' = NO. \qquad\qquad\qquad\qquad\qquad \text{(Q.E.D.)}$$

---

[9] As mentioned in Sect. 3.4, the NT name is assumed to be invariant under the application of NT operations.

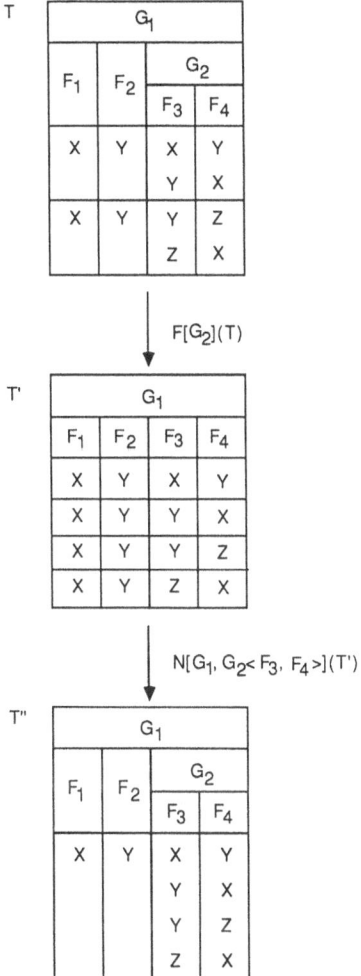

Fig. 3.23. Irreversible FLAT operation

This proposition assures that the NEST operation is always reversible by the FLAT operation. However, the inverse does not always hold. Namely, some transformations by the FLAT operation are not reversible by the NEST operation. A very simple case is illustrated in Fig. 3.23. The FLAT operation $F[G_2]$ is applied to T to give T', and then the NEST operation $N[G_1, G_2\langle F_3, F_4\rangle]$ is applied to T'. T'' is the result and its NT occurrence is different from that of T.

Before showing the condition assuring reversibility of the FLAT operation, we clarify the LFDs automatically generated by the NEST operation.

Proposition 3.8. Let G_i be a group of an NT T, $C_i = cc(G_i)$, $C_j \subseteq C_i$, $C_j \neq \emptyset$, $G_j\langle C_j\rangle$ be a new group schema, and $T' = N[G_i, G_j\langle C_j\rangle](T)$. Then, LFD $C_i - C_j \rightarrow G_j$ holds in T'.

Proof. By the definition of the NEST operation, every occurrence O' of G_i in T' can be specified as

$$O' = \{(t[C_i - C_j], FN(t)) \mid t \in O\}$$

$$FN(t) = \{u[C_j] \mid u \in O \wedge u[C_i - C_j] = t[C_i - C_j]\}$$

for some occurrence O of G_i in T. Therefore, if $v[C_i - C_j] = w[C_i - C_j]$ for some G_i clusters v and w in O',

$$v[G_j] = \{u[C_j] \mid u \in O \wedge u[C_i - C_j] = v[C_i - C_j]\}$$
$$= \{u[C_j] \mid u \in O \wedge u[C_i - C_j] = w[C_i - C_j]\}$$
$$= w[G_j]. \tag{Q.E.D.}$$

The following proposition gives a necessary and sufficient condition which assures reversibility of transformation by the FLAT operation:

Proposition 3.9. Let G_i be a group of an NT T, G_j be the parent of G_i, $C_i = cc(G_i)$, $C_j = cc(G_j)$, and $T' = F[G_i](T)$. Iff LFD $C_j - G_i \rightarrow G_i$ holds in T, $T = N[G_j, G_i \langle C_i \rangle](T')$.

Proof.
[$\rightarrow$] Let $T = (NN, NS, NO)$, $T' = (NN, NS', NO')$, and $T'' = N[G_j, G_i \langle C_i \rangle]$ $(T') = (NN, NS'', NO'')$. Then, by definition

$$NS' = (NS - \{G_i \langle C_i \rangle, G_j \langle C_j \rangle\}) \cup \{G_j \langle (C_j - G_i)C_i \rangle\}$$
$$NS'' = (NS' - \{G_j \langle (C_j - G_i)C_i \rangle\}) \cup \{G_j \langle C_j \rangle, G_i \langle C_i \rangle\}.$$

By substitution,

$$NS'' = NS.$$

Regarding NT occurrence, by definition,

$$NO' = REP(NO, O, G_j, O')$$
$$O' = \{(t[C_j - G_i], u) \mid t \in O \wedge u \in t[G_i]\}$$
$$NO'' = REP(NO', O', G_j, O'')$$
$$O'' = \{(v[C_j - G_i], FN(v)) \mid v \in O'\}$$
$$FN(v) = \{w[C_i] \mid w \in O' \wedge w[C_j - G_i] = v[C_j - G_i]\}.$$

Therefore,

$$O'' = \{(t[C_j - G_i], FN((t[C_j - G_i], u))) \mid t \in O \wedge u \in t[G_i]\},$$

and

$$FN((t[C_j - G_i], u))$$
$$= \{w[C_i] \mid w \in O' \wedge w[C_j - G_i] = t[C_j - G_i]\}$$
$$= \{r \mid s \in O \wedge r \in s[G_i] \wedge s[C_j - G_i] = t[C_j - G_i]\}.$$

If LFD $C_j - G_i \rightarrow G_i$ holds in T,

$$O'' = O,$$

since $s[C_j - G_t] = t[C_j - G_t]$ implies $s[G_t] = t[G_t]$ and

$$FN((t[C_j - G_t], u)) = \{r \mid r \in t[G_t]\} = t[G_t].$$

Thus, we obtain

$$NO'' = NO.$$

[$\leftarrow$] Assume LFD $C_j - G_t \rightarrow G_t$ does not hold in T,

$$T'' \neq T,$$

since LFD $C_j - G_t \rightarrow G_t$ holds in T'' (by Proposition 3.8). Since we have proved the contraposition, $T'' = T$ implies LFD $C_j - G_i \rightarrow G_t$ in T.   (Q.E.D.)

Note that in the example shown in Fig. 3.23, $F_1 F_2 \rightarrow G_2$ does not hold in T, since two root clusters have the same F_1 and F_2 values.

Definition 3.8. Let G_i be a group of an NT T, G_j be the parent of G_i, $C_i = cc(G_i)$, and $C_j = cc(G_j)$. If LFD $C_j - G_i \rightarrow G_t$ holds in T, $F[G_i]$ is said to be a *reversible* FLAT operation for T.

Proposition 3.10. Let G_i and G_j be distinct groups other than the root in an NT T. Then, $F[G_j]F[G_i](T) = F[G_i]F[G_j](T)$.

Proof. Suppose

$$T = (NN, NS, NO)$$

$$T^{(1)} = F[G_t](T), \quad T^{(2)} = F[G_j]F[G_t](T)$$

$$T^{(3)} = F[G_j](T), \quad T^{(4)} = F[G_i]F[G_j](T)$$

$$T^{(\alpha)} = (NN, NS^{(\alpha)}, NO^{(\alpha)}) \; (1 \leq \alpha \leq 4).$$

Let G_k and G_m be the parents of G_t and G_j in T, respectively; $G_j^{(1)} = G_j$; $G_m^{(1)}$ be the parent of $G_j^{(1)} (= G_j)$ in $T^{(1)}$; $G_i^{(3)} = G_i$; $G_k^{(3)}$ be the parent of $G_i^{(3)} (= G_i)$ in $T^{(3)}$; C_β be $cc(G_\beta)$ in T; and $C_\beta^{(\alpha)}$ be $cc(G_\beta^{(\alpha)})$ in $T^{(\alpha)}$. Symbols O_β and $O_\beta^{(\alpha)}$ stand for occurrences of G_β in T and $T^{(\alpha)}$, respectively. In the following, we can assume that G_k is not a descendant of G_m without losing generality, since we consider the equivalent case that G_m is a descendant of G_k.

Proof of $NS^{(2)} = NS^{(4)}$. By definition,

$$NS^{(2)} = (NS^{(1)} - \{G_j \langle C_j^{(1)} \rangle, G_m^{(1)} \langle C_m^{(1)} \rangle\}) \cup \{G_m^{(1)} \langle (C_m^{(1)} - G_j)C_j^{(1)} \rangle\}$$

$$= (((NS - \{G_t \langle C_i \rangle, G_k \langle C_k \rangle\}) \cup \{G_k \langle (C_k - G_t)C_t \rangle\})$$

$$- \{G_j \langle C_j^{(1)} \rangle, G_m^{(1)} \langle C_m^{(1)} \rangle\}) \cup \{G_m^{(1)} \langle (C_m^{(1)} - G_j)C_j^{(1)} \rangle\}.$$

Similarly,

$$NS^{(4)} = (((NS - \{G_j \langle C_j \rangle, G_m \langle C_m \rangle\}) \cup \{G_m \langle (C_m - G_j)C_j \rangle\})$$

$$- \{G_i \langle C_i^{(3)} \rangle, G_k^{(3)} \langle C_k^{(3)} \rangle\}) \cup \{G_k^{(3)} \langle (C_k^{(3)} - G_i)C_i^{(3)} \rangle\}.$$

(Case 1) $G_m = G_k$

In this case, $C_m = C_k$, $C_j^{(1)} = C_j$, $G_m^{(1)} = G_k$, $C_m^{(1)} = (C_k - G_i)C_i$, $C_i^{(3)} = C_i$, $G_k^{(3)}$
$= G_k$, and $C_k^{(3)} = (C_k - G_j)C_j$. Therefore,

$$NS^{(2)} = (NS - \{G_i\langle C_i\rangle, G_j\langle C_j\rangle, G_k\langle C_k\rangle\}) \cup \{G_k\langle (C_k - G_i - G_j)C_iC_j\rangle\}$$

$$= NS^{(4)}.$$

(Case 2) $G_m = G_i$

In this case, $C_m = C_i$, $C_j^{(1)} = C_j$, $G_m^{(1)} = G_k$, $C_m^{(1)} = (C_k - G_i)C_i$, $C_i^{(3)} = (C_i$
$- G_j)C_j$, $G_k^{(3)} = G_k$, and $C_k^{(3)} = C_k$. Therefore,

$$NS^{(2)} = (NS - \{G_i\langle C_i\rangle, G_j\langle C_j\rangle, G_k\langle C_k\rangle\}) \cup \{G_k\langle (C_k - G_i)(C_i - G_j)C_j\rangle\}$$

$$= NS^{(4)}.$$

(Case 3) Otherwise

Since $C_j^{(1)} = C_j$, $G_m^{(1)} = G_m$, $C_m^{(1)} = C_m$, $C_i^{(3)} = C_i$, $G_k^{(3)} = G_k$, and $C_k^{(3)} = C_k$,

$$NS^{(2)} = (NS - \{G_i\langle C_i\rangle, G_k\langle C_k\rangle, G_j\langle C_j\rangle, G_m\langle C_m\rangle\})$$

$$\cup \{G_k\langle (C_k - G_i)C_i\rangle, G_m\langle (C_m - G_j)C_j\rangle\}$$

$$= NS^{(4)}.$$

Therefore, we have shown

$$NS^{(2)} = NS^{(4)}.$$

Proof of $NO^{(2)} = NO^{(4)}$. Next, we prove

$$NO^{(2)} = NO^{(4)}.$$

(Case 1) $G_m = G_k$ or $G_m = G_i$

By definition, $NO^{(\alpha)}$ is formulated as

$$NO^{(\alpha)} = REP(NO, O_\beta, G_\beta, O_\beta^{(\alpha)}) \qquad ((\alpha, \beta) = (1, k), (3, m)),$$

where

$$O_k^{(1)} = \{(t[C_k - G_i], u) \mid t \in O_k \wedge u \in t[G_i]\}$$

$$O_m^{(3)} = \{(t[C_m - G_j], u) \mid t \in O_m \wedge u \in t[G_j]\}.$$

In this case, $G_m^{(1)} = G_k$, $G_k^{(3)} = G_k$, and

$$NO^{(\alpha)} = REP(NO^{(\alpha-1)}, O_k^{(\alpha-1)}, G_k, O_k^{(\alpha)}) \qquad (\alpha = 2, 4),$$

where

$$O_k^{(2)} = \{(v[(C_k - G_i)C_i - G_j], w) \mid v \in O_k^{(1)} \wedge w \in v[G_j]\}$$

$$O_k^{(4)} = \{(v[C_k^{(3)} - G_i], w) \mid v \in O_k^{(3)} \wedge w \in v[G_i]\}.$$

(Subcase 1) $G_m = G_k$

By substitution, we obtain

$$O_k^{(2)} = \{(v[(C_k - G_i)C_i - G_j], w) \mid v \in O_k^{(1)} \wedge w \in v[G_j]\}$$
$$= \{(t[C_k - G_i - G_j], u, w) \mid t \in O_k \wedge u \in t[G_i] \wedge w \in t[G_j]\}.$$

Similarly, we obtain

$$O_k^{(4)} = \{(t[C_k - G_i - G_j], w, u) \mid t \in O_k \wedge w \in t[G_i] \wedge u \in t[G_j]\}.$$

Thus, we can conclude $NO^{(2)} = NO^{(4)}$.

(*Subcase* 2) $G_m = G_i$

In this case,

$$O_k^{(2)} = \{(v[(C_k - G_i)C_i - G_j], w) \mid v \in O_k^{(1)} \wedge w \in v[G_j]\}$$
$$= \{(t[C_k - G_i], u[C_i - G_j], w) \mid t \in O_k \wedge u \in t[G_i] \wedge w \in u[G_j]\}$$
$$O_k^{(3)} = \{(t[C_k - G_i], O_i^{(3)}(t)) \mid t \in O_k\},$$

where

$$O_i^{(3)}(t) = \{(u[C_i - G_j], w) \mid u \in t[G_i] \wedge w \in u[G_j]\}.$$

Therefore, by substitution, we finally obtain

$$O_k^{(4)} = \{(t[C_k - G_i], u[C_i - G_j], w) \mid t \in O_k \wedge u \in t[G_i] \wedge w \in u[G_j]\}.$$

Thus, we can conclude $NO^{(2)} = NO^{(4)}$.

(*Case* 2) Otherwise

In general, the FLAT operation is a mapping MAP_G from NTs to NTs such that $MAP_G(T)$ is obtained by applying some function $FUN_G: dom(G) \rightarrow R$ (R is a new domain of G) to every occurrence O of group G and replacing it with $FUN_G(O)$. For the FLAT operation $F[G_j]$, group G is the parent G_m of G_j. In Case 2, which we are currently considering, G_m is neither G_i nor the parent G_k of G_i. We show here that the NT occurrences of $MAP_{G_m}(F[G_i](T))$ and $F[G_i](MAP_{G_m}(T))$ coincide in this case. By definition,

$$NO^{(1)} = REP(NO, O_k, G_k, O_k^{(1)})$$
$$O_k^{(1)} = \{(t[C_k - G_i], u) \mid t \in O_k \wedge u \in t[G_i]\},$$

where $F[G_i](T) = T^{(1)} = (NN, NS^{(1)}, NO^{(1)})$.

(*Subcase* 1) $G_m \in cg(G_i)$

$$MAP_{G_m}(O_k^{(1)}) = \{(t[C_k - G_i], MAP_{G_m}(u)) \mid t \in O_k \wedge u \in t[G_i]\}^{10}$$
$$= \{(t[C_k - G_i], u) \mid t \in O_k \wedge u \in MAP_{G_m}(t[G_i])\}$$
$$= \{(t[G_k - G_i], u) \mid t \in MAP_{G_m}(O_k) \wedge u \in t[G_i]\}$$

---

[10] $MAP_{G_m}(O_k^{(1)})$ means the result of applying the mapping procedure to $O_k^{(1)}$. This notation is used for occurrences and clusters.

Therefore,

$$MAP_{G_m}(NO^{(1)}) = REP(MAP_{G_m}(NO), O_k, G_k, O_k^{(1)}).$$

(*Subcase* 2) $G_m \in cg(G_k)$, $G_m \neq G_i$

$$MAP_{G_m}(O_k^{(1)}) = \{(MAP_{G_m}(t[C_k - G_i]), u) \mid t \in O_k \wedge u \in t[G_i]\}$$
$$= \{(t[C_k - G_i], u) \mid t \in MAP_{G_m}(O_k) \wedge u \in t[G_i]\}$$

Therefore,

$$MAP_{G_m}(NO^{(1)}) = REP(MAP_{G_m}(NO), O_k, G_k, O_k^{(1)}).$$

(*Subcase* 3) $G_m \in cg(G_p)$, $G_k \in dg(G_p)$ for some G_p

Obviously, MAP_{G_m} and $F[G_i]$ can be applied independently without interacting with one another. Therefore,

$$MAP_{G_m}(NO^{(1)}) = REP(MAP_{G_m}(NO), O_k, G_k, O_k^{(1)}).$$

(*Subcase* 4) Otherwise

Mapping MAP_{G_q} equivalent to MAP_{G_m} can always be defined for some group G_q meeting the condition for one of the above three subcases. Therefore,

$$MAP_{G_m}(NO^{(1)}) = REP(MAP_{G_m}(NO), O_k, G_k, O_k^{(1)}).$$

Since $F[G_j]$ is a special case of the above-mentioned mapping MAP_{G_m}, we have proved $NO^{(2)} = NO^{(4)}$ for Case 2.   (Q.E.D.)

This proposition assures that successive applications of FLAT operations are always commutative. On the contrary, the NEST operation does not have this property, as exemplified in Fig. 3.24. Although the resultant NTs have the same NT schema, their NT occurrences are different.

Proposition 3.11. Let G_k and G_m be groups of an NT T, $X_i \subseteq cc(G_k)$, $X_j \subseteq cc(G_m)$, $X_i \neq \emptyset$, and $X_j \neq \emptyset$. Then, $N[G_m^{(1)}, G_j\langle X_j^{(1)}\rangle]N[G_k, G_i\langle X_i\rangle](T)$ and $N[G_k^{(3)}, G_i\langle X_i^{(3)}\rangle]N[G_m, G_j\langle X_j\rangle](T)$, where

$$(G_m^{(1)}, X_j^{(1)}, G_k^{(3)}, X_i^{(3)})$$

$$= \begin{cases} (G_i, X_j, G_k, (X_i - X_j)G_j) & (G_k = G_m \text{ and } X_j \subseteq X_i) \\ (G_k, (X_j - X_i)G_i, G_j, X_i) & (G_k = G_m \text{ and } X_i \subseteq X_j) \\ (G_m, X_j, G_k, X_i) & (\text{otherwise}), \end{cases}$$

have an identical NT schema. However, their NT occurrences are not always identical.

Proof. Suppose

$$T = (NN, NS, NO)$$

$$T^{(1)} = N[G_k, G_i\langle X_i\rangle](T)$$

$$T^{(2)} = N[G_m^{(1)}, G_j\langle X_j^{(1)}\rangle]N[G_k, G_i\langle X_i\rangle](T)$$

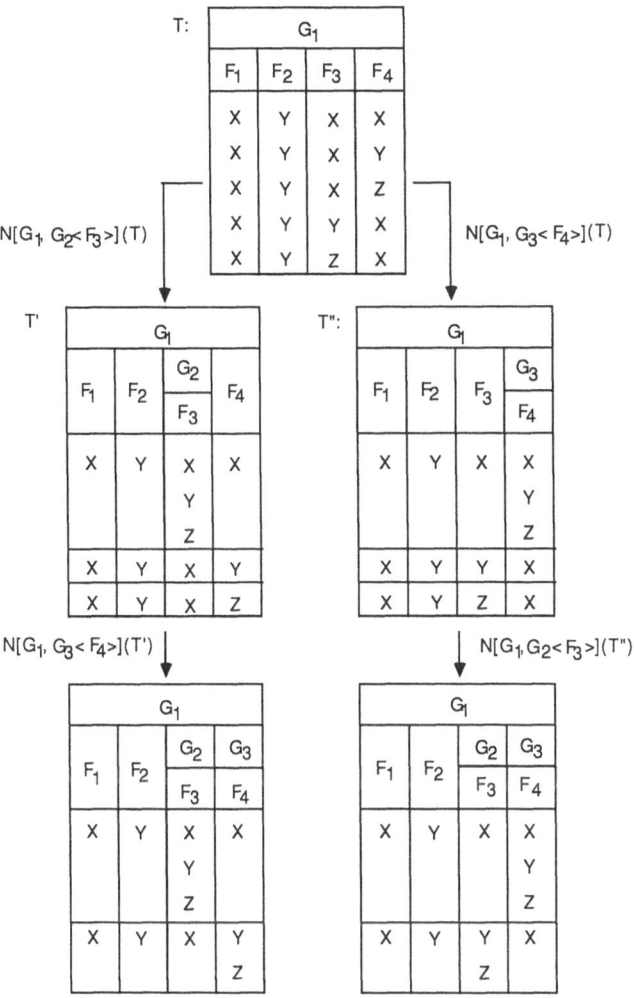

Fig. 3.24. Incommutable NEST operations

$$T^{(3)} = N[G_m, G_j\langle X_j\rangle](T)$$

$$T^{(4)} = N[G_k^{(3)}, G_i\langle X_i^{(3)}\rangle]N[G_m, G_j\langle X_j\rangle](T)$$

$$T^{(\alpha)} = (NN, NS^{(\alpha)}, NO^{(\alpha)}) \qquad (1 \le \alpha \le 4).$$

Let C_β be $cc(G_\beta)$ in T and $C_\beta^{(\alpha)}$ be $cc(G_\beta^{(\alpha)})$ in $T^{(\alpha)}$. By definition,

$$NS^{(2)} = (NS^{(1)} - G_m^{(1)}\langle C_m^{(1)}\rangle) \cup \{G_m^{(1)}\langle(C_m^{(1)} - X_j^{(1)})G_j\rangle, G_j\langle X_j^{(1)}\rangle\}$$

$$= (((NS - G_k\langle C_k\rangle) \cup \{G_k\langle(C_k - X_i)G_i\rangle, G_i\langle X_i\rangle\}) - G_m^{(1)}\langle C_m^{(1)}\rangle)$$

$$\cup \{G_m^{(1)}\langle(C_m^{(1)} - X_j^{(1)})G_j\rangle, G_j\langle X_j^{(1)}\rangle\}.$$

Similarly,

$$NS^{(4)} = (((NS - G_m\langle C_m\rangle) \cup \{G_m\langle(C_m - X_j)G_j\rangle, G_j\langle X_j\rangle\}) - G_k^{(3)}\langle C_k^{(3)}\rangle)$$
$$\cup \{G_k^{(3)}\langle(C_k^{(3)} - X_i^{(3)})G_i\rangle, G_i\langle X_i^{(3)}\rangle\}.$$

(*Case* 1) $G_k = G_m$ and $X_j \subseteq X_i$

In this case, $C_m = C_k$, $G_m^{(1)} = G_i$, $X_j^{(1)} = X_j$, $C_m^{(1)} = X_i$, $G_k^{(3)} = G_k$, $X_i^{(3)} = (X_i - X_j)G_j$, and $C_k^{(3)} = (C_k - X_j)G_j$. Therefore,

$$NS^{(2)} = (NS - G_k\langle C_k\rangle) \cup \{G_k\langle(C_k - X_i)G_i\rangle, G_i\langle(X_i - X_j)G_j\rangle, G_j\langle X_j\rangle\}$$

$$= NS^{(4)}.$$

(*Case* 2) $G_k = G_m$ and $X_i \subseteq X_j$

In this case, $C_m = C_k$, $G_m^{(1)} = G_k$, $X_j^{(1)} = (X_j - X_i)G_i$, $C_m^{(1)} = (C_k - X_i)G_i$, $G_k^{(3)} = G_j$, $X_i^{(3)} = X_i$, and $C_k^{(3)} = X_j$. Therefore,

$$NS^{(2)} = (NS - G_k\langle C_k\rangle) \cup \{G_k\langle(C_k - X_j)G_j\rangle, G_j\langle(X_j - X_i)G_i\rangle, G_i\langle X_i\rangle\}$$

$$= NS^{(4)}.$$

(*Case* 3) $G_k = G_m$ and $X_i \cap X_j = \emptyset$

In this case, $C_m = C_k$, $G_m^{(1)} = G_k$, $X_j^{(1)} = X_j$, $C_m^{(1)} = (C_k - X_i)G_i$, $G_k^{(3)} = G_k$, $X_i^{(3)} = X_i$, and $C_k^{(3)} = (C_k - X_j)G_j$. Therefore,

$$NS^{(2)} = (NS - G_k\langle C_k\rangle) \cup \{G_k\langle(C_k - X_i - X_j)G_iG_j\rangle, G_i\langle X_i\rangle, G_j\langle X_j\rangle\}$$

$$= NS^{(4)}.$$

(*Case* 4) Otherwise

Since $G_m^{(1)} = G_m$, $X_j^{(1)} = X_j$, $G_k^{(3)} = G_k$, and $X_i^{(3)} = X_i$,

$$NS^{(2)} = (NS - G_k\langle C_k\rangle - G_m\langle C_m\rangle) \cup$$

$$\{G_k\langle(C_k - X_i)G_i\rangle, G_i\langle X_i\rangle, G_m\langle(C_m - X_j)G_j\rangle, G_j\langle X_j\rangle\}$$

$$= NS^{(4)}.$$

Therefore, we have shown

$$NS^{(2)} = NS^{(4)}.$$

$\dot{N}O^{(2)} = NO^{(4)}$ does not always hold, as exemplified in Fig. 3.24.   (Q.E.D.)

The following proposition gives a sufficient condition for the commutativity of NEST operations:

Proposition 3.12. Let $G_k, G_m, X_i, X_j, G_i, G_j, G_m^{(1)}, X_j^{(1)}, G_k^{(3)}, X_i^{(3)}$ be the same as Proposition 3.11. Then, $N[G_m^{(1)}, G_j\langle X_j^{(1)}\rangle]N[G_k, G_i\langle X_i\rangle](T) = N[G_k^{(3)}, G_i\langle X_i^{(3)}\rangle]N[G_m, G_j\langle X_j\rangle](T)$, if
a) $G_k = G_m$, $X_i \cap X_j = \emptyset$, and $cc[G_k] - X_i - X_j \twoheadrightarrow X_i$ holds in T,
b) $G_k = G_m$ and $X_i \subseteq X_j$,
c) $G_k = G_m$ and $X_j \subseteq X_i$, or
d) $G_k \neq G_m$.

Proof. Suppose

$$T=(NN,\ NS,\ NO)$$

$$T^{(1)}=N[G_k,\ G_i\langle X_i\rangle](T)$$

$$T^{(2)}=N[G_m^{(1)},\ G_j\langle X_j^{(1)}\rangle]N[G_k,\ G_i\langle X_i\rangle](T)$$

$$T^{(3)}=N[G_m,\ G_j\langle X_j\rangle](T)$$

$$T^{(4)}=N[G_k^{(3)},\ G_i\langle X_i^{(3)}\rangle]N[G_m,\ G_j\langle X_j\rangle](T)$$

$$T^{(\alpha)}=(NN,\ NS^{(\alpha)},\ NO^{(\alpha)})\quad(1\leq\alpha\leq4).$$

Let C_β be $cc(G_\beta)$ in T. Symbols O_β and $O_\beta^{(\alpha)}$ stand for occurrences of G_β in T and $T^{(\alpha)}$, respectively.

(*Case* 1) $G_k=G_m$

By definition, $NO^{(\alpha)}$ ($\alpha=1,\ 3$) is formulated as

$$NO^{(\alpha)}=REP(NO,\ O_k,\ G_k,\ O_k^{(\alpha)})\quad(\alpha=1,\ 3),$$

where

$$O_k^{(1)}=\{(t[C_k-X_i],\ O_i^{(1)}(t))\,|\,t\in O_k\}$$

$$O_i^{(1)}(t)=\{u[X_i]\,|\,u\in O_k\wedge t[C_k-X_i]=u[C_k-X_i]\}$$

$$O_k^{(3)}=\{(t[C_k-X_j],\ O_j^{(3)}(t))\,|\,t\in O_k\}$$

$$O_j^{(3)}(t)=\{u[X_j]\,|\,u\in O_k\wedge t[C_k-X_j]=u[C_k-X_j]\}.$$

(*Subcase* 1) $X_i\cap X_j=\varnothing$ and $cc[G_k]-X_i-X_j\twoheadrightarrow X_i$ holds in T

In this case, $G_m^{(1)}=G_k$, $X_j^{(1)}=X_j$, $G_k^{(3)}=G_k$, $X_i^{(3)}=X_i$, and

$$NO^{(\alpha)}=REP(NO^{(\alpha-1)},\ O_k^{(\alpha-1)},\ G_k,\ O_k^{(\alpha)})\quad(\alpha=2,\ 4),$$

where

$$O_k^{(2)}=\{(t[(C_k-X_i)G_i-X_j],\ O_j^{(2)}(t))\,|\,t\in O_k^{(1)}\}$$

$$O_j^{(2)}(t)=\{u[X_j]\,|\,u\in O_k^{(1)}\wedge t[(C_k-X_i)G_i-X_j]=u[(C_k-X_i)G_i-X_j]\}$$

$$O_k^{(4)}=\{(t[(C_k-X_j)G_j-X_i],\ O_i^{(4)}(t))\,|\,t\in O_k^{(3)}\}$$

$$O_i^{(4)}(t)=\{u[X_i]\,|\,u\in O_k^{(3)}\wedge t[(C_k-X_j)G_j-X_i]=u[(C_k-X_j)G_j-X_i]\}.$$

By substitution,

$$O_k^{(2)}=\{(t[C_k-X_i-X_j],\ O_i^{(1)}(t),\ O_j^{(2)}((t[C_k-X_i],\ O_i^{(1)}(t))))\,|\,t\in O_k\}$$

$$O_k^{(4)}=\{(t[C_k-X_i-X_j],\ O_i^{(4)}((t[C_k-X_j],\ O_j^{(3)}(t))),\ O_j^{(3)}(t))\,|\,t\in O_k\}.$$

Here,

$$O_j^{(2)}((t[C_k-X_i],\ O_i^{(1)}(t)))$$

$$=\{u[X_j]\,|\,u\in O_k^{(1)}\wedge t[C_k-X_i-X_j]=u[C_k-X_i-X_j]\wedge O_i^{(1)}(t)=u[G_i]\}$$

$$=\{v[X_j]\,|\,v\in O_k\wedge t[C_k-X_i-X_j]=v[C_k-X_i-X_j]\wedge O_i^{(1)}(t)=O_i^{(1)}(v)\}.$$

Since $C_k - X_j - X_j \twoheadrightarrow X_i$ holds in T, $O_i^{(1)}(t) = O_i^{(1)}(v)$ is implied by $t[C_k - X_i - X_j] = v[C_k - X_i - X_j]$. Thus,

$$O_j^{(2)}((t[C_k - X_i], O_i^{(1)}(t))) = \{v[X_j] \mid v \in O_k \wedge t[C_k - X_i - X_j] = v[C_k - X_i - X_j]\}.$$

When $C_k - X_i - X_j \twoheadrightarrow X_i$ holds in T, $C_k - X_i - X_j \twoheadrightarrow X_j$ also holds in T. This is easily derived from the definition of local multivalued dependency by analogy with multivalued dependency in the relational data model [38]. Thus,

$$O_j^{(3)}(t) = \{u[X_j] \mid u \in O_k \wedge t[C_k - X_j] = u[C_k - X_j]\}$$
$$= \{u[X_j] \mid u \in O_k \wedge t[C_k - X_i - X_j] = u[C_k - X_i - X_j]\}.$$

Therefore,

$$O_j^{(2)}((t[C_k - X_i], O_i^{(1)}(t))) = O_j^{(3)}(t).$$

Similarly, we can derive

$$O_i^{(4)}((t[C_k - X_i], O_j^{(3)}(t))) = O_i^{(1)}(t).$$

Therefore,

$$O_k^{(2)} = O_k^{(4)}.$$

Thus, we can conclude

$$NO^{(2)} = NO^{(4)}.$$

(*Subcase* 2) $X_i \subseteq X_j$

In this case, $G_m^{(1)} = G_k$, $X_j^{(1)} = (X_j - X_i)G_i$, $G_k^{(3)} = G_j$, $X_i^{(3)} = X_i$, and

$$NO^{(2)} = REP(NO^{(1)}, O_k^{(1)}, G_k, O_k^{(2)})$$
$$NO^{(4)} = REP(NO^{(3)}, O_j^{(3)}, G_j, O_j^{(4)}),$$

where

$$O_k^{(2)} = \{(t[C_k - X_j], O_j^{(2)}(t)) \mid t \in O_k^{(1)}\}$$
$$O_j^{(2)}(t) = \{u[(X_j - X_i)G_i] \mid u \in O_k^{(1)} \wedge t[C_k - X_j] = u[C_k - X_j]\}$$
$$O_j^{(4)} = \{(t[X_j - X_i], O_i^{(4)}(t)) \mid t \in O_j^{(3)}]$$
$$O_i^{(4)}(t) = \{u[X_i] \mid u \in O_j^{(3)} \wedge t[X_j - X_i] = u[X_j - X_i]\}.$$

By substitution,

$$O_k^{(2)} = \{(t[C_k - X_j], O_j^{(2)}((t[C_k - X_i], O_i^{(1)}(t)))) \mid t \in O_k\}$$
$$O_j^{(2)}((t[C_k - X_i], O_i^{(1)}(t)))$$
$$= \{u[(X_j - X_i)G_i] \mid u \in O_k^{(1)} \wedge t[C_k - X_j] = u[C_k - X_j]\}$$
$$= \{(v[X_j - X_i], O_i^{(1)}(v)) \mid v \in O_k \wedge t[C_k - X_j] = v[C_k - X_j]\}$$
$$O_i^{(1)}(v) = \{u[X_i] \mid u \in O_k \wedge v[C_k - X_i] = u[C_k - X_i]\}.$$

By the way,

$$O_k^{(4)} = \{(t[C_k - X_j], O_j^{(4)}(t)) \mid t \in O_k\},$$

where

$$O_j^{(4)}(t) = \{(u[X_j - X_i], O_i^{(4)}(t, u)) | u \in O_j^{(3)}(t)\}$$
$$O_i^{(4)}(t, u) = \{v[X_i] | v \in O_j^{(3)}(t) \wedge u[X_j - X_i] = v[X_j - X_i]\}.$$

By substitution,

$$O_j^{(4)}(t) = \{(v[X_j - X_i], O_i^{(4)}(t, v)) | v \in O_k \wedge t[C_k - X_j] = v[C_k - X_j]\}$$
$$O_i^{(4)}(t, v) = \{w[X_i] | w \in O_k \wedge t[C_k - X_j] = w[C_k - X_j] \wedge v[X_j - X_i] = w[X_j - X_i]\}$$
$$= \{w[X_i] | w \in O_k \wedge v[C_k - X_i] = w[C_k - X_i]\}.$$

Therefore,

$$O_k^{(2)} = O_k^{(4)}.$$

Thus, we can conclude

$$NO^{(2)} = NO^{(4)}.$$

(*Subcase 3*) $X_i \supseteq X_j$

We can derive

$$NO^{(2)} = NO^{(4)}.$$

as in Subcase 2.

(*Case 2*) $G_k \neq G_m$

In general, the NEST operation is a mapping MAP_G from NTs to NTs such that $MAP_G(T)$ is obtained by applying some one-to-one function $FUN_G: dom(G) \rightarrow R$ (R is a new domain of G) to every occurrence O of group G and replacing it with $FUN_G(O)$. (The one-to-one property is implied by Proposition 3.7.) For the NEST operation $N[G_m, G_j\langle X_j\rangle]$, group G is G_m. In Case 2, which we are currently considering, G_m is not G_k. We show here that the NT occurrences of $MAP_{G_m}(N[G_k, G_i\langle X_i\rangle](T))$ and $N[G_k, G_i\langle X_i\rangle](MAP_{G_m}(T))$ coincide in this case. By definition,

$$NO^{(1)} = REP(NO, O_k, G_k, O_k^{(1)})$$
$$O_k^{(1)} = \{(t[C_k - X_i], O_i^{(1)}(t)) | t \in O_k\}$$
$$O_i^{(1)}(t) = \{u[X_i] | u \in O_k \wedge t[C_k - X_i] = u[C_k - X_i]\},$$

where $N[G_k, G_i\langle X_i\rangle](T) = T^{(1)} = (NN, NS^{(1)}, NO^{(1)})$. In the following discussion, we can assume that G_k is not a descendant of G_m without losing generality, since we consider the equivalent case that G_m is a descendant of G_k.

(*Subcase 1*) $G_m \in cg(G_k)$ and $G_m \in X_i$

$$MAP_{G_m}(O_k^{(1)}) = \{(t[C_k - X_i], MAP_{G_m}(O_i^{(1)}(t))) | t \in O_k\}^{11}$$

---

[11] $MAP_{G_m}(O_k^{(1)})$ means the result of applying the mapping procedure to $O_k^{(1)}$. This notation is used for occurrences and clusters.

$$MAP_{G_m}(O_i^{(1)}(t)) = \{MAP_{G_m}(u[X_i]) | u \in O_k \wedge t[C_k - X_i] = u[C_k - X_i]\}$$

$$= \{u[X_i] | u \in MAP_{G_m}(O_k) \wedge t[C_k - X_i] = u[C_k - X_i]\}$$

Thus,

$$MAP_{G_m}(O_k^{(1)}) = \{(t[C_k - X_i], M_i^{(1)}(t)) | t \in MAP_{G_m}(O_k)\}$$

$$M_i^{(1)} = \{u[X_i] | u \in MAP_{G_m}(O_k) \wedge t[C_k - X_i] = u[C_k - X_i]\}.$$

Therefore,

$$MAP_{G_m}(NO^{(1)}) = REP(MAP_{G_m}(NO), O_k, G_k, O_k^{(1)}).$$

(*Subcase* 2) $G_m \in cg(G_k)$ and $G_m \notin X_i$

$$MAP_{G_m}(O_k^{(1)}) = \{(MAP_{G_m}(t[C_k - X_i]), O_i^{(1)}(t)) | t \in O_k\}$$

$$O_i^{(1)}(t) = \{u[X_i] | u \in O_k \wedge t[C_k - X_i] = u[C_k - X_i]\}.$$

Since MAP_{G_m} is based on the one-to-one function FUN_{G_m},

$$O_i^{(1)}(t) = \{u[X_i] | u \in O_k \wedge MAP_{G_m}(t[C_k - X_i]) = MAP_{G_m}(u[C_k - X_i])\}$$

$$= \{u[X_i] | u \in MAP_{G_m}(O_k) \wedge MAP_{G_m}(t[C_k - X_i]) = u[C_k - X_i]\}.$$

Thus,

$$MAP_{G_m}(O_k^{(1)}) = \{(t[C_k - X_i], M_i^{(1)}(t)) | t \in MAP_{G_m}(O_k)\}$$

$$M_i^{(1)}(t) = \{u[X_i] | u \in MAP_{G_m}(O_k) \wedge t[C_k - X_i] = u[C_k - X_i]\}.$$

Therefore,

$$MAP_{G_m}(NO^{(1)}) = REP(MAP_{G_m}(NO), O_k, G_k, O_k^{(1)}).$$

(*Subcase* 3) $G_m \in cg(G_p)$, $G_k \in dg(G_p)$ for some G_p

Obviously, MAP_{G_m} and $N[G_k, G_i\langle X_i\rangle]$ can be applied independently without interacting with one another. Therefore,

$$MAP_{G_m}(NO^{(1)}) = REP(MAP_{G_m}(NO), O_k, G_k, O_k^{(1)}).$$

(*Subcase* 4) Otherwise

Mapping MAP_{G_q} equivalent to MAP_{G_m} can always be defined for some group G_q meeting the condition for one of the above three subcases. Therefore,

$$MAP_{G_m}(NO^{(1)}) = REP(MAP_{G_m}(NO), O_k, G_k, O_k^{(1)}).$$

Since $N[G_m, G_j\langle X_j\rangle]$ is a special case of the above-mentioned mapping MAP_{G_m}, we have proved $NO^{(2)} = NO^{(4)}$ for Case 2.   (Q.E.D.)

The above basic properties of the NEST and FLAT operations were discussed in [70]. Later some other researchers also investigated properties of NEST and FLAT. However, the context here is very general, since NEST and FLAT can be applied at any hierarchical levels in our definition. If we replace condition (a) of Proposition 3.12 with

(a') $G_k = G_m$, $X_i \cap X_j = \emptyset$, and $cc[G_k] - X_i - X_j - (w) \twoheadrightarrow X_i$ holds in T, where "$\xrightarrow{(w)}$" denotes *weak multivalued dependency* defined in [60], then Proposition 3.12 gives the necessary and sufficient condition for commutativity of the NEST operation. Here, we do not go into discussion of the weak multivalued dependency. It is studied in [42].

So far, we have considered sequences of two NEST operations or FLAT operations. We can also consider sequences of NEST or FLAT to derive a complicated NT from a flat NT and vice versa.

Definition 3.9. Given at NT T with groups $G_R, G_1, \ldots, G_n$ $(n \geq 0, G_R$ is the root), we define $F_{P_n}{}^* = F_{P_n(1)} \ldots F_{P_n(n)}$ as a *flattening* for T. Here, F_i $(1 \leq i \leq n)$ is the FLAT to destroy group G_i and P_n is a permutation of $(1, \ldots, n)$. $(F_{P_n}{}^*(T) = F_{P_n(1)} \ldots F_{P_n(n)} (T)$ means $F_{P_n(1)}(\ldots (F_{P_n(n)}(T)) \ldots).)$

From Proposition 3.10, we obtain the following corollary:

Corollary 3.1. Given an NT T,

$$FT = F_{P_n}{}^*(T)$$

is same for any flattening $F_{P_n}{}^*$ for T.

Similarly, we can define a sequence of NEST operations.

Definition 3.10. Given two NT schemas NS_1 and NS_2, if NS_1 and NS_2 are interchangeable with sequences of NEST and/or FLAT, they are said to be *NF-translatable*.

Definition 3.11. Given a flat NT FT and an NT schema NS which has groups G_R, $G_1, \ldots, G_n$ $(n \geq 0, G_R$ is the root) and is NF-translatable into the NT schema of FT, we define $N_{P_n}{}^* = N_{P_n(1)} \ldots N_{P_n(n)}$ as a *nesting* for FT. Here, N_i $(1 \leq i \leq n)$ is the NEST to construct group G_i and P_n is a permutation of $(1, \ldots, n)$. $(N_{P_n}{}^*(T) = N_{P_n(1)} \ldots N_{P_n(n)}(T)$ means $N_{P_n(1)}(\ldots (N_{P_n(n)}(T)) \ldots).)$

From Proposition 3.11, we obtain the following corollary:

Corollary 3.2. Given a flat NT FT and an NF-translatable NT schema NS,

$$N_{P_n}{}^*(FT) = N_{P'_n}{}^*(FT)$$

does not always hold for different nestings $N_{P_n}{}^*$ and $N_{P'_n}{}^*$.

From Propositions 3.7 and 3.9, we derive the following corollaries:

Corollary 3.3. Given a flat NT FT and a nesting $N_{P_n}{}^*$ for FT, let $T = N_{P_n}{}^*(FT)$. Then, $FT = F_{P_n{}^t}{}^*(T).$[12]

Corollary 3.4. Given an NT T and a flattening $F_{P_n}{}^*$ for T, let $FT = F_{P_n}{}^*(T)$. Then, $T = N_{P_n{}^t}{}^*(FT)$ does not always hold.

---

[12] $P_n{}^t$ means $(P_n(n), \ldots, P_n(1))$, where $P_n = (P_n(1), \ldots, P_n(n))$.

Now we define a class of NTs called *Canonical NTs* for which the property stated in Corollary 3.4 holds.

Definition 3.12. Given an NT T with groups $G_R, G_1, \ldots, G_n$ ($n \geq 0$, G_R is the root), T is a *Canonical NT (CNT)*, if $n=0$ or there exists at least one flattening for T $F_{P_n}{}^*$ $= F_{P_n(1)} \cdots F_{P_n(n)}$ such that every $F_{P_n(i)}$ is reversible for $F_{P_n(i+1)} \cdots F_{P_n(n)}(T)$ ($1 \leq i \leq n$). $F_{P_n}{}^*$ is called a *reversible flattening* for T.

Proposition 3.13. If T is a CNT,

$$T = N_{P_n}{}^*(FT)$$

for some nesting $N_{P_n}{}^* = N_{P_n(1)} \cdots N_{P_n(n)}$ and a uniquely determined flat NT FT. Conversely, if T is defined in the above expression for some nesting $N_{P_n}{}^*$ and flat NT FT, then T is a CNT.

Proof. In the case where $n=0$, the proposition is self-evident. We prove the proposition for $n \geq 1$.

First half. Assume T is a CNT with groups $G_R, G_1, \ldots, G_n$ ($n \geq 1$, G_R is the root). By definition, there exists some reversible flattening $F_{Q_n}{}^*$ for T. Let $N_{P_n}{}^*$ be $N_{Q_n}{}^*$ and FT be $F_{Q_n}{}^*(T)$. Then,

$$N_{P_n}{}^*(FT) = N_{Q_n}{}^*(F_{Q_n}{}^*(T)) = N_{Q_n(n)} \cdots N_{Q_n(1)} F_{Q_n(1)} \cdots F_{Q_n(n)}(T).$$

Since $F_{Q_n}{}^*$ is reversible flattening for T,

$$N_{Q_n(i)} F_{Q_n(i)} \cdots F_{Q_n(n)}(T) = F_{Q_n(i+1)} \cdots F_{Q_n(n)}(T)$$

for $1 \leq i \leq n$. Therefore, we finally obtain

$$N_{P_n}{}^*(FT) = T.$$

Assume $T = N_{P'_n}{}^*(FT')$ holds for some nesting $N_{P'_n}{}^*$ and flat NT FT',

$$
\begin{aligned}
FT' &= F_{P'_n t}{}^*(T) && \text{(by Corollary 3.3)} \\
&= F_{P_n t}{}^*(T) && \text{(by Corollary 3.1)} \\
&= FT && \text{(by Corollary 3.3)}
\end{aligned}
$$

Therefore, FT is uniquely determined for T.

Last half. Assume $T = N_{P_n}{}^*(T)$ for some nesting $N_{P_n}{}^* = N_{P_n(1)} \cdots N_{P_n(n)}$ and flat NT FT. Then we prove by induction on n that $F_{P_n t}{}^* = F_{P_n(n)} \cdots F_{P_n(1)}$ is a reversible flattening for T.

Basis of induction. Let $T = N_1(FT)$. Then,

$$
\begin{aligned}
N_1 F_1(T) &= N_1 F_1 N_1(FT) \\
&= N_1(FT) && \text{(by Proposition 3.7)} \\
&= T.
\end{aligned}
$$

Therefore, F_1 is a reversible flattening for T.

Induction step. Assume $F_{P_n t}{}^* = F_{P_n(n)} \dots F_{P_n(1)}$ is a reversible flattening for $T_n = N_{P_n(1)} \dots N_{P_n(n)}(FT)$ in the case where $n \le k$. Let $T_{k+1} = N_{P_{k+1}(1)} \dots N_{P_{k+1}(k+1)}(FT)$. Then,

$$T_{k+1} = N_{P_{k+1}(1)} N_{P_{k+1}(2)} \dots N_{P_{k+1}(k+1)}(FT) = N_{P_{k+1}(1)}(T_k),$$

where

$$T_k = N_{P_{k+1}(2)} \dots N_{P_{k+1}(k+1)}(FT).$$

From the above assumption, $F_{P_{k+1}(k+1)} \dots F_{P_{k+1}(2)}$ is a reversible flattening for T_k. Therefore, for $1 \le i \le k$,

$$N_{P_{k+1}(i+1)} F_{P_{k+1}(i+1)} \dots F_{P_{k+1}(1)}(T_{k+1})$$

$$= N_{P_{k+1}(i+1)} F_{P_{k+1}(i+1)} F_{P_{k+1}(i)} \dots F_{P_{k+1}(2)} F_{P_{k+1}(1)} N_{P_{k+1}(1)}(T_k)$$

$$= N_{P_{k+1}(i+1)} F_{P_{k+1}(i+1)} F_{P_{k+1}(i)} \dots F_{P_{k+1}(2)}(T_k) \quad \text{(by Proposition 3.7)}$$

$$= F_{P_{k+1}(i)} \dots F_{P_{k+1}(2)}(T_k) \quad \text{(by assumption)}.$$

From $T_{k+1} = N_{P_{k+1}(1)}(T_k)$ and Proposition 3.7,

$$T_k = F_{P_{k+1}(1)}(T_{k+1}).$$

Therefore, for $1 \le i \le k$,

$$N_{P_{k+1}(i+1)} F_{P_{k+1}(i+1)} \dots F_{P_{k+1}(1)}(T_{k+1}) = F_{P_{k+1}(i)} \dots F_{P_{k+1}(1)}(T_{k+1}).$$

In case $i = 0$,

$$N_{P_{k+1}(1)} F_{P_{k+1}(1)}(T_{k+1})$$

$$= N_{P_{k+1}(1)} F_{P_{k+1}(1)} N_{P_{k+1}(1)}(T_k)$$

$$= N_{P_{k+1}(1)}(T_k) \quad \text{(by Proposition 3.7)}$$

$$= T_{k+1}.$$

At this point, we have proved that $F_{P_{k+1} t}{}^*$ is a reversible flattening for $T = N_{P_{k+1}}{}^*(FT)$. Therefore, by induction on n, we have completed the proof that T is a CNT.   (Q.E.D.)

As shown in Proposition 3.13, CNTs are always translatable to flat NTs by FLAT operations, while the inverse translation is accomplished by NEST operations. NTs with this property play an important role when we consider mapping between a general NT world and a restricted NT world consisting only of flat NTs (or equivalently, the world of the relational data model) as explained in the next subsection. In the remaining part of this subsection, we consider dependencies which assure the canonicality of NTs.

Definition 3.13. Let G be a group in an NT T. G is a *well-classified group*, if LFD $cf(G) \to G_i$ holds in T for every child group $G_i \in cg(G)$.

Definition 3.14. An NT T is a *Well-classified NT (WNT)*, if every group G in T is a well-classified group.

To clarify this concept: in a WNT, two clusters in any occurrence of group G differ from each other by some field value. Most of the NTs hitherto used in our explanations are WNTs. The NTs shown in Figs. 3.20, 3.23, and 3.24 include examples of NTs that are not WNTs. Data structures considered in the Verso model [1] are essentially equivalent to WNTs.

Proposition 3.14. If T is a WNT, every flattening $F*$ for T is a reversible flattening, and therefore T is a CNT.

Proof. Let $\#g(T)$ be the number of groups in T. If $\#g(T)=1$, T is a flat NT, and the proposition is self-evident. We prove it by induction on $\#g(T)$ for $\#g(T)\geq 2$. Let G_i be a group other than the root in T, and let G be the parent of G_i. Since T is a WNT, LFD $cf(G)\rightarrow G_i$ holds in T. Therefore, LFD $cc(G)-G_i\rightarrow G_i$ also holds in T. Then, by Proposition 3.9, the FLAT operation $F[G_i]$ is reversible for T.

Basis of induction. If $\#g(T)=2$, G_i is the only group other than the root in T. Therefore, $F[G_i](T)$ is a flat NT. Then, $F[G_i]$ is the only applicable flattening for T, and is reversible.

Induction step. Assume that the proposition holds for NTs T' with $\#g(T')\leq k$. Let $\#g(T)=k+1$ for T. Then, $\#g(F[G_i](T))=k$. We show that $F[G_i](T)$ is a WNT. Let G_p be a group in $F[G_i](T)$.

(Case 1) $G_p\not\in ag+(G)$

Every occurrence of G_p in $F[G_i](T)$ is inherited from T. Therefore, every LFD among components of G_p is preserved. Thus, G_p is a well-classified group in $F[G_i](T)$.

(Case 2) $G_p=G$

Let O' be an occurrence of G in $F[G_i](T)$. Let $C=cc(G)$, $F=cf(G)$, and $F_i=cf(G_i)$ all in T. Then, O' can be represented by

$$O'=\{(t[C-G_i], u)|t\in O \wedge u\in t[G_i]\}$$

for some occurrence O of G in T. Let G_q be a child group of either G or G_i in T. In the former case, for any cluster $w\in O'$, there exists some cluster $t\in O$ such that $w[G_q]=t[G_q]$ and $w[F]=t[F]$. Since G is a well-classified group in T, any G_q-value in w is determined by an F-value in w. Therefore, LFD $F\rightarrow G_q$ holds in $F[G_i](T)$. In the latter case, for any cluster $w\in O'$, there exists some clusters $t\in O$ and $u\in t[G_i]$ such that $w[G_q]=u[G_q]$, $w[F]=t[F]$, and $w[F'_i]=u[F_i]$, where F'_i is the set of fields in $F[G_i](T)$ inherited from F_i. Since G and G_i are well-classified groups in T, any G_q-value in w is determined by F-value and F'_i-value in w. Therefore, LFD $F\cup F'_i\rightarrow G_q$ holds in $F[G_i](T)$. Thus, in either case, $F\cup F'_i\rightarrow G_q$ holds in $F[G_i](T)$, and therefore G_p is a well-classified group in $F[G_i](T)$.

(Case 3) $G_p\in ag(G)$

We can regard $F[G_i](T)$ as the result of applying some function $FUN_G: dom(G)\rightarrow R$ (R is a new domain of G) to every occurrence O of G and replacing it with $FUN_G(O)$. Because of this functional property of $F[G_i]$, group G_p is a well-classified group in $F[G_i](T)$.

Since G_p has been proved to be a well-classified group in each of the above three cases, we can conclude that $F[G_i](T)$ is a WNT. Thus, by assumption, any flattening $F_{Q_k}^*$ consisting of k FLAT operations for $F[G_i](T)$ is reversible. Note that $F[G_i]$ is reversible for T as stated at the beginning of the proof. Therefore, $F_{Q_k}^* F[G_i]$ is a reversible flattening for T. Any flattening $F_{P_{k+1}}^*$ consisting of $k+1$ FLAT operations for T can be formulated as $F_{P_{k+1}}^* = F_{Q_k}^* F[G_i]$, since $F_{Q_k}^*$ and G_i are arbitrarily selected in the above proof. Therefore, any flattening $F_{P_{k+1}}^*$ for T is reversible. Thus, by induction on $\#g(T)$, we have completed the proof of the proposition. (Q.E.D.)

The converse of Proposition 3.14 does not hold. For example, the two NTs at the bottom in Fig. 3.24 are not WNTs, though they are CNTs, since they are derived by NEST operations from the flat NT.

3.6.2 Data Manipulation Capability

In this subsection, the data manipulation capability of NT operations is considered. As mentioned before, flat NTs, as special cases of NTs, are equivalent to relations which are data objects in the relational data model. In the relational data model, relational algebra operations are defined, and their data manipulation capability is referred to as *relational completeness* [25]. Among them, Projection, Selection, Cartesian product, Set union, and Set difference are usually referred to as primitive relational algebra operations [148]. In NTD, NT operations are provided, and also, XR operations are defined so that they are extensions of the primitive relational algebra operations. Therefore, we can derive the following proposition:

Proposition 3.15. NT operations have the relational complete capability for manipulating flat NTs.

Proof. Let T and T' be flat NTs with the roots G_R and G'_R, respectively. As shown below, we have NT operations equivalent to five primitive relational algebra operations. The term "equivalent" means that the flat NT structure which results from the NT operation on the right hand side applied to T (and T') is same as that obtained by using the corresponding relational algebra operation on the left hand side:

Relational algebra	NT operation
Projection	PROJECTION: $P[G_R\langle C\rangle]$
Selection	SELECTION: $S[G_R, SC]$
Cartesian product	CARTESIAN_PRODUCT: $CX[G_R] = F[G'_R]X[G_R]$
Set union	UNION: $\cup[G_R]$
Set difference	DIFFERENCE: $D[G_R]$

Therefore, we can state that NT operations have the relational complete capability for manipulating flat NTs.   (Q.E.D.)

Definition 3.15. NT operations listed as equivalent to primitive relational algebra operations in the proof of Proposition 3.15 are referred to as *primitive relational equivalent NT operations*. Operations combining one or more primitive relational equivalent NT operations are called *relational equivalent NT operations*.

Now, we define a concept related to the capability of operations for the manipulation of NTs in general.

Definition 3.16. The NT manipulation capability provided by NEST, FLAT, and primitive relational equivalent NT operations is referred to as *NFR-expressiveness*.

Proposition 3.16. NT operations have at least the capability of NFR-expressiveness for manipulating NTs.

Proof. NT operations include NEST and FLAT, and all primitive relational equivalent NT operations are special cases of NT operations.   (Q.E.D.)

Suppose NT manipulation by an XR operation is always representable as a sequence consisting of NEST, FLAT, and relational equivalent NT operations. In other words, suppose, for any XR operation Φ applicable to an NT T, there exists a sequence Θ of NEST, FLAT, and relational equivalent NT operations such that

$$\Phi(T) = \Theta(T).$$

If the assumption were true, we could conclude that the capability of NT operations is restricted to NFR-expressiveness, and that essential data manipulation may be performed using only the NEST, FLAT, and relational equivalent NT operations. In fact, this assumption is false. In other words, in general, NT operations provide data manipulation capability more extensive than NFR-expressiveness. However, with some restrictions, the above translation is possible. Here, we study the translation into a sequence consisting of flattening(s), a relational equivalent NT operation, and a nesting.

Definition 3.17. Let Φ be an XR operation applicable to NT(s) T (and T'). Φ is *NFR decomposable* for T (and T'), if

$$\Phi(T) = N_{P_n}^* \Psi F_{Q_m}^*(T) \quad \text{(if } \Phi \text{ is unary)}$$

$$\Phi(T, T') = N_{P_n}^* \Psi(F_{Q_m}^*(T), F_{R_k}^*(T')) \quad \text{(if } \Phi \text{ is binary)}$$

for some nesting $N_{P_n}^*$, flattening(s) $F_{Q_m}^*$ (and $F_{R_k}^*$), and relational equivalent NT operation Ψ.

Proposition 3.17. If an XR operation Φ is NFR decomposable for T (and T'), then $\Phi(T)$ (or $\Phi(T, T')$) is a CNT.

Proof. Assume Φ is unary. Then, by definition,

$$\Phi(T) = N_{P_n}^* \Psi F_{Q_m}^*(T)$$

for some $N_{P_n}^*$, Ψ, and $F_{Q_m}^*$. By definition, $F_{Q_m}^*(T)$ is a flat NT. Since Ψ is a relational equivalent NT operation, $\Psi F_{Q_m}^*(T)$ is also a flat NT. Therefore, we can conclude $\Phi(T) = N_{P_n}^*(\Psi F_{Q_m}^*(T))$ is a CNT by Proposition 3.13. Similarly, we can prove the proposition in the case where Φ is binary. (Q.E.D.)

The converse of Proposition 3.17 does not necessarily hold unless some restrictions are imposed. Before we proceed, let us prove the following lemma:

Lemma 3.1. Let T, Φ, Ψ, $N_{P_n}^*$, $F_{Q_m}^*(, T', F_{R_k}^*)$ be the same as in Definition 3.17. If $\Phi(T)$ (or $\Phi(T, T')$) is a CNT,

$$\Phi(T) = N_{P_n}^* \Psi F_{Q_m}^*(T)$$

$$\longleftrightarrow F_{S_n}^* \Phi(T) = \Psi F_{Q_m}^*(T)$$

$$\Phi(T, T') = N_{P_n}^* \Psi(F_{Q_m}^*(T), F_{R_k}^*(T'))$$

$$\longleftrightarrow F_{S_n}^* \Phi(T, T') = \Psi(F_{Q_m}^*(T), F_{R_k}^*(T')),$$

where $F_{S_n}^*$ is some flattening for $\Phi(T)$ (or $\Phi(T, T')$).

Proof. Assume Φ is unary.

[$\rightarrow$] If we apply $F_{P_{n'}}^*$ to both sides of

$$\Phi(T) = N_{P_n}^* \Psi F_{Q_m}^*(T),$$

we obtain

$$F_{P_{n'}}^* \Phi(T) = \Psi F_{Q_m}^*(T)$$

by Corollary 3.3.

[$\leftarrow$] Since $\Phi(T)$ is a CNT, by Proposition 3.13, $\Phi(T) = N_{P_n}^*(FT)$ for some nesting $N_{P_n}^*$ and flat NT FT. Therefore, the left hand side of the given equation can be rewritten as follows:

$$F_{S_n}^* \Phi(T) = F_{P_{n'}}^* \Phi(T) \qquad \text{(by Corollary 3.1)}$$

$$= F_{P_{n'}}^* N_{P_n}^*(FT)$$

$$= FT \qquad \text{(by Corollary 3.3)}$$

Then, we apply $N_{P_n}^*$ to both sides to get

$$\Phi(T) = N_{P_n}^*(FT) = N_{P_n}^* \Psi F_{Q_m}^*(T).$$

In a similar way, we can prove the lemma in the case where Φ is binary. (Q.E.D.)

Now, we consider whether the converse of Proposition 3.17 generally holds for an XR operation. Given an NT T, let F^* be a flattening for T. By Corollary 3.1, $F^*(T)$ is the same flat NT for any flattening F^*. For a field F_i in T, the field in $F^*(T)$ inherited from F_i is denoted by $\omega^*(F_i)$. For group G_i in T, let

$$\omega^*(G_i) = \{\omega^*(F_j) \mid F_j \in cf(G_k) \wedge G_k \in dg + (G_i) \text{ for some group } G_k \text{ in } T\}.$$

In addition, for a set $C_i = CF_i \cup CG_i$, where CF_i is a set of fields in T and CG_i is a set of groups in T, let

$$\omega^*(C_i) = \{\omega^*(F_{ij}) \mid F_{ij} \in CF_i\} \cup \{\omega^*(G_{ij}) \mid G_{ij} \in CG_i\}.$$

Proposition 3.18. Let Φ be a PROJECTION $P[G_i\langle C_{ij}\rangle]$ applicable to an NT T. If $\Phi(T)$ is a CNT, Φ is NFR decomposable for T.

Sketch of Proof. Let $F_{Q_m}^*$ and $F_{S_n}^*$ be arbitrary flattenings for T and $\Phi(T)$, respectively, and let G_R be the root of T. In the case where $\Phi = P[G_i\langle C_{ij}\rangle]$, let $\Psi = P[G_R\langle \omega^*(G_R) - \omega^*(cc(G_i) - C_{ij})\rangle]$. Then, Ψ is a relational equivalent NT operation, and $F_{S_n}^*\Phi(T) = \Psi F_{Q_m}^*(T)$ obviously holds from the definition of PROJECTION. Therefore, by Lemma 3.1, we conclude that Φ is NFR decomposable for T. (Q.E.D.)

Proposition 3.19. Let Φ be a SELECTION $S[G_i, SC_i]$ applicable to an NT T. If $\Phi(T)$ is a CNT and the selection condition SC_i does not include set references (denoted by $\langle \text{s\_reference}\rangle$ in the syntax description for SC_i in Sect. 3.3), then Φ is NFR decomposable for T.

Sketch of Proof. Let $F_{Q_m}^*$ and $F_{S_n}^*$ be arbitrary flattenings for T and $\Phi(T)$, respectively, and let G_R be the root of T. Since SC_i does not include set references, all references to occurrences in SC_i are primitive references (denoted by $\langle \text{p\_reference}\rangle$ in the syntax description) of the form $G_j[F_{jk}]$. Now, replace every primitive reference $G_j[F_{jk}]$ in SC_i with $G_R[\omega^*(F_{jk})]$ to get the modified selection condition SC_i^*, and let $\Psi = S[G_R, SC_i^*]$. Since a primitive reference refers to each occurrence of field, $S[G_R, SC_i^*]$ is a relational equivalent NT operation evaluatable for $F_{Q_m}^*(T)$, and $F_{S_n}^*\Phi(T) = \Psi F_{Q_m}^*(T)$ obviously holds from the definition of SELECTION. Therefore, by Lemma 3.1, we conclude that Φ is NFR decomposable for T. (Q.E.D.)

Fig. 3.8 shows three sample SELECTION operations. SELECTION $S[G_2, G_2[F_3] = X]$ (shown in Fig. 3.8) can be mapped to SELECTION $S[G_1, G_1[F_3] = X]$ (shown in Fig. 3.25) applicable to the flat NT. However, for SELECTION operations which generally include set references, the formulation of relational equivalent NT operations is not straightforward.

Proposition 3.20. Let Φ be PRODUCT $X[G_i]$ or UNION $\cup[G_i]$ applicable to NTs T and T'. If $\Phi(T, T')$ is a CNT, Φ is NFR decomposable for T and T'.

Sketch of Proof. Let $F_{Q_m}^*$, $F_{R_k}^*$, and $F_{S_n}^*$ be arbitrary flattenings for T, T', and $\Phi(T, T')$, respectively. And let $\Psi(T_1, T_2)$ be as follows:

$$\Psi(T_1, T_2) = \begin{cases} CX[G_R](T_1, T_2) & \text{if } \Phi = X[G_i], \\ \cup[G_R](T_1, CX[G_R](P[G_R\langle C'_R\rangle](T_1), T_2)) & \text{if } \Phi = \cup[G_i], \end{cases}$$

where G_R is the root of T_1, and C'_R is the set of fields of T_1 excluding those corresponding to fields of T_2. Then, in either case Ψ is a relational equivalent NT operation, and $F_{S_n}^*\Phi(T, T') = \Psi(F_{Q_m}^*(T), F_{R_k}^*(T'))$ obviously holds from the definitions of PRODUCT, UNION, CARTESIAN_PRODUCT, and PROJECTION. Therefore, by Lemma 3.1, we conclude that Φ is NFR decomposable for T and T'. (Q.E.D.)

Definition 3.18. Let G_i be a group in an NT N, and $CG = cg(G_i)$. Given clusters t and u in $cdom(G_i)$, t and u are said to *have an intersection*, if:
a) $t[cf(G_i)] = u[cf(G_i)]$, and
b) if $CG \neq \phi$, for every $G_j \in CG$, there exist clusters $v \in t[G_j]$ and $w \in u[G_j]$ such that v and w have an intersection.

Proposition 3.21. Let Φ be a DIFFERENCE $D[G_i]$ applicable to NTs T and T', and let $F_{Q_m}^*$, $F_{R_k}^*$, and $F_{S_n}^*$ be arbitrary flattenings for T, T', and $\Phi(T, T')$, respectively. And let $\Psi(T_1, T_2)$ be as follows:

$$\Psi(T_1, T_2) = D[G_R](T_1, CX[G_R](P[G_R\langle C'_R\rangle](T_1), T_2)),$$

where G_R is the root of T_1, and C'_R is the set of fields of T_1 excluding those corresponding to fields of T_2. Iff T and T' meet the following difference condition,

$$F_{S_n}^* \Phi(T, T') = \Psi(F_{Q_m}^*(T), F_{R_k}^*(T')).$$

Difference Condition. For every G_i cluster t of T, if t has an intersection with any root cluster u of T', there exists a root cluster v (not necessarily distinct from u) of T' such that $t = v$.

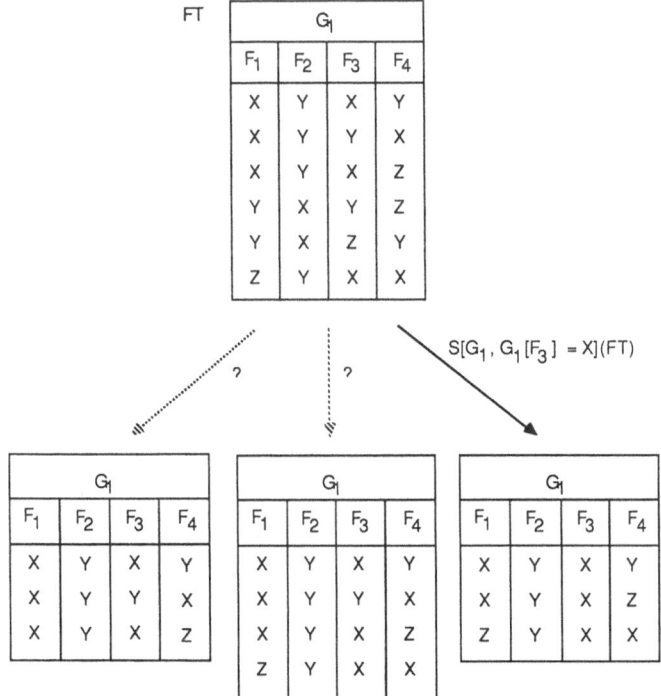

Fig. 3.25. SELECTION

Proof. Let C'_i be the fields $\omega^*(G_i)$ of $F_{Q_m}{}^*(T)$.

[→] First, we show

$$F_{S_n}{}^*\Phi(T, T') \supseteq \Psi(F_{Q_m}{}^*(T), F_{R_k}{}^*(T')).$$

Assume t is a root cluster of $\Psi(F_{Q_m}{}^*(T), F_{R_k}{}^*(T'))$. Then, $t \in F_{Q_m}{}^*(T)$ and $t \notin CX[G_R](P[G_R\langle C'_R\rangle](F_{Q_m}{}^*(T), F_{R_k}{}^*(T'))$. This means that $t[C'_i]$ is obtained from some G_i cluster u of T in the flattening, while $t[C'_i]$ is not obtained from any root cluster of T' in the flattening. Therefore, u appears as a G_i cluster of $\Phi(T, T')$, and t also appears in $F_{S_n}{}^*\Phi(T, T')$. Thus,

$$F_{S_n}{}^*\Phi(T, T') \supseteq \Psi(F_{Q_m}{}^*(T), F_{R_k}{}^*(T')).$$

Next, we show

$$F_{S_n}{}^*\Phi(T, T') \subseteq \Psi(F_{Q_m}{}^*(T), F_{R_k}{}^*(T')).$$

Assume t is a root cluster of $F_{S_n}{}^*\Phi(T, T')$. Then, t is obtained from some root cluster of $\Phi(T, T')$ in the flattening. This means that $t[C'_i]$ is obtained from some G_i cluster u such that $u \notin T'$. If we assume that u has an intersection with any root cluster of T', $u \in T'$ since T and T' meet the difference condition. This is a contradiction. Therefore, u has an intersection with no root cluster of T'. Thus, $t \notin CX[G_R](P[G_R\langle C'_R\rangle](F_{Q_m}{}^*(T), F_{R_k}{}^*(T'))$ while $t \in F_{Q_m}{}^*(T)$. Therefore,

$$t \in \Psi(F_{Q_m}{}^*(T), F_{R_k}{}^*(T'))$$

and

$$F_{S_n}{}^*\Phi(T, T') \subseteq \Psi(F_{Q_m}{}^*(T), F_{R_k}{}^*(T')).$$

We have proved that

$$F_{S_n}{}^*\Phi(T, T') = \Psi(F_{Q_m}{}^*(T), F_{R_k}{}^*(T')).$$

[←] Assume T and T' do not meet the difference condition. Then, there exists a G_i cluster t of T which has an intersection with some root cluster u of T', but there exists no root cluster v of T' such that $t = v$. Then, t appears in some G_i occurrence of $\Phi(T, T')$. Therefore, $F_{S_n}{}^*\Phi(T, T')$ has a root cluster w such that $w[C'_i] = x$, where x is a cluster obtained from u in the flattening. However, $\Psi(F_{Q_m}{}^*(T), F_{R_k}{}^*(T'))$ does not have such a cluster w. Therefore,

$$F_{S_n}{}^*\Phi(T, T') \neq \Psi(F_{Q_m}{}^*(T), F_{R_k}{}^*(T')).$$

Since we have proved the contraposition, we have completed the proof. (Q.E.D.)

In Proposition 3.21, the difference condition is essential. Figure 3.26 shows NTs which do not meet the condition. In Fig. 3.26,

$$F[G_2](D[G_1](T, T')) \neq D[G_1](F[G_2](T), F[G_2](T')).$$

Such incommutativity was also cited by Fischer and Thomas [41] in the context of their extended relational algebra.

From Proposition 3.21 and Lemma 3.1, we can derive the following proposition:

Proposition 3.22. Let Φ be a DIFFERENCE $D[G_i]$ applicable to NTs T and T'. If $\Phi(T, T')$ is a CNT, and T and T' meet the difference condition, Φ is NFR decomposable for T and T'.

Proof. Straightforward from Proposition 3.21 and Lemma 3.1. (Q.E.D.)

From Propositions 3.17, 3.18, 3.19, 3.20, and 3.22, we obtain the following proposition:

Proposition 3.23. Let Φ be an XR operation. In the case where Φ is the SELECTION or DIFFERENCE operation, assume the constraints of Propositions 3.19 and 3.22 are satisfied. Then, Φ is NFR decomposable for NT(s) T (and T'), iff $\Phi(T)$ (or $\Phi(T, T')$) is a CNT.

Proof. Straightforward from Propositions 3.17, 3.18, 3.19, 3.20, and 3.22. (Q.E.D.)

From Propositions 3.14 and 3.23, we obtain the following corollary:

Corollary 3.5. Let Φ be an XR operation. In the case where Φ is the SELECTION or DIFFERENCE operation, assume the constraints of Propositions 3.19 and 3.22 are satisfied. Then, Φ is NFR decomposable for NT(s) T (and T'), if $\Phi(T)$ (or $\Phi(T, T')$) is a WNT.

Proposition 3.23 gives a condition under which NT manipulations by NT operations can be translated into flat NT manipulations by relational equivalent NT operations. This proposition has the practically important implications. There

T

G1			
F1	F2	G2	
		F3	F4
X	Y	X	Y
		Y	X
		X	Z
Z	Y	X	X

T'

G1			
F1	F2	G2	
		F3	F4
X	Y	X	Y
		Y	X
Z	Y	X	X

F[G2](D[G1](T, T'))

G1			
F1	F2	F3	F4
X	Y	X	Y
X	Y	Y	X
X	Y	X	Z

D[G1](F[G2](T), F[G2](T'))

G1			
F1	F2	F3	F4
X	Y	X	Z

Fig. 3.26. DIFFERENCE and FLAT

are several possible approaches toward the implementation of NTD. Among them, one approach is to support it simply as a view to the flat relational storage structures by means of the mapping functions NEST and FLAT. In such a scheme, the actual data objects are relations or flat NTs, and hierarchical views associated with NTs are constructed "on the fly" by NEST operations. Proposition 3.23 mentions the limitation of this approach—that manipulations of NTs are not always translatable to manipulations of underlying relations, at least, in a straight-forward way. This theoretical result has contributed to our design of a form document workbench based on NTD.

3.7 Summary

In this chapter, the nested table data model (NTD) has been defined as an abstract data model for form documents, and some of its most important properties have been clarified.

A brief introduction to NTD was first given in Sect. 3.1. NTD provides constructs for modeling both data definition and manipulatin. A more precise definition of NTD was given in Sects. 3.2, 3.3, and 3.4, together with related terminology. Sect. 3.2 was concerned with the definition of data in NTD, and Sects. 3.3 and 3.4 were devoted to the modeling of data manipulation in NTD. Firstly, data objects named NTs were defined in Sect. 3.2. It was claimed that relations in the relational data model are special cases of NTs. Next, a number of "static" data manipulation primitives named NT handles were defined in Sect. 3.3. Then, a number of algebraic operations named NT operations were introduced in Sect. 3.4 for modeling "dynamic" NT manipulation. There, NEST and FLAT operations, generically referred to as NF operations, were defined for handling hierarchical data structures in NTs. The remaining five primitive NT operations, referred to as XR operations, were defined so that they were natural extensions of primitive relational algebra operations.

In Sect. 3.5, functional dependency and multivalued dependency in NTD were formulated. For both types of dependency, local and global dependencies were identified. In addition, Normalized NT was defined, based on the dependencies.

In the first part of Sect. 3.6, basic properties of NF operations were studied. In particular, reversibility and commutativity of NF operations were clarified, and special types of NTs such as Canonical NTs (CNTs) and Well-Classified NTs (WNTs) were introduced on the basis of the reversibility and commutativity properties. Then, the data manipulation capabilities of NT operations were considered, taking as a starting basis the relational completeness concept in the relational data model. First, it was shown that NT operations provide relational complete data-manipulation capability for the handling of flat NTs. Then, an NT manipulation capability, referred to as NFR-expressiveness, was formulated. NFR-expressiveness is assured by a special subclass of NT operations. Finally, the limitation of NFR-expressiveness for handling NTs in general was studied based on the properties of NT operations.

This chapter provides a sound theoretical basis for modeling form documents and their manipulation. Definitions and discussions in this chapter are referred to extensively in more practical contexts in Chaps. 4 and 5.

Comment on Some Examples

To demonstrate the capability of FORMDOQ in handling any characters including idiographics and phonetic symbols as well as pictures, we show the cases of Kanji characters and Japanese phonetics as examples in Figs. 4.15, 4.23, 4.25-4.31.

Authors

4 Form Document Workbench

4.1 Overview

In this chapter, we present the design and implementation of a form document workbench *FORMDOQ*. FORMDOQ is a powerful automation facility for manipulation of conventional form-based documents (abbreviated as *form documents*) in offices. Here, the term *office* refers to any office where paper work is done, and the term *form* refers to any sheet of paper which has a predetermined purpose of documentation.

FORMDOQ manipulates form documents which may contain text, drawings, diagrams, and tables, as well as traditional alphanumeric data. The user of the workbench can interactively handle various types of documents on the screen. FORMDOQ internally manages the document data, utilizing the nested table data model (NTD) defined in Chap. 3. Therefore, FORMDOQ exemplifies a practical use of NTD.

A prototype system of FORMDOQ has been implemented in UNIX environments on a VAX11/780.[1] The prototype FORMDOQ was developed as the basis of a software specification and documentation system. The prototype has been used experimentally for computer-aided preparation and management of system specification documents in software engineering offices.

This chapter is composed of nine sections. In Sect. 4.2, the basic requirements for the form document workbench are clarified, and features of FORMDOQ meeting the requirements are outlined. In Sect. 4.3, a hierarchical system structure consisting of three levels is presented, and building blocks at each hierarchical level are explained. In Sect. 4.4, a document manipulation model is described, highlighting features of FORMDOQ from the user's point of view. In Sect. 4.5, the global system architecture of FORMDOQ is shown, and the function of each system module is explained. Section 4.6 details external features of FORMDOQ. First, the design of the graphics-based man-machine interface is discussed. Then, examples of interactive document handling in the prototype FORMDOQ are shown. In Sect. 4.7, issues concerning the implementation of the prototype FORMDOQ are discussed. Section 4.8 explores the application of FORMDOQ in software engineering offices. There, FORMDOQ is used for the manipulation of various system specification documents which are developed on standardized forms. Finally, Sect. 4.9 summarizes the chapter.

---

[1] VAX is a trademark of Digital Equipment Corporation.

4.2 Requirements and Features

4.2.1 Requirements for Form Document Workbench

As mentioned in Chap. 1, innumerable kinds of forms have been devised and utilized up to the present to facilitate a variety of information-processing activities in offices. A form document workbench is a system which provides the office workers with friendly computer-aided environments for interactively handling documents based on the forms. As shown in Fig. 4.1, such environments must at least include facilities for:
a) Form definition
b) Form document development
c) Form document storage and retrieval
d) Report generation from form document repository
e) Application data processing on form documents
Here, we do not precisely define these functions of a form document workbench; in the context of FORMDOQ a more precise functional specification is given in Sect. 4.4. Rather, we consider more generic requirements for workbench capability in the following discussion. The requirements described below, although not explicitly represented in Fig. 4.1, are generically important for a form document workbench designed to support office information processing.

Requirement 1: Variety in Document Types

In practice, a variety of form documents are used in office activities, and they differ from office to office depending on factors such as the type of activity, the structure of

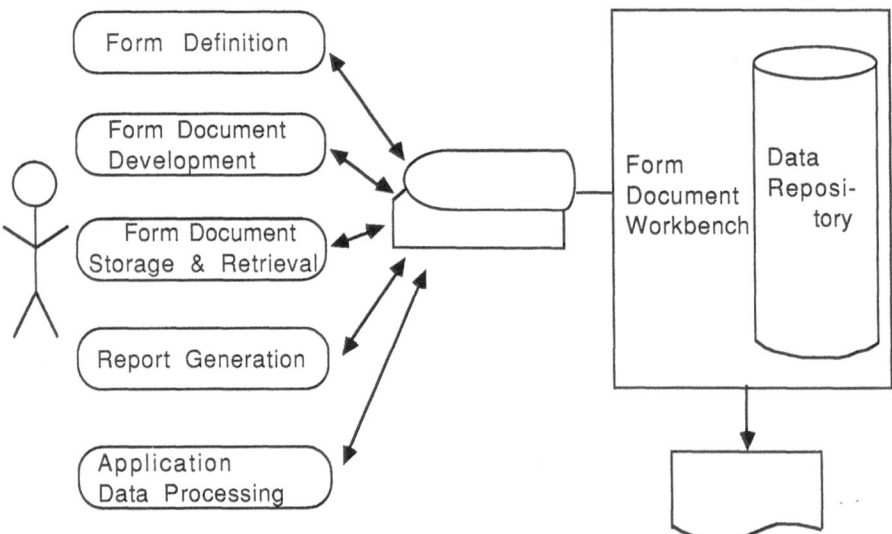

Fig. 4.1. Form document workbench

an organization, business customs, and working environments. In addition, the types of data items included in the form documents are usually not limited to the numeric data and character strings conventionally manipulated in computer data-processing systems. Text, graphics, and images are often included in the documents. In particular, the manipulation of graphics such as drawings and diagrams is inevitably required in most engineering offices. Therefore, to facilitate the present manual document handling, the form document workbench has to be capable of manipulating a variety of form documents combining data items of such extended data types as graphics and text.

Requirement 2: Uniform Data Management

Although the form document workbench handles various types of form documents from the user's viewpoint, it has to manage document data uniformly in its internal structure. In other words, external heterogeneity should be managed universally within the system under some discipline rather than in an ad hoc way. Such uniform data management is necessary, for example, to facilitate logical analysis of data embedded in form documents. It is often the case that data included in multiple form documents are interrelated, and that cross-references and restructuring of logical data structures are required for generating other documents. When document data are not uniformly modeled and managed within the system, machine processing of such document manipulation can only be accomplished by developing a set of ad hoc programs strongly dependent on both application requirements and low-level storage structures.

Requirement 3: User-Friendliness

User-friendliness is one of the most essential requirements for most office information systems. Users of the form document workbench are usually end-users, though they are experts in their own fields. Therefore, they have little computer background, if any, and most of them cannot afford to spend their time on learning such subjects as complicated data structures, formal syntax of data manipulation languages, and so on. Thus, the form document workbench has to meet users' demands for manipulation of data, as if handling conventional paper form documents, while requiring minimal learning effort.

Requirement 4: Open-Endedness for Application Development

Much information manipulated in offices is conventionally represented in form documents. Thus, the data repository in the form document workbench includes valuable information to be shared by many application programs developed to perform, for example, traditional batch-oriented data-processing activities. The incorporation of additional application programs is sometimes necessary to implement application-oriented processing of document data, even in interactive environments for handling form documents. Therefore, the workbench should be organized to be open-ended for application development and resource sharing with other application programs. Uniform data management (Requirement 2) is essential to make the application interface clear-cut.

In the next subsection, features of FORMDOQ are explained, and our approaches to fulfil the above requirements are clarified.

4.2.2 Features of FORMDOQ

The most important feature of FORMDOQ is the uniform modeling and management of form documents in terms of the nested table data model (NTD). In other words, FORMDOQ embodies the blueprint illustrated in Fig. 3.3, in which external form documents are internally mapped down into NT structures. The usefulness of NTs as abstract form document representations was discussed in Sect. 3.2. FORMDOQ exploits those features of NTs within its architecture. Here, we explain our solutions in FORMDOQ to the four generic requirements itemized in the previous subsection.

Requirement 1: Variety in Document Types

As explained in Sect. 3.2, NTs are suitable for canonical[2] models of various form documents. Conventional form documents usually have hierarchical data structures such as nests of data items, tabular clustering of data, and repeating groups. Those form document data structures are readily represented as NTs. In addition, FORMDOQ is designed so that occurrences of extended data types such as graphics and text can be stored directly in NTs. Therefore, a variety of form documents combining multiple types of data items are manipulatable in FORMDOQ to meet the first requirement.

Requirement 2: Uniform Data Management

As mentioned above, the use of NTD indeed contributes to uniform management of form document data. Once data included in form documents are extracted as NTs, they can be manipulated as pure data objects independently from their external presentation format. Therefore, for example, it is possible to modify the external presentation format of documents without changing embedded data occurrences, so long as no change is required in the underlying NT structures. In addition, FORMDOQ provides a module which directly executes NT operations for NTs. Therefore, document data can be dynamically edited to generate the desired target document structures. This feature is explained in detail in the next section.

Requirement 3: User-Friendliness

FORMDOQ provides graphics-based user-friendly environments for interactive document manipulation. The screen displays a virtual desktop, and form documents combining various types of data items can be manipulated on it, as if they were conventional paper documents. An icon-based interface design is utilized to represent data and procedure objects [126, 132]. Data handling is performed under the principle of "direct manipulation" [125]. Most commands for data manipulation are issued by first positioning the graphics cursor on the appropriate position and then pressing a function key. Overlapping multiple windows can be opened on the desktop to manipulate more than one object within these environments. An integrated form document editor is provided for creating and editing

---

[2] The term "canonical" is used as a common adjective here and not associated with "Canonical NT" defined in Chap. 3.

form documents. Facilities for handling text, graphics, Japanese character strings, etc. are automatically triggered in the form document editor, depending on the type of data item which the user selects with the graphics cursor. Also, the user can use a cabinet as a metaphor for an organized filing structure with indexing facilities for document storage and retrieval.

Requirement 4: Open-Endedness for Application Development

FORMDOQ has an interface to allow users to code their own programs to exploit its resources such as form document definition and document data. The interface is implemented as a set of library functions to be linked with user application programs. Therefore, any user programs can have access to the data repository in FORMDOQ through the library functions. In addition, with certain restrictions, user programs may be incorporated into the interactive FORMDOQ environments and activated from the desktop to perform an application-oriented procedure on document data. Customization of FORMDOQ functions can be achieved by the addition of such user application programs. Another approach to form-based application development is discussed in Chap. 5.

4.3 Three Level System Hierarchy

The basic structure of FORMDOQ consists of three hierarchical levels similar to the ANSI/X3/SPARC information system framework [22, 78, 160] as shown in Fig. 4.2. It is composed of *external*, *logical*, and *internal* levels. The external level handles various form documents complying with the users' requirements. The logical level manipulates NTs as canonical representations of form document data. The internal level corresponds to physical implementation on machines. The basic building blocks at each level and mapping among them are explained, to delineate the framework of FORMDOQ.

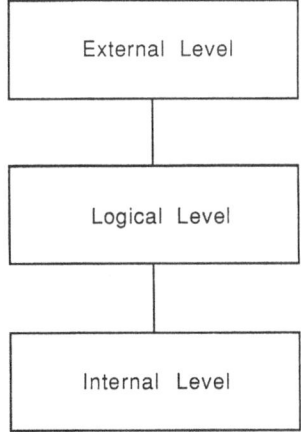

Fig. 4.2. Three hierarchical levels

4.3.1 External Level

The end-user's interactive data handling is performed at the external level. The basic objects manipulated at the external level are *form documents*. A form document is a combination of a skeleton named a *form schema* and a set of data occurrences embedded in the skeleton. A form schema determines the logical document data structure and its presentation to the user. In the terminology of paper document handling, a form schema corresponds to a preprinted format on the form sheet, and a form document corresponds to a filled-in form sheet. In the following part of this chapter, we use the term *form* as an abbreviation for form schema, and the term *form sheet* to mean the form schema instanciated in a form document. Here, we define form schemas and form documents in more detail as external objects of FORMDOQ.

A form schema at the external level of FORMDOQ is composed of units called *form section schemas*. In the simplest case, a form schema consists of a form section schema. An example of a form section schema is given in Fig. 4.3. As shown in this figure, a form section schema is concerned with information usually included in a "page" of the presentation medium such as screen or paper. A form section schema includes *areas* for which data occurrences are provided when the user fills in the form. An area is either a *box* or a *table*. A table usually consists of a number of *columns*. A table may have internal sub-tables, conventionally referred to as repeating groups. Several lines and character strings can be combined to achieve the desired appearance on a form section schema. They will serve as useful guidelines

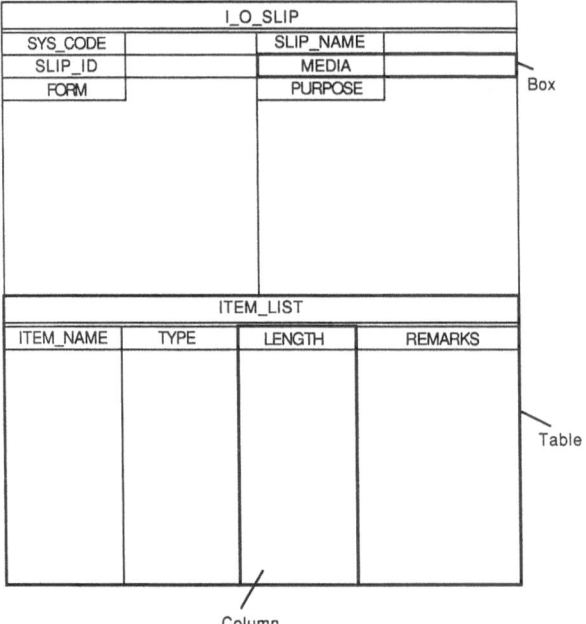

Fig. 4.3. Form section schema

reinforcing the meanings of the areas and their semantic relationships, when the user fills them in. An instance of a form section schema, such as that shown in Fig. 4.4, is called a *form section*. A form document is an instance of a form schema. In the situation where a form schema simply consists of a form section schema, form sections are just form documents manipulated at the external level of FORMDOQ.

It is often the case that a form schema is composed of just one form section schema, as assumed above. However, more complex data structures can be incorporated in form documents. Namely, a form schema may be defined as a tree of form section schemas as shown in Fig. 4.5. In such cases, a child form section schema is associated with a box or a column in the parent form section schema, and is usually used for storing logically elaborated data. A sample form document based on the form schema of Fig. 4.5 is shown in Fig. 4.6. In this case, the form document is a tree of form sections. A collection of "sibling" form sections, that is, form sections sharing the same parent form section, is called a *form section heap*. In Fig. 4.6, a form section heap is indicated by the symbol '*'.

To summarize, the structural expansion of a form schema can be represented in the following BNF expression:

$$\langle form\_schema \rangle ::= \langle form\_section\_schema \rangle$$
$$\langle form\_section\_schema \rangle ::= [\langle area \rangle]^+$$
$$\langle area \rangle ::= \langle box \rangle | \langle table \rangle$$
$$\langle box \rangle ::= \langle terminal\_box \rangle | \langle non\_terminal\_box \rangle$$
$$\langle table \rangle ::= [\langle column \rangle]^+$$
$$\langle column \rangle ::= \langle terminal\_column \rangle | \langle non\_terminal\_column \rangle$$

I_O_SLIP			
SYS_CODE	103467	SLIP_NAME	Order Slip
SLIP_ID	FRDEX101	MEDIA	Paper
FORM		PURPOSE	

ORDER

Order ID
Date
Customer ID
Customer Name

This business slip is used for identification of each customer order

Commodity ID	Q'ty	Price	Sub-Total
	Total		

ITEM_LIST			
ITEM_NAME	TYPE	LENGTH	REMARKS
OID	9	5	-
DATE	9	6	-
CID	9	8	-
CNAME	x	30	-
COID	9	8	-
QTY	9	5	-
PRICE	9	8	-
SUB-TOTAL	9	16	-
TOTAL	9	16	-

Fig. 4.4. Form section

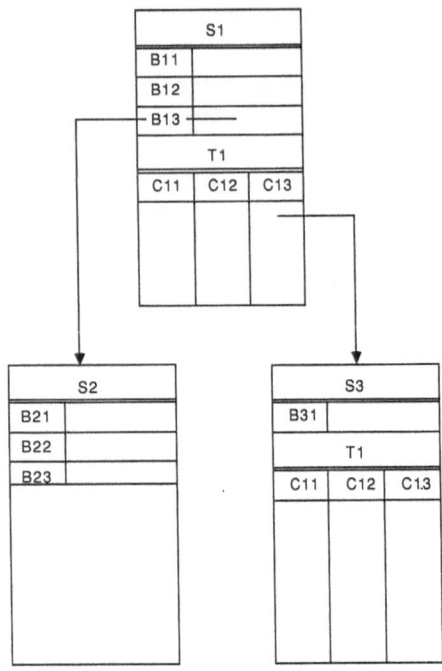

Fig. 4.5. Tree of form section schemas

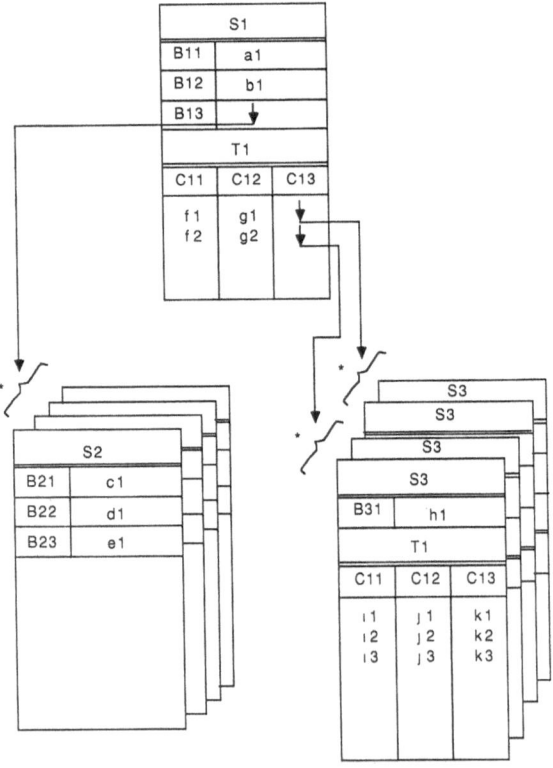

Fig. 4.6. Tree of form sections in a form document

⟨non_terminal_box⟩ ::= ⟨form_section_schema⟩

⟨non_terminal_column⟩ ::= ⟨table⟩ | ⟨form_section_schema⟩

Here, $[A]^+$ means a non-empty sequence of objects designated by A.

The form schema in Fig. 4.5 is composed of three form section schemas *S1*, *S2*, and *S3*. Box *B13* in *S1* is a non-terminal box and associated with *S2*. Column *C13* in table *T1* is a non-terminal column and associated with *S3*. Only terminal boxes and terminal columns may directly include data occurrences in form documents. A domain of data occurrences is given for each terminal box and terminal column. In FORMDOQ, the user may choose the domain from integer, float, character string, kanji/kana character string, text, kanji/kana text, and graphics.

A form document is a basic unit for document development and storage at the external level of FORMDOQ. Both form schemas and form documents are interactively developed by graphics-based editors. An organized storage structure and indexing facilities are provided for them, as explained in Sect. 4.5.

Although each form document is an independent object for document manipulation, it is sometimes useful to manipulate as a batch, documents developed on the same form schema. In the sense that data on a member form document can be viewed as if it were a member record in the traditional file, this concept also coincides with requirements of conventional data processing. For this reason, a group of one or more form documents having an identical form schema is also defined as an object manipulatable at this level. Such a group is called a *form document heap*. A simple form document heap is illustrated in Fig. 4.7. At the external level of FORMDOQ, the user can only temporarily construct form document heaps to perform manipulation of batches of form documents.

I_O_SLIP			
SYS_CODE	103467	SLIP_NAME	Order Slip
SLIP_ID	FRDEX101	MEDIA	Paper
FORM		PURPOSE	

ORDER

Order ID
Date
Customer ID
Customer Name

This business slip is used for identification of each customer order

Commodity ID	Q'ty	Price	Sub-Total
	Total		

ITEM_LIST			
ITEM_NAME	TYPE	LENGTH	REMARKS
OID	9	5	-
DATE	9	6	-
CID	9	8	-
CNAME	x	30	-
COID	9	8	-
QTY	9	5	-
PRICE	9	8	-
SUB-TOTAL	9	16	-
TOTAL	9	16	-

Fig. 4.7. Form document heap

4.3.2 Logical Level

As stated before, NTD is a basis for data management at the logical level. An intensive discussion on NTD itself was given in Chap. 3. Fig. 3.3 gives a simple example of a mapping in which a form document at the external level is translated into an NT at the logical level. The more complicated form document shown in Fig. 4.6 corresponds to an NT shown in Fig. 4.8. For generating an NT schema from a given from schema, the following general mapping rule applies:

Mapping rule. For each form section schema S_i and table T_i in a given form schema, generate a group schema $G_i\langle C_i\rangle$, where $C_i = CF_i \cup CG_i$ and CF_i and CF_i are determined as follows:

a) For a form section schema S_i
   CF_i: fields corresponding to terminal boxes in S_i
   CG_i: groups corresponding to tables and non-terminal boxes in S_i
b) For a table T_i
   CF_i: fields corresponding to terminal columns in T_i
   CG_i: groups corresponding to non-terminal columns in T_i

Given a form document, the NT schema of an underlying NT is readily obtained from its associated form schema by applying this mapping rule. Once the mapping between the form schema and the NT schema is established, the mapping of data occurrences is straightforward.

This is a general rule for external/logical mapping in FORMDOQ. In practice, the external level has two types of objects, namely form documents and form document heaps. Hence, there are two types of NTs at the logical level. As illustrated previously, the set of data occurrences included in a form document actually corresponds to one root cluster in the underlying NT. Therefore, each form

S1										
S2							T1			
B11	B12							S3		
		B21	B22	B23	C11	C12	B31	T2		
								C21	C22	C23
a1	b1	c1	d1	e1	f1	g1	h1	i1	j1	k1
		c2	d2	e2				i2	j2	k2
		c3	d3	e3				i3	j3	k3
		c4	d4	e4			h2	i4	j4	k4
								i5	j5	k5
					f2	g2	h3	i6	j6	k6
								i7	j7	k7
							h4	i8	j8	k8

Fig. 4.8. Underlying NT for the form document of Fig. 4.6

document is mapped to an NT having only one root cluster at the logical level. Such NTs are called *D-NTs*, where "D" stands for "document." In contrast, when a form document heap is constructed at the external level, an NT usually having multiple root clusters is organized at the logical level. Such NTs are called *H-NTs*, where "H" stands for "heap." An H-NT includes root clusters corresponding to member form documents in the form document heap. The number of root clusters in an H-NT is equal to the number of form documents included in the form document heap. Examples of a D-NT and an H-NT are given in Fig. 4.9. The mapping between the external and logical levels is summarized in Fig. 4.10.

In Chap. 3, NT operations were defined for manipulating NTs. From the viewpoint of document handling in FORMDOQ, NT operations may be used for

I_O_SLIP						ITEM_LIST			
SYS _CODE	SLIP _NAME	SLIP _ID	MEDIA	FORM	PURPOSE	ITEM_NAME	TYPE	LENGTH	REMARKS
103467	Order Slip	FRDEX 101	Paper	Order Order ID Date Customer ID Customer Name	This business slip is used for identification of each customer order	OID DATE CID CNAME COID QTY PRICE SUB-TOTAL TOTAL	9 9 9 X 9 9 9 9 9	5 6 8 30 8 5 8 16 16	- - - - - - - - -

D-NT

I_O_SLIP						ITEM_LIST			
SYS _CODE	SLIP _NAME	SLIP _ID	MEDIA	FORM	PURPOSE	ITEM_NAME	TYPE	LENGTH	REMARKS
103467	Order Slip	FRDEX 101	Paper	Order Order ID Date Customer ID Customer Name	This business slip is used for identification of each customer order	OID DATE CID CNAME COID QTY PRICE SUB-TOTAL TOTAL	9 9 9 X 9 9 9 9 9	5 6 8 30 8 5 8 16 16	- - - - - - - - -
103467	Shipping Instr Slip	FRDEX 102	Paper	Shipping Instruction Instruction ID Customer ID Customer Name Customer Address Order ID	This business slip is used to initiate goods delivery processing	IID CID CADR CNAME COID QTY OID	9 9 X X 9 9 9	5 8 50 30 8 5 5	- - - - - - -
				.	.				

H-NT

Fig. 4.9. D-NT and H-NT

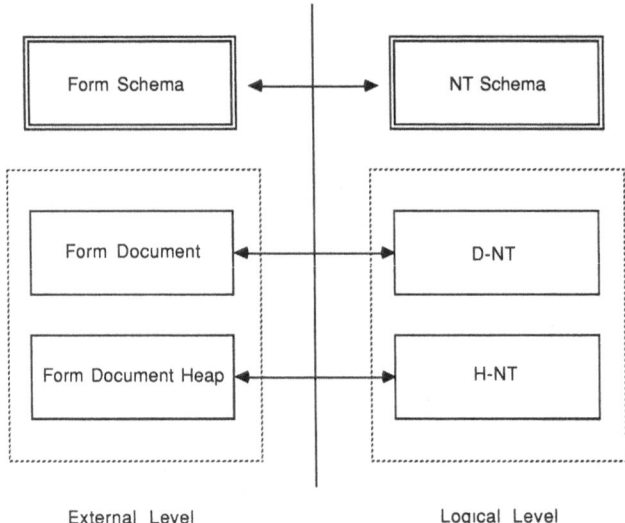

Fig. 4.10. Mapping between external and logical levels

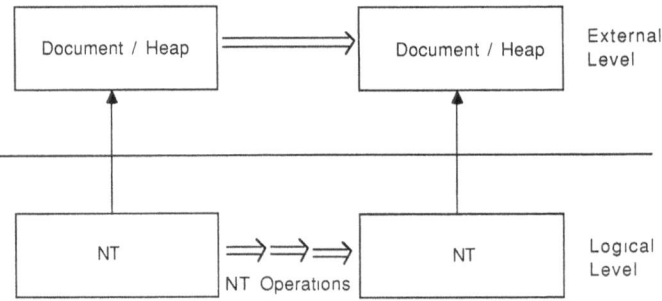

Fig. 4.11. Data manipulation by NT operations

expressing form document manipulation procedures in a highly abstract manner. In particular, data in form document heaps can be effectively handled by NT operations. As illustrated in Fig. 4.11, data manipulation can be accomplished independently from external presentation of data. FORMDOQ has a system module which can directly execute NT operations for NTs at the logical level. Reconstructing of stored form documents and report generation from them are typical cases in which the NT operations are very effective for data handling.

Here, we explain the use of NT operations with a simple report generation example. The example outlines the generation of a report document heap consisting of SLIP_SUM documents, shown in Fig. 4.12, from another document heap consisting of I_O_SLIP documents, shown in Fig. 4.7. The SLIP_SUM document

SLIP_SUM			
SYS_CODE	103467		
SLIP_LIST			
MEDIA	SLIP		
	ID	NAME	PURPOSE
Paper	FRDEX101	Order Slip	xxxxxxxx xxxxxx
	FRDEX102	Shipping Instr Slip	xxxxxx xxxxxx
	FRDEX103	Shipping Slip	xxxxxx xxxxxxxxx xxx
Screen	FRDEX121	Out of Order Notification	xxxx xxxxxxxx
	FRDEX122	Stock Report	xxx xxxxxxxx xxxxxx
	FRDEX123	Stock Warning Notification	xxxx xxxxxxxxx xx

Fig. 4.12. SLIP_SUM document help

heap includes summary information on i/o-slips each of which is specified in an I_O_SLIP specification document. Data in the I_O_SLIP document heap are first grouped by SYS_CODE, then a SLIP_SUM report document is generated to list i/o-slips for each SYS_CODE. In the list of i/o-slips within each SLIP_SUM document, entries are grouped by MEDIA. At the logical level, generation of this report is specified merely by a combination of PROJECTION and NEST operations. First, the PROJECTION operation is performed on data in the I_O_SLIP document heap to select the five fields necessary for the generation of this report, namely SYS_CODE, MEDIA, SLIP_ID, SLIP_NAME, and PURPOSE. Then, the NEST operation is applied to group I_O_SLIP to make a new child group SLIP_LIST consisting of fields MEDIA, SLIP_ID, SLIP_NAME, and PURPOSE. Finally, the NEST operation is applied to SLIP_LIST to make another new group, SLIP. (Actually, a number of operations for changing group and field names will also be applied). Of course, the external presentation of SLIP_SUM documents as shown in Fig. 4.12 has to be specified separately by the user. However, the data manipulation necessary for the report generation is completely specified at the logical level by the above NT operations. In FORMDOQ, both the NT operation sequences and the external presentation forms for target document heaps can be stored. Therefore, once these are registered, they can be reused without worrying about such NT operation sequences.

4.3.3 Internal Level

The organization of the internal level is tightly related to implementation issues. Therefore, only a brief overview is given here, and a more extensive discussion is presented in Sect. 4.7.

The prototype FORMDOQ was implemented on UNIX, and its internal level is built on a basis of UNIX file structures. Given an NT at the logical level, its NT schema and the NT occurrence are stored in separate files at the internal level. The NT schema is stored in a file called an *S-file*. Usually, there are multiple NTs having an identical NT schema at the logical level. In fact, the NT schema is identical for D-NTs associated with form documents sharing the same form schema. Thus, an S-file is shared by those NTs. If the NT of concern is a D-NT, a file called a *D-file* is assigned to it to store its NT occurrences. UNIX files are basically character arrays of variable length. Therefore, they are useful for storing text and graphics data items in NTs. Similarly, if the NT is an H-NT, one file is created at the internal level. This is called an *H-file*. Data occurrences in the H-NT are stored in pointer-chained record structures in the H-file. As explained in Sect. 4.5, an H-NT is always constructed by copying data from D-NTs in FORMDOQ. Thus, data in an H-NT have their originals in D-NTs. Therefore, to reduce the size of a potentially large H-file and to attain more efficient data manipulation, the H-file includes only logical pointers to actual data occurrences stored in D-NTs, when the data items are raw text or graphics.

4.4 Form Document Manipulation Model

In this section, a form document manipulation model (FDM) is presented to specify activities performed in FORMDOQ environments. The model is described in the terminology of the external level, since the external level is most closely tuned to human understanding of document handling, so that the explanation becomes more reader-friendly at this level. However, needless to say, activities at the external level are successively translated into activities at the logical and internal levels through the mapping scheme explained in Sect. 4.3, and finally executed on the machine.

Figure 4.13 gives an illustrative overview of the model. The model includes the following six phases represented by rectangles in the figure:
a) Form schema design
b) Form schema base manipulation
c) Form document development
d) Form document base manipulation
e) Form document heap handling
f) Application processing
Activities in these six phases are explained below.

Form Schema Design

Form schemas are interactively designed in this phase. An interactive editor for designing form schemas is used for this purpose. The user can design a form schema

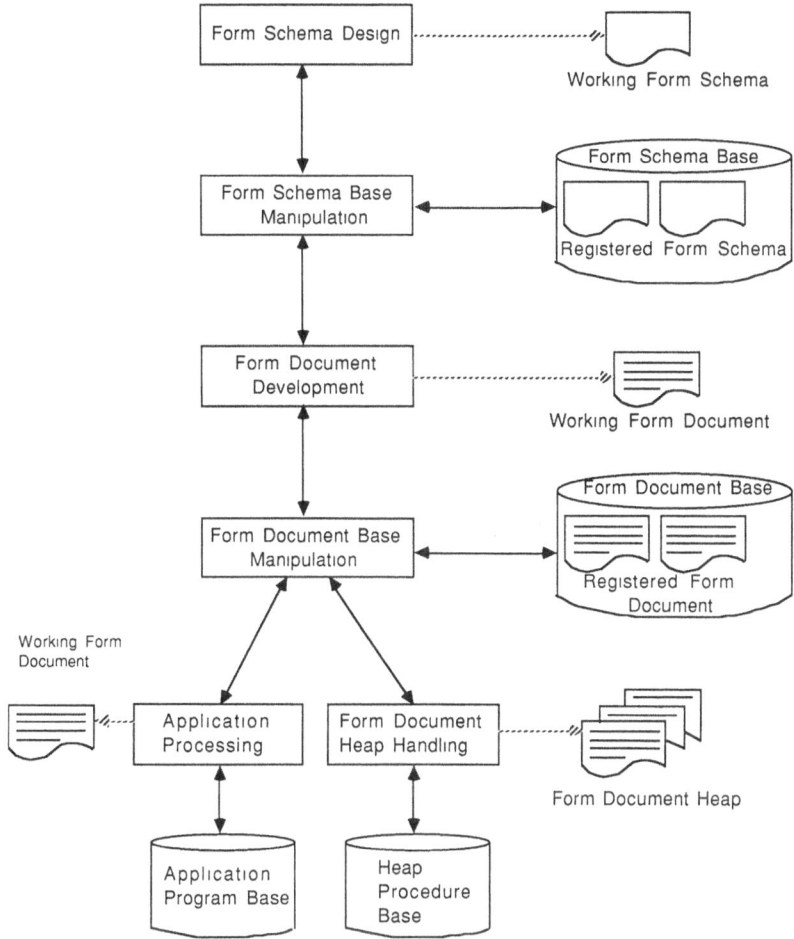

Fig. 4.13. Form Document Manipulation Model (FDM)

from scratch or modify a form schema already existing in the system to create another. In either case, a new form schema is defined in this phase.

Form Schema Base Manipulation

Form schemas designed in the form schema design phase are tagged with form schema identifiers and stored in a depository called the *form schema base*. Form schemas stored in the form schema base are called *registered form schemas*. The others are called *working form schemas*. In other words, working form schemas are basically under development with the editor, and have not yet completed the form schema design phase. Facilities are provided in this phase for storage and retrieval of form schemas to and from the form schema base.

Form Document Development

Form documents are interactively developed in this phase. An interactive editor is used for developing form documents. Before starting, the user gets a form sheet designating a registered form schema. Then, the image of the form sheet is displayed on the screen. The editor facilitates the entry of data occurrences by the user to make a form document. Graphics and text data can be handled as data occurrences. The user can develop documents by cutting and pasting data occurrences from other documents. In this way, he can make a new document based on other documents at hand, as is the case with form schemas in the form schema design phase.

Form Document Base Manipulation

Form documents developed in the form document development phase are tagged with form document identifiers and stored in a depository called the *form document base*. Form documents stored in the form document base are called *registered form documents*. The others are called *working form documents*. Facilities are provided in this phase for storage and retrieval of form documents to and form the form document base.

Form Document Heap Handling

As mentioned in Sect. 4.3, the user can temporarily construct form document heaps to manipulate batches of documents. The handling of form document heaps is performed in this phase. Form documents generated as the result of document heap handling in this phase are treated in exactly the same manner as other form documents developed in the form document development phase. Therefore, for example, they can be interactively edited with the same editor, to augment the form description. In this way, the user can achieve the optimum combination of automatic procedures performed in the form document heap handling phase and interactive document manipulation with the editor.

The procedures for document heap handling are called *heap procedures*, and they are specified in sequences of NT operations. Heap procedures are stored in a repository called the *heap procedure base*. Therefore, once they are stored, the user has only to select the desired heap procedure for execution, without worrying about actual sequences of NT operations. Facilities are provided for the definition and execution of heap procedures in this phase.

Application Processing

Registration and execution of add-in application programs are performed in this phase, for processing document data. Add-in application programs are developed by the user to provide document data handling for specific applications. FORMDOQ provides a set of library functions to facilitate the development of application programs by the user. A variety of such programs can be constructed using the library functions. Some programs may automatically generate new documents based on data occurrences in other documents, and others may validate the integrity of data entries in interactively developed documents. All application programs to be executed in this phase must be registered in a depository called an *application program base*. To execute one of them, the user first chooses the desired program from the application program base, and gives required parameters, if any, via the keyboard or the graphics cursor. Facilities are provided in this phase for the registration and execution of application programs.

Figure 4.13 includes a number of arcs in addition to the nodes explained above. A solid arc represents information flow and a dotted arc represents information generation. Actually, most of the information flows among the above six phases as form schemas and form documents. For example, a working form schema generated in the form schema design phase is passed to the form schema base manipulation phase. Conversely, a registered form schema may be passed from the form schema base manipulation phase to the form schema design phase, to allow the design of a new form schema modifying it. Similar flows of form documents occur along other solid arcs in the figure.

4.5 System Architecture

Figure 4.14 shows the global system architecture of FORMDOQ. There are eleven modules represented by rectangles in the figure. The system manager (SM) is the kernel in the architecture. The other ten system modules are located around the SM to form a star-like configuration. In the following part of this section, the function of each system module is explained.

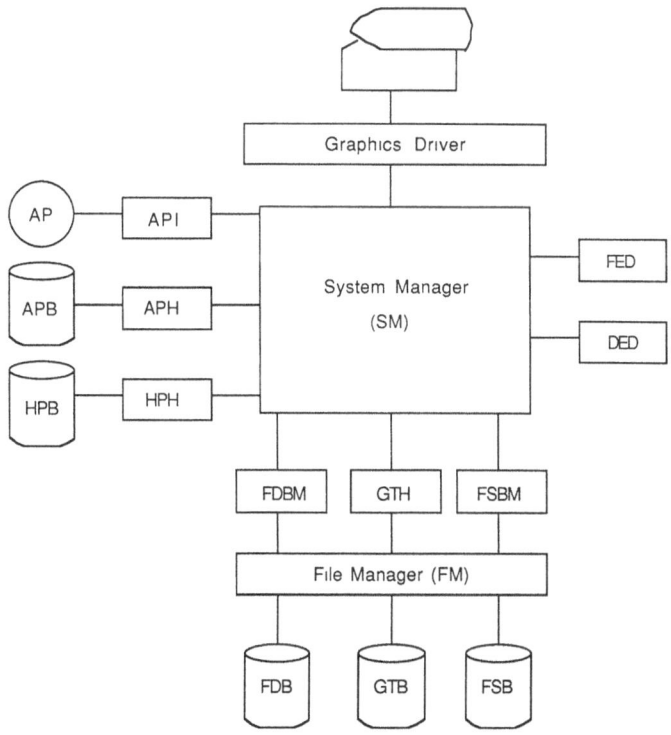

Fig. 4.14. Architecture of FORMDOQ

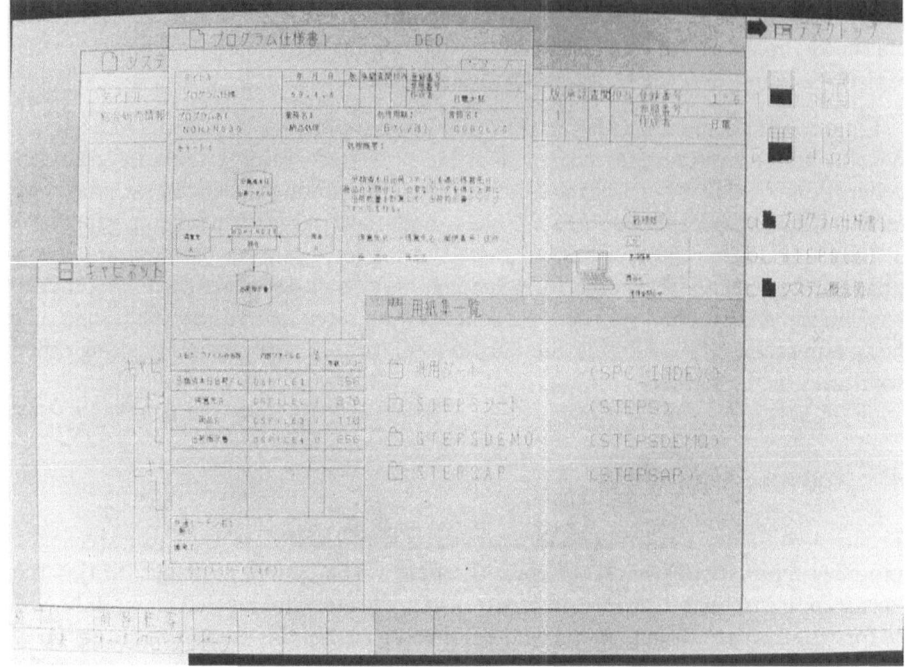

Fig. 4.15. Screen sample

4.5.1 Graphics Driver

As mentioned in Sect. 4.2, FORMDOQ has a graphics-based man-machine interface. The *graphics driver* provides a set of common functions for driving the screen, windows, and graphics objects. It also includes functions for receiving interactive graphics input from the user. A screen sample of the prototype FORMDOQ is shown in Fig. 4.15. The FORMDOQ screen features icon-based object representation and multiple windows. All data handling on the screen is implemented using functions of the graphics driver. A more detailed explanation of the FORMDOQ man-machine interface is given in Sect. 4.6.

4.5.2 System Manager

The *system manager (SM)* manages the system status at the top level. In other words, the major function of SM is to coordinate the other system modules. Communications among the other system modules are basically accomplished through SM.

Management of multiple windows and icons is included in the top level system management functions performed by SM. For this purpose, SM logically maintains the following tables:[3]

---

[3] Detailed items are omitted here.

WINDOW (window-id, window-type, left-x, left-y, right-x, right-y, process-id)
PROCESS (process-id, process-type, object-type, object-id)
ICON (icon-id, object-type, object-id).

The table WINDOW has an entry for each window maintaining the identifier, type, position on the screen, and the identifier of an associated process. The table PROCESS stores the identifier and type of each process executed in a window. The process type designates one of the following system modules explained later:

FED: Form Schema Editor
FSBM: Form Schema Base Manager
DED: Form Document Editor
GTH: Graphics Type Handler
FDBM: Form Document Base Manager
HPH: Heap Procedure Handler
APH: Application Program Handler

The identifiers and types of data objects are also maintained, when the process type is FED or DED. The table ICON stores the identifier and type of object represented by each icon displayed on the screen.

4.5.3 Form Schema Editor

The *form schema editor (FED)* is used to define form schemas. In other words, with FED, the user performs work in the form schema design phase of the form document manipulation model (FDM) explained in Sect. 4.4. FED is completely interactive, and runs in a window provided by SM. The user can select boxes of desired types and determine their sizes and positions interactively in the window. Similarly, he can decide areas for tables and freely design the column arrangement within the tables. In addition, FED provides the user with the capability to place arbitrary lines and character strings on the form schema. Therefore, he can use FED to give the most appropriate external appearance to form schemas. The FED window is primarily devoted to the design of the form schema section at the top level. If necessary, the user can define a tree of form schema sections such as that shown in Fig. 4.5.

When defining a form schema, the user has to specify a domain of data occurrences for each non-terminal box and non-terminal column. As stated in Sect. 4.3, a domain may be integer, float, character string, kanji/kana character string, text, kanji/kana text, or graphics. Internal identifiers for form schema sections, boxes, tables, and columns are also given by the user, and they are used for NT schema generation. An optional facility for the automatic generation of such internal identifiers is also available, in case the user does not care which internal identifiers are given to fields and groups of NTs.

4.5.4 Form Document Editor

The *form document editor (DED)* is used to develop form documents. In other words, with DED, the user performs work in the form document development phase of the FDM. Before executing DED, the user designates a registered form schema. Then, a window is provided by SM, and a form sheet corresponding to the designated form

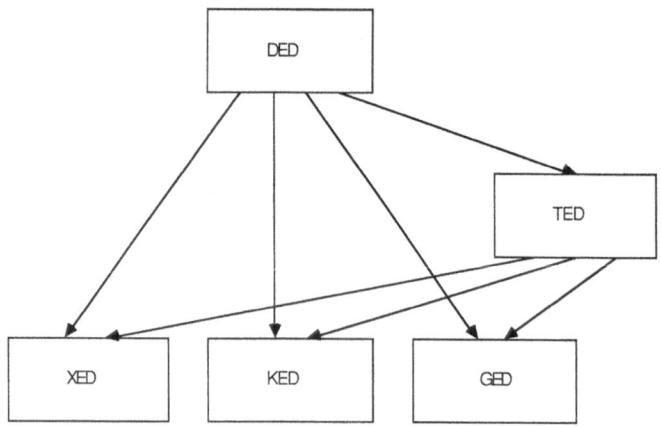

Fig. 4.16. Sub-editors of document editor

schema is displayed in the window. A form document is developed by filling in the form sheet in the window. Data occurrences in other documents can be copied to a new document. DED is used for manipulating data in both working and registered form documents.

As shown in Fig. 4.15, data occurrences of several domains can be used in combination to fill in the form sheet. Entry or modification of a data occurrence is done simply by positioning the graphics cursor in the area and pressing the appropriate function key. As shown in Fig. 4.16, four sub-editors, namely the table editor (TED), text editor (XED), kanji/kana text editor (KED), and graphics editor (GED), are internally called from DED to perform editing oriented to domains and/or data structures. When GED is executed, a template of graphics symbols automatically appears on the screen. The user can freely move, magnify, shrink, rotate, copy and delete graphics elements on the screen. As stated in Sect. 4.2, graphics data handling is also one of the features of FORMDOQ. Therefore, we explain the graphics data items manipulated in FORMDOQ in more detail here.

The logical structure of a graphics data item G is specified as the following tuple:

$$G = (N,\ A,\ af,\ C,\ TYPE,\ ntf,\ atf,\ nsf,\ asf),$$

where N is a set of *nodes*, A is a set of *arcs*, *af* is *arc function*

$$af:\ A \rightarrow N \times N,$$

and C is a set of *comments*, that is to say, graphics elements not classified into nodes, arcs, and their labels.

Nodes and arcs have types. A node type associated with a node is given by a *node type function nft*, and an arc type associated with an arc is given by an *arc type function atf*. Namely,

$$ntf:\ N \rightarrow NTYPE,$$

and

$$atf:\ A \rightarrow ATYPE,$$

where *NTYPE* and *ATYPE* are the *node type set* and *arc type set*, respectively. *NTYPE* and *ATYPE* produce a *graphics type* denoted by *TYPE*, namely

$$TYPE = (NTYPE, ATYPE).$$

Each *node type ntype* as an element in *NTYPE* is the following tuple:

$$ntype = (ID, S, A_1, \ldots, A_n) \ (n \geq 0),$$

where *ID* is an identifier, *S* is a *node symbol*, such as a rectangle, triangle, or circle, for visual presentation of nodes of this type, and $A_1, \ldots, A_n$ are user-defined *attributes*. Attributes are used for describing properties of entities to be represented by nodes of the node type. The user can assign domains of attribute values, denoted by $d(A_i)$ $(1 \leq i \leq n)$, to those attributes. Attribute values are represented in node and arc labels. The *semantics domain* of node type *ntype*, denoted by $nsd(ntype)$, is the Cartesian product of domains $d(A_1), \ldots, d(A_n)$, namely

$$nsd(ntype) = d(A_1) \times \ldots \times d(A_n).$$

Arc types and *arc semantics domains* are defined analogously to the node types and node semantics domains, respectively.

The *node semantics function* (*nsf*) associates an element in a node semantic domain $nsd(ntf(n))$ with a node n. Similarly, the *arc semantics function asf* associates an element in an arc semantic domain $asd(atf(a))$ with an arc a. Therefore,

$$nsf: \ N \to \cup_{n \in N} nsd(ntf(n)),$$

and

$$asf: \ A \to \cup_{a \in A} asd(atf(a)).$$

For example, Fig. 4.17 shows a diagram termed a PND (Program Network Diagram). Elements in node and arc types for the graphic-type PND are given in Table 4.1. Four node types are defined, to represent modules, files, screens, and reports; two arc types are defined to represent control and data flows. A number of user-defined attributes are also given. For example, a module node has attributes MID to represent the module identifier and MNAME to represent the module name.

In fact, some graphics data items are associated with no graphic type. In other words, they are only composed of comments, and $N = \varnothing$ and $A = \varnothing$. Graphics drawings used just for illustrative purposes can be classified into this category. To have the system handle logical information represented by graphics data, a user must designate a graphics type. Then, the logical meaning of graphics data representable by the functions *af, ntf, atf, nsf,* and *asf* can be recognized by GED. This information is stored in the system, and can be utilized in form document heap manipulation and application processing, as explained later.

Actually, when a box of a graphics domain is defined in the form schema design phase with FED, a graphics type can be also assigned to the box. In this sense, the graphics type associated with a graphics data box is a part of the form schema information. If a graphics type is assigned to a graphics data box, GED presents a template consisting of node and arc symbols on the screen, just before the input or editing of the graphics data is started. The definition of graphics types is performed with the graphics type handler as explained later.

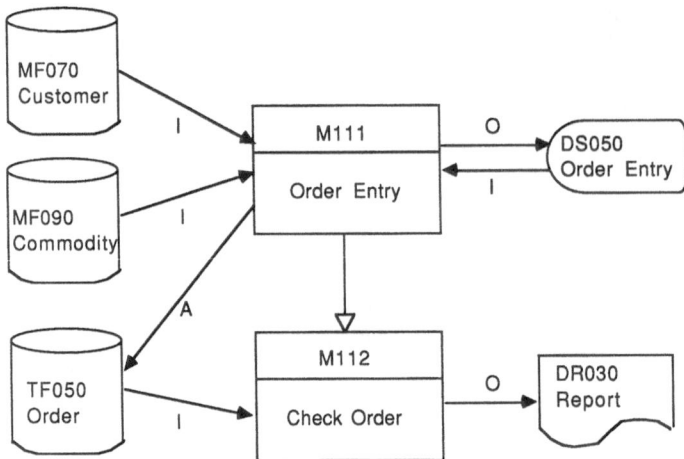

Fig. 4.17. PND (Program Network Diagram)

Table 4.1. Node types and arc types in PND

	Object	ID	Symbol	User-defined attribute
Node				
	Module	1		MID, MNAME
	File	2		FID, FNAME
	Screen	3		SID, SNAME
	Report	4		RID, RNAME
Arc				
	Control flow	1	⟶▷	none
	Data flow	2	⟶▶	MODE

4.5.5 Form Schema Base Manager

The *form schema base manager* (*FSBM*) manages the *form schema base* (*FSB*), which stores registered form schemas. Therefore, access requests to FSB are always passed to FSBM and coordinated. Such requests to FSBM may be issued by other system modules or directly by the user. In the latter case, a window is given by SM, and FSBM runs in the window. For example, activities in the form schema base manipulation phase of the FDM are performed in the window associated with FSBM. In the window, working form schemas can be stored in FSB, and registered form schemas can be retrieved. The form schema identifier assigned to each registered form schema is given by the user. Its uniqueness is checked by FSBM.

   In addition, FSBM manages the storage area for working form schemas, which are not registered in FSB. The form schema identifier assigned to each working form schema is automatically given by FSBM.

4.5.6 Graphics Type Handler

The *graphics type handler* (*GTH*) manages the *graphics type base* (*GTB*), which stores definitions of graphics types. When GED manipulates graphics data items of some graphics type, it needs to refer to the type definition. Such access requests to GTB are handled by GTH. At that time, some graphics type information has to be loaded into the graphics workstation to allow interactive graphics manipulation on the terminal. The loading and unloading of graphics types are also performed by GTH.

   In addition, interactive sessions for defining graphics types are handled by GTH. When a new graphics type is defined using GTH, a window is assigned by SM, and GTH runs in the window. Node and arc symbols are interactively designed in the window. As in GED, the user is provided with a template of primitive graphics symbols, and can freely move, magnify, shrink, rotate, copy, and delete those primitive graphics symbols to construct desired node and arc symbols. He can also combine them with several types of lines and various sizes of character strings in the design. Attributes of nodes are also defined in this window.

4.5.7 Form Document Base Manager

The *form document base manager* (*FDBM*) manages the *form document base* (*FDB*), which stores registered form documents. The organization of FDB is outlined in Fig. 4.18. Form documents are stored in units called *holders*. Form documents with different form schemas can be mixed in a holder. Holders are created and destroyed by the user, and they may be nested as shown in Fig. 4.18. Two facilities for document indexing are provided. The first one is the *key word index*. Key words are grouped into *key word classes*. Key word classes can be created and destroyed by the user at any time. Key word classes are usually used for systematic categorization of key words. Therefore, the key word index has a key word class table at the first level, and a key word table is associated with each key word class entry. The registration of key words into key word tables and the indexing of documents are performed directly by the user. The second indexing facility is the *link index*. The

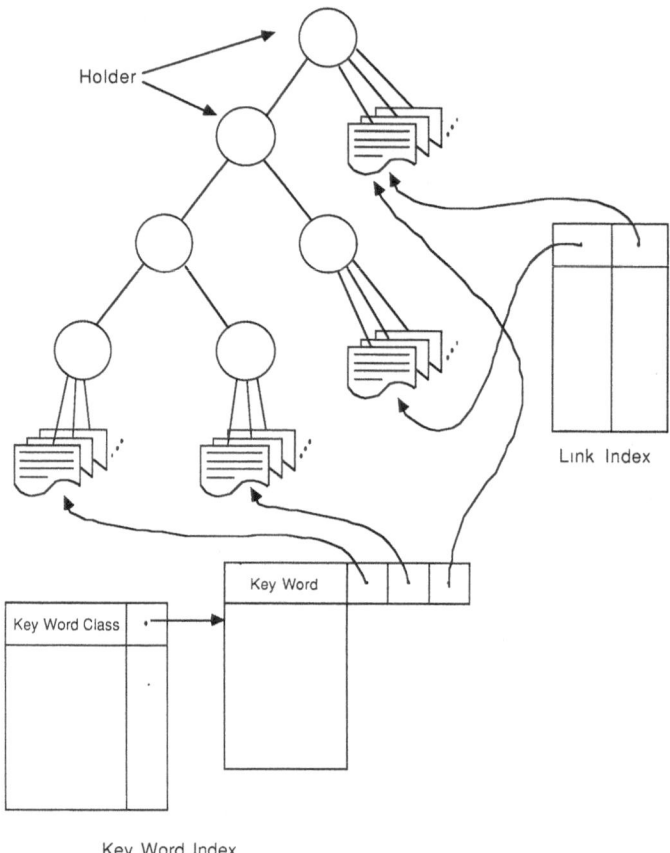

Fig. 4.18. Organization of form document base

link index is used to register a bi-directional relationship between two documents. Once a pair of documents is registered in the link index, either document may be readily retrieved from the other through the link index. Documents stored in different holders may be linked using the link index as shown in Fig. 4.18. Entries in the link index are also maintained by the user.

Access requests to FDB are always passed to FDBM and coordinated. Such requests to FDBM may be issued by other system modules or directly by the user. In the latter case, a window is provided by SM, and FDBM runs in the window. For example, activities in the form document base manipulation phase are performed in the window associated with FDBM. In the window, working form documents can be stored in FDB, and registered form documents can be retrieved either by traversing the holder hierarchy or by utilizing key word and link indexes. The form document identifier assigned to each registered form document is allocated by the user. Its uniqueness is checked by FDBM. Traversal and maintenance of the holder hierarchy and index maintenance are also accomplished in this window.

   Documents registered in FDB can be retrieved by a conditional search. This is accomplished with the *query-by-form* (*QBF*) facility. QBF is inspired by query-by-example (QBE), which was developed for relational database manipulation [161, 163]. However, the target objects, which in QBE are mere flat tables, are extended in QBF to naturally displayed form documents. In QBF, the user first designates a form schema for documents to be retrieved. Then, a blank form sheet appears in the window, and the user fills it with example elements to specify a query condition. When the query is executed, a list of form documents meeting the query condition appears in the window.

   FDBM also manages the storage area for working form documents, which are not registered in FDB. The storage area is called the *working holder*. The form document identifier assigned to each working form document is automatically given by FDBM. No indexing facility is available for working form documents.

4.5.8 File Manager

FSB, FDB, and GTB are constructed on the UNIX file system. For example, D-files are created for form documents, as mentioned in Sect. 4.3, and they are organized into FDB structures as indicated in Fig. 4.18. The *file manager* (*FM*) provides other system modules with a set of primitives for manipulating such file structures. The principal primitives provided by FM are listed below:

FSB Primitive

FSB primitives are used to manipulate S-files constituting FSB. As explained later in Sect. 4.7, an S-file includes a form schema, namely the logical-level NT schema together with information on external presentation of form documents. The manipulation of S-files underlying working form schemas is also done by FSB primitives.
a) Open S-file list
b) Close S-file list
c) Create S-file
d) Delete S-file
e) Open S-file
f) Close S-file

FDB Primitive

FDB primitives are used to manipulate D-files which make up FDB. A D-file includes data occurrences in a form document. They are also used to handle holders, the key word index, and the link index in FDB. The manipulation of D-files underlying working form documents is also done by FDB primitives.
a) Open holder list
b) Close holder list
c) Create holder
d) Delete holder
e) Open holder
f) Close holder
g) Create D-file

h) Delete D-file
i) Open D-file
j) Close D-file
k) Open key word index
l) Close key word index
m) Create key word class
n) Delete key word class
o) Cretate key word
p) Delete key word
q) Create key word index entry
r) Delete key word index entry
s) Open link index
t) Close link index
u) Create link index entry
v) Delete link index entry

GTB Primitive

GTB primitives are used to manipulate G-files in GTB. A G-file includes information on a graphics type.
a) Open G-file list
b) Close G-file list
c) Create G-file
d) Delete G-file
e) Open G-file
f) Close G-file

FM could also provide primitives for reading and writing data items in files such as S-files, D-files, and G-files. For example, primitives for D-file access could be constructed based on the NT handles defined in Sect. 3.3. Such primitives hide implementation-dependent layout of data items from modules accessing the files, and enhance the modularity of the system. In particular, in most database systems, complicated data storage structures are usually implemented to improve time and space efficiency in handling large files. In such cases, manipulation of data without those data item access primitives is, of course, too burdensome. In the context of FORMDOQ, the primitives explained here are not directly utilized by user application programs but by a limited number of system modules. In addition, as far as D-files are concerned, under typical conditions of use of FORMDOQ, it can be assumed that they contain fewer data items than the data files in traditional databases. Therefore, a rather simple scheme for storing data items works well in FORMDOQ environments. For this reason, the current version of FORMDOQ is so designed that those files are manipulated directly by relevant system modules to accomplish flexible and efficient data handling. As explained later in this section, a set of primitives for D-file data item access is provided by the application program interface (API) module at the interface with user application programs.

4.5.9 Heap Procedure Handler

The *heap procedure handler* (*HPH*) is a module used to perform document manipulation in the form document heap handling phase. In this phase, the user can temporarily construct form document heaps as batches of documents and apply *heap procedures* for their manipulation. Heap procedures are defined as sequences of *heap procedure primitives* and stored in the *heap procedure base* (*HPB*). A list of heap procedure primitives is given in Table 4.2. As illustrated in Fig. 4.19, heaps are constructed from documents stored in holders in FDB, and documents generated from a heap procedure are put into the working holder as working documents. Data restructuring of form documents in heap procedures is specified at the logical level independently from external presentations. For this reason, heap procedure primitives are defined to manipulate NTs which logically represent document data included in form document heaps. The NT operations defined in Sect. 3.4 have corresponding heap procedure primitives. Therefore, form document manipulation expressible as a combination of NT operations can be formulated as a heap procedure. The following primitives are additionally introduced in Table 4.2 to enhance the usability of heap procedures in FORMDOQ environments:

Get

This primitive is usually specified at the beginning of a heap procedure. The primitive receives a holder identifier and a form schema identifier as parameters. Then, it constructs a form document heap consisting of documents registered in the designated holder and having the specified form schema. Precisely speaking, copies

Table 4.2. Heap procedure primitives

Primitive	Function
nest	NEST
flat	FLAT
project	PROJECTION
take	INNER_PROJECTION
select	SELECTION
union	UNION
diff	DIFFERENCE
inter	INTERSECTION
embed	Integration of PRODUCT, CARTESIAN_PRODUCT, EMBED, NATURAL_EMBED, JOIN, and NATURAL_JOIN
get	
put	
rename	
add	See descriptions in Sect. 4.5.9
sort	
rmdup	
table	
graphic	

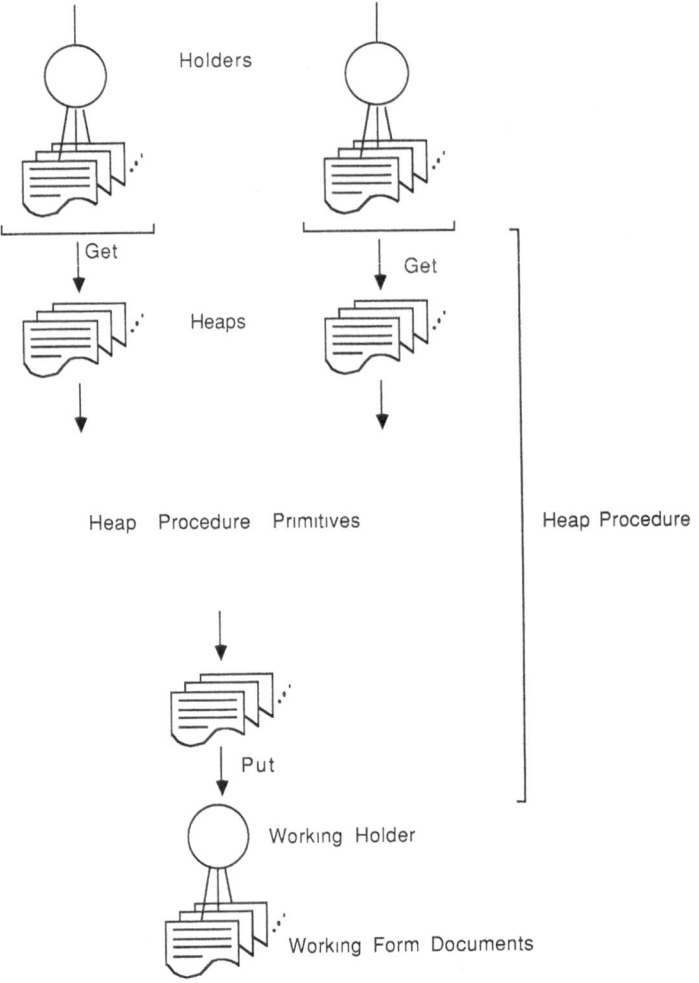

Fig. 4.19. Heap procedure

of these documents are created and included in the heap. Therefore, manipulation of the heap is independent from the original form documents. Although Fig. 4.19 implies that this primitive outputs a form document heap, the actual output is an NT underlying the form document heap. In other words, information on external presentation is not associated with the output.

Put

This primitive is usually specified at the end of a heap procedure (Fig. 4.19). It inputs an NT and receives a form schema identifier as a parameter. It first attaches the form schema to the NT to generate a form document heap which can be represented externally. Then, it puts the form documents included in the heap under the working holder, the storage area for working form documents. The form schema given as a parameter has to be compatible with the NT schema of the inputed NT.

Rename

This primitive is used to change names of groups and fields in an NT.

Add

This primitive is used to add new groups and fields to an NT.

Sort

Clusters in NTs have a sequential order in FORMDOQ. This is a practical modification to the set theoretical definition of NTs shown in Sect. 3.2. Clusters in an NT are sorted by this primitive.

Rmdup

Duplicated clusters are allowed in NTs in FORMDOQ. This is another practical modification to the NT definition in Sect. 3.2. Therefore, when duplicated clusters are generated in a heap procedure, they are not automatically removed. Duplicates are removed only if the **rmdup** primitive is explicitly specified.

Table

This primitive has been introduced for media conversion. As mentioned before, graphics data can be stored in NTs as primitive data items. For example, the PND diagram shown in Fig. 4.17 is stored as an occurrence of field DIAGRAM in an NT shown in the upperpart of Fig. 4.20. However, its logical graphics structure—represented by arc function, node semantic function, and arc semantic function—is captured by GED and actually embedded in the stored information. This information can also be expanded in a tabular structure termed a *G-structure* as shown in the lower part of Fig. 4.20. The G-structure is determined by the graphics type associated with the graphics field. It is composed of a field *GTYPE* and two groups *NODE* and *ARC*. Fields A_1, A_2, ... in groups *NODE* and *ARC* correspond to attributes to node and arc types defined in the graphics type.[4] The primitive **table** is used to convert a graphics field to such a G-structure. This primitive has not been implemented in the prototype FORMDOQ.

Graphic

This primitive is the inverse of the above **table** primitive. That is, it converts a group consisting of a G-structure into a graphics field. Missing information required for visually presenting graphics data, such as x, y-coordinates, scaling factors, and rotation angles, must be appropriately supplemented by some heuristic rules depending on the specified graphics type or layout algorithms defined by the user. This primitive has not been implemented in the prototype FORMDOQ, either.

An example of a specification for a heap procedure is shown in Fig. 4.21. Since a heap procedure is regarded as a pipeline consisting of heap procedure primitives as shown in Fig. 4.19, a notation similar to that in UNIX shell script is used for the

---

[4] A rule for associating fields A_1, A_2, ... with attributes of nodes and arcs has to be supplied as a parameter to the primitive **table**.

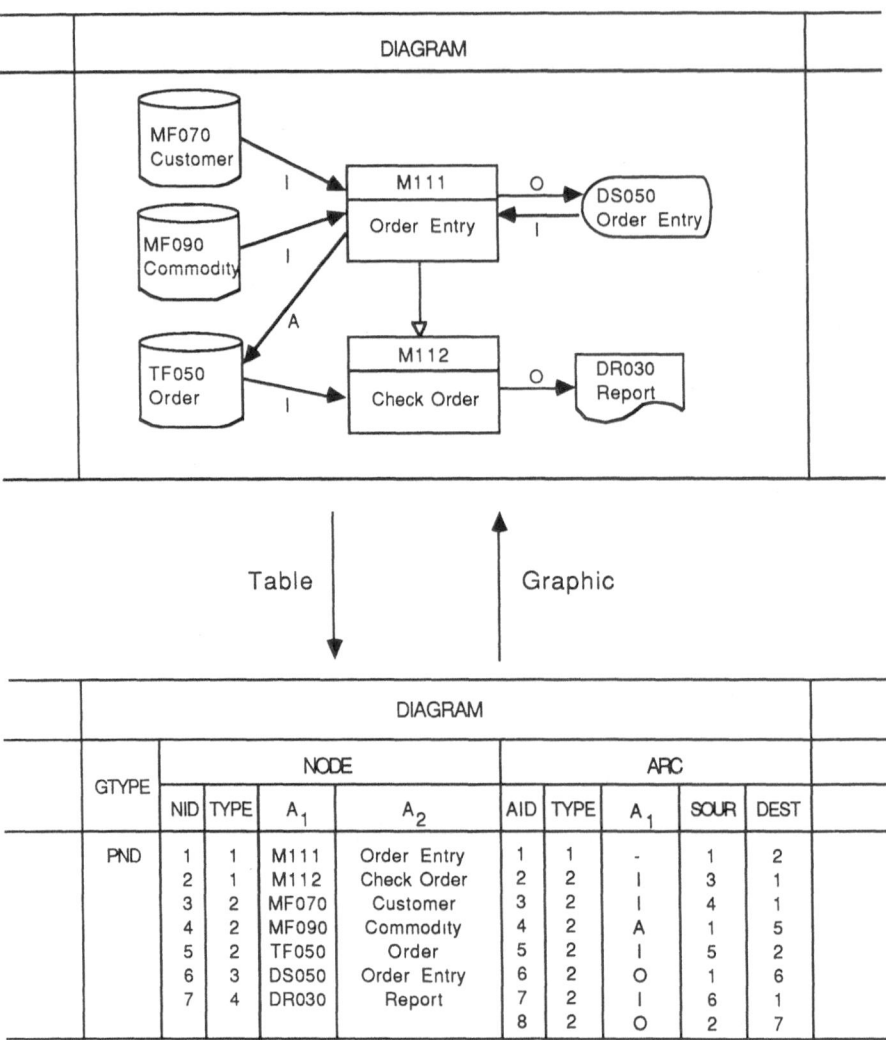

Fig. 4.20. Table and graphic primitives

```
get $1 I_O_SLIP |

project I_O_SLIP (SYS_CODE MEDIA SLIP_ID SLIP_NAME PURPOSE) |

nest I_O_SLIP SLIP_LIST (MEDIA SLIP_ID SLIP_NAME PURPOSE) |

nest SLIP_LIST SLIP (SLIP_ID SLIP_NAME PURPOSE) |

rename I_O_SLIP = SLIP_SUM |

put SLIP_SUM ,
```

Fig. 4.21. Sample heap procedure specification

specification. Namely, heap procedure primitives can be connected by the pipe denoted by "|", and names for temporarily generated NTs can be omitted. Explicit names can be assigned to them by the following specification:

$$(pipeline) > NT \ name.$$

Input from an explicitly named NT is specified as follows:

$$NT \ name > (pipeline).$$

All temporarily generated NTs are removed from the system after the execution of the heap procedure, even if they are explicitly named in this way.

As mentioned in Sect. 4.3, once heap procedures are specified and stored in HPB, there is no need to be aware of such sequences of heap procedure primitives. In addition, we have proposed the use of a QBF-like language for example-oriented specification of heap procedures. It is named a *language for office form processing* (*OFP*) [74]. Specifications in OFP will be more user-friendly than those consisting of heap procedure primitives. Some examples of OFP specifications are given in the paper [74]. The OFP technique can be used in combination with external presentations of form documents, as in QBF. Consequently, definition of a heap procedure could be accomplished at the external level without regard to NT structures at the logical level.

4.5.10 Application Program Handler/Interface

The *application program handler* (*APH*) is used to execute application programs in FORMDOQ. Therefore, its use corresponds to the application processing phase of FDM. Application programs to be executed in this phase are developed utlizing functions of another system module named the *application program interface* (*API*). API is a set of library functions to be linked with application programs. Application programs are basically developed by the user. However, some utility programs have also been developed as application programs taking advantage of API. Application programs are compiled and linked, and their load module files are registered in the *application program base* (*APB*). Although the execution of an application program is triggered by APH, its communication with other system modules is done through API and SM, as indicated by the diagram shown in Fig. 4.14. The following three classes of functions are included in API:

Screen Management

Functions in this class allow application programs to perform interactive input and output through the graphics screen. The following requests can be issued with these functions:
a) Open window
b) Close window
c) Display form document
d) Put message to screen
e) Receive message from screen
f) Receive icon pick up
g) Set function key
h) Receive function key input

Form Document Management

Functions in this class are for manipulating and accessing holders and D-files in the form document base FDB. They are restricted versions of FDB primitives provided by the file manager FM. D-files underlying working form documents are also accessed using functions in this class. Functions for manipulating key word and link indexes are omitted here:

a) Get holder list
b) Create holder
c) Delete holder
d) Open holder
e) Close holder
f) Get D-file list
g) Create D-file
h) Delete D-file
i) Open D-file
j) Close D-file

File Access

Functions in this class are for manipulating data items stored in D-files. Using functions from the form document management class, application programs open D-files storing form document data. Functions in this class enable application programs to manipulate open D-files as if they were NTs. In other words, application programs can access data items in D-files but their data item layout is invisible to the application programs. In this sense, the interface of FORMDOQ to application programs is set at the logical level. Functions in this class are based on the NT handles defined in Sect. 3.3. They include the following primitives:

a) Read occurrence
b) Modify occurrence
c) Insert cluster
d) Delete cluster

Although these are based on primitive NT handles (GET, MODIFY, INSERT, and DELETE, respectively), there are a number of restrictions enforced by limitations on their implementation. The sequential cluster number is assigned according to the internal ordering of clusters and used for the cluster address. This number may vary depending on insertion and deletion of other clusters. At each execution of the **read occurrence** primitive, the calling program can read the sequence of field occurrences of basic domains (integer, float, and string) or a field occurrence of extended domain (text and graphics), designating a cluster number. In the former case (basic domains), data transported between the **read occurrence** primitive and calling programs is passed through buffers allocated in the working memory area of the calling programs. In the latter case (extended domain), temporary files are used for passing data to get rid of the limitation on the amount of transferable data imposed by buffer size. Accesses to group occurrences are performed by nested executions of the **read occurrence** primitive. Similarly, in the **modify occurrence** primitive, a sequence of field occurrences of basic domains and a field occurrence of extended domain are the units of modification. At the execution of the **insert cluster** primitive, the calling program can designate the insertion position. The **insert cluster** primitive can only set field occurrences of basic domains for the inserted cluster. To input an occurrence of extended domain, the application program creates a temporary file including the occurrence. Then, it executes the **modify occurrence** primitive designating the file name. Modification of occurrences of extended domain is performed in the same way.

4.6 Interactive Document Handling

As mentioned in Sect. 4.2, FORMDOQ features a graphics-based user-friendly interface between man and machine. The man-machine interface is designed to implement the form document manipulation model (FDM), utilizing the direct manipulation technique for man-machine interaction. In Sect. 4.6.1, the basic design of the FORMDOQ man-machine interface is explained. Then, in Sect. 4.6.2, screen samples from typical interactive sessions in the prototype FORMDOQ are shown.

4.6.1 Basic Man-Machine Interface

Fig. 4.22 shows a standard screen layout in FORMDOQ. The screen is divided into five regions, termed the *main region*, *side region*, *key-top region*, *kanji/kana input region*, and *dialog region*. A graphics cursor is displayed on the screen. In the prototype FORMDOQ, the thumbwheels serve as a pointing device. Most commands are issued by positioning the graphics cursor and pressing one of the function keys. The role of each of these regions is explained below.

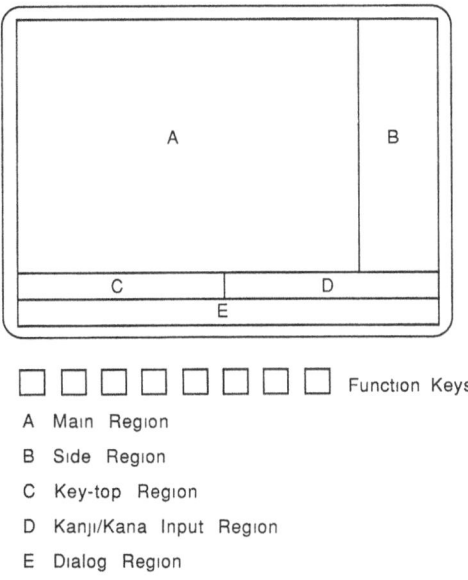

A Main Region
B Side Region
C Key-top Region
D Kanji/Kana Input Region
E Dialog Region

Fig. 4.22. Screen layout

Main Region

The main region serves the user as a "desktop." In other words, it is the main
working area. Several types of activities are performed on the desktop. They include
activities for six phases of document handling which were defined in Sect. 4.4. It is
usually the case with document handling that one document is manipulated with
reference to others. For this reason, we have decided to support a multiple window
mechanism within the main region. In the prototype FORMDOQ, the multiple
window mechanism was implemented using only the primitive window manipulation features of the target graphics terminals.

A screen sample from the prototype FORMDOQ (Fig. 4.15) shows that
overlapping windows can be set at any position within the main region. Each
window is associated with an activity for one of the six phases of the FDM. Each
window has a *header*, and the activity type is displayed in it as a title. Even if more
than one window is opened in the main region, only one is an *active window* at one
time. The overlapping windows are controlled so that the active window always
appears in front. The user can zoom in on any portion of the contents in a window.
Then, only the selected part is enlarged and displayed in the window. The window
size is not changed during zooming. For example, four windows are open in
Fig. 4.15. A portion of the document displayed in the middle window is zoomed in
on the screen shown in Fig. 4.23. In the prototype FORMDOQ, the window sizes
available for each type of activity are predetermined. For example, for form schema
definition, a form sheet may be placed in a vertical or horizontal position, and two

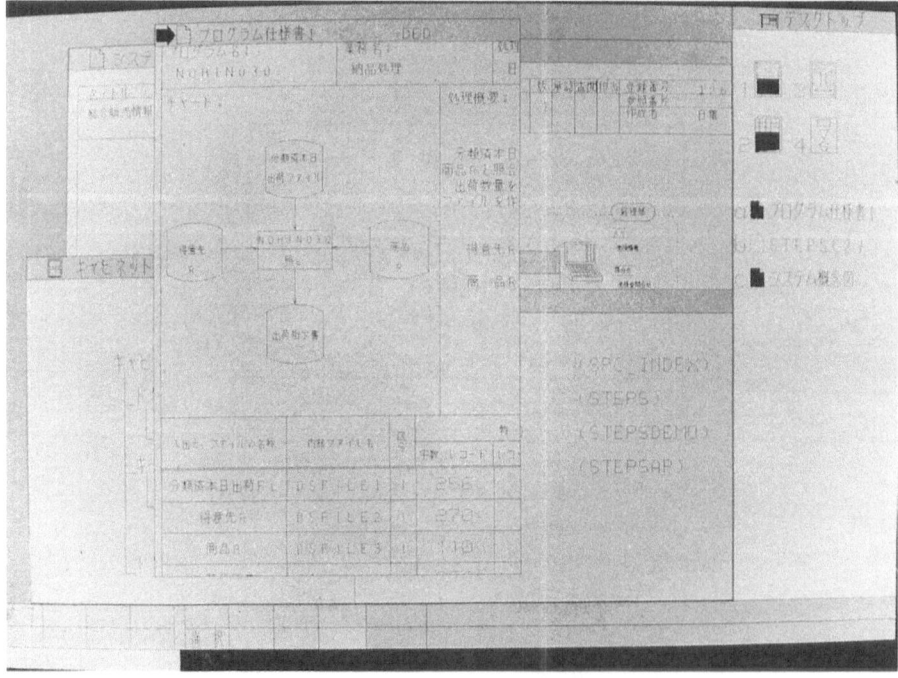

Fig. 4.23. Zooming in a window

window sizes are available in either case. Therefore, four types of window are selected when defining a form schema.

Side Region

The side region has two important roles. The first role is to display icons which graphically represent objects in the system. They are used to select an activity for one of six phases defined in the FDM. More precisely, the icons displayed in the side region in Fig. 4.15 are metaphors representing the following resources:

icon # 1:	Form Document Base
icon # 2:	Form Schema Base
icon # 3:	Application Program Base
icon # 4:	Graphics Type Base
icon # 5:	Heap Procedure Base[5]
icon # a– # z:	(Working and Registered) Form Schemas
	(Working and Registered) Form Documents

In Fig. 4.15, icons # a and # c represent form documents, and icon # b represents a form schema. Each of the above objects has an associated activity defined in the FDM as follows:

Form Document Base:	Form Document Base Manipulation
Form Schema Base:	Form Schema Base Manipulation
Application Program Base:	Application Processing
Graphics Type Base:	Graphics Type Handling[6]
Heap Procedure Base:	Form Document Heap Handling
Form Schema:	Form Schema Design
Form Document:	Form Document Development

As explained in Sect. 4.5, these activities are actually performed with system modules FDBM, FSBM, APH, GTH, HPH, FED, and DED. To start one of the activities, the user has only to select an appropriate icon in the side region and to set a window at a desirable position in the main region. For example, if an icon representing a form document is selected, the form document editor DED is activated in the window, and activity in the form document development phase is started for the selected form document. If, instead, the icon representing the form document base is selected, activity in the form document base manipulation phase, including document storage and retrieval, becomes possible for the form document base.

The second role of the side region is to hold temporarily information passed among windows. As mentioned in Sect. 4.4, form schemas are transferred among the form schema design, form schema base manipulation, and form document development phases. Similarly, form documents are transferred among the form document development, form document base manipulation, form document heap handling, and application processing phases. These form schemas and documents are transferred from one phase to another via the side region as illustrated in Fig.

---

[5] Heap Procedure Base is not installed in the version depicted in Fig. 4.15.
[6] Although the original FDM does not include the graphics type handling phase for simplicity, it can be defined in accordance with activity performed with the graphics type handler (GTH).

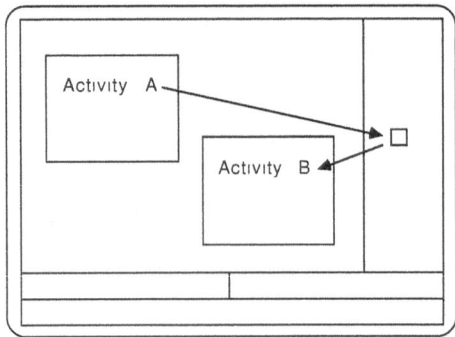

Fig. 4.24. Data passing among windows

4.24. For example, let the activities performed in windows A and B in Fig. 4.24 be form document development and form document base manipulation, respectively. After activity in the form document development phase performed in window A is finished and the window is closed, an icon representing the manipulated form document remains in the side region. Therefore, the document can be stored in the form document base by picking it up from the side region and placing it in window B.

We have introduced working form schemas and working form documents in Sect. 4.4. In the context of the above explanation, working form documents mean form documents which have been placed in the side region but not yet registered in the form document base. A similar view can be taken for working form schemas.

Key-top Region

A set of eight function keys is used for issuing commands, often in combination with positioning the graphics cursor. The function assigned to each key changes depending on which type of activity is performed in the active window and what status the activity is in. Therefore, the key-top region is used to display a set of function labels temporarily assigned to the function keys. As shown in Fig. 4.15, key-top labels displayed in the region can be in Japanese.

Kanji/Kana Input Region

The prototype FORMDOQ handles the JIS standard set of Japanese kanji/kana characters. They can appear in data occurrences in form documents, display formats in form schemas, form document names, form schema names, and so on. As its name indicates, the kanji/kana input region is used for their input. Their input is performed with a romaji-to-kanji/kana translation method. Namely, the user first inputs phonetic symbols (called romaji) for target kanji/kana characters from the keyboard. Then, a number of candidate kanji/kana characters are displayed in this area based on dictionary information stored in the system. The reason is that kanji/kana character strings often have homonyms. The user chooses the desired one from the candidate list, and assembles the input kanji/kana character strings in this region. The region is automatically activated when the system requests an input of a kanji/kana character string from the user.

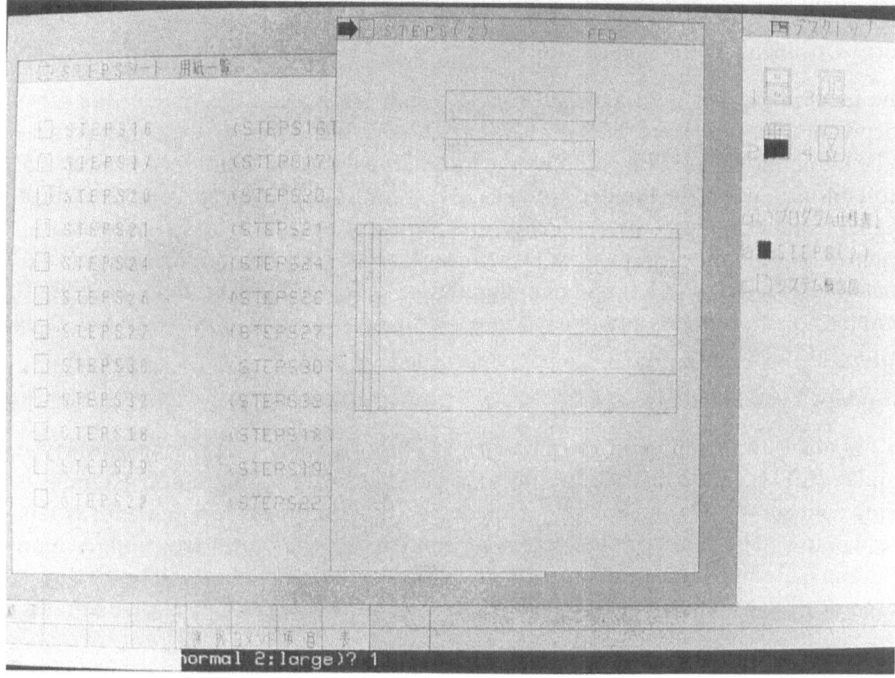

Fig. 4.25. Form schema design and form schema base manipulation

Dialog Region

The dialog region is for passing messages from the system to the user. Error messages are displayed in this region. This region is also used to give auxiliary information for command input.

4.6.2 Session Examples

Screen samples from the prototype FORMDOQ, reproduced here, show snapshots of interactive sessions using on the man-machine interface explained above.

Form Schema Design

The screen shown in Fig. 4.25 includes a session for form schema design. The window at the right shows an execution of the form schema editor (FED). The user can interactively design boxes and tables in this window. In the figure, two boxes and a table have been defined, and column and row layout within the table is being done. Area titles and column and row names will be given later, as character strings. The character strings can be kanji/kana character strings inputted through the kanji/kana input region.

Form Schema Base Manipulation

In Fig. 4.25, the left window, partially overlapped by the window of FED, shows a list of registered form schemas. This window is associated with the form schema base manager (FSBM), and interactive storage and retrieval of form schemas are performed in it.

Form Document Development

The left window on the screen in Fig. 4.26 shows a session example of the form
document editor (DED) for the development of a form document. Data occurrences
to be manipulated are picked up by the graphics cursor. As mentioned in Sect. 4.5,
sub-editors, namely the table editor (TED), text editor (XED), kanji/kana text editor
(KED), and graphics editor (GED), are initiated by DED to perform editing
oriented to domains and/or data structures. In Fig. 4.26, the graphics data in the
document is selected as a target of manipulation and GED is executed. Therefore, a
template of graphics symbols associated with the graphics type for the data is
displayed in the side region.

Graphics Type Handling

In Fig. 4.27, the window at the lower right shows a session of the graphics type
handler (GTH). In the figure, a graphics type for hardware configuration diagrams is
being defined. A node symbol for representing a certain type of terminal is drawn in
the window. The side region displays a template for the hardware configuration
diagram including node symbols defined in this way. This template will be displayed
in the side region when GED is activated to edit hardware configuration diagrams.

Form Document Base Manipulation

In Fig. 4.28, the right window is associated with the form document base manager
(FDBM). Interactive storage and retrieval of form documents, traversal and main-

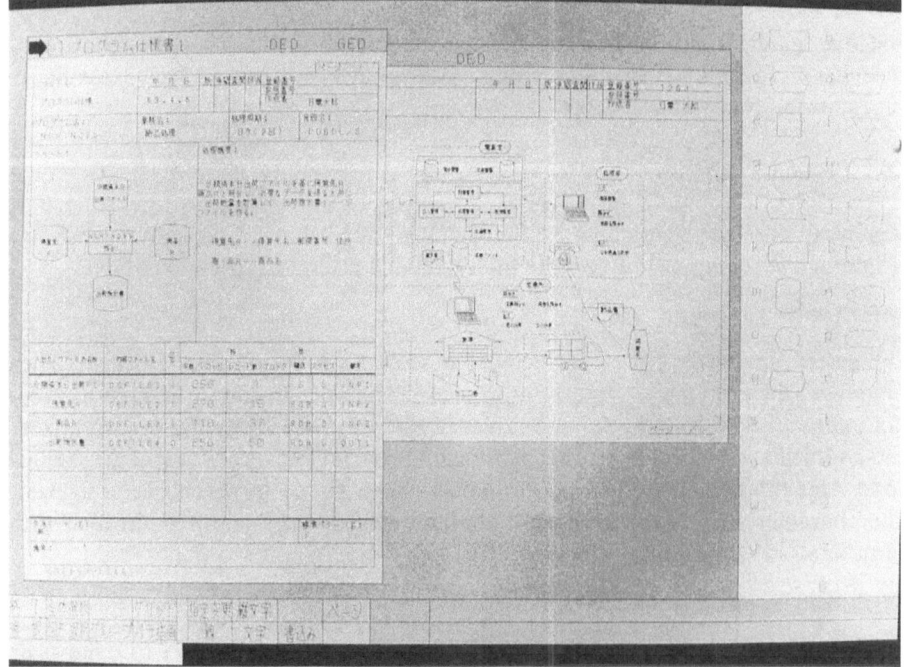

Fig. 4.26. Form document development

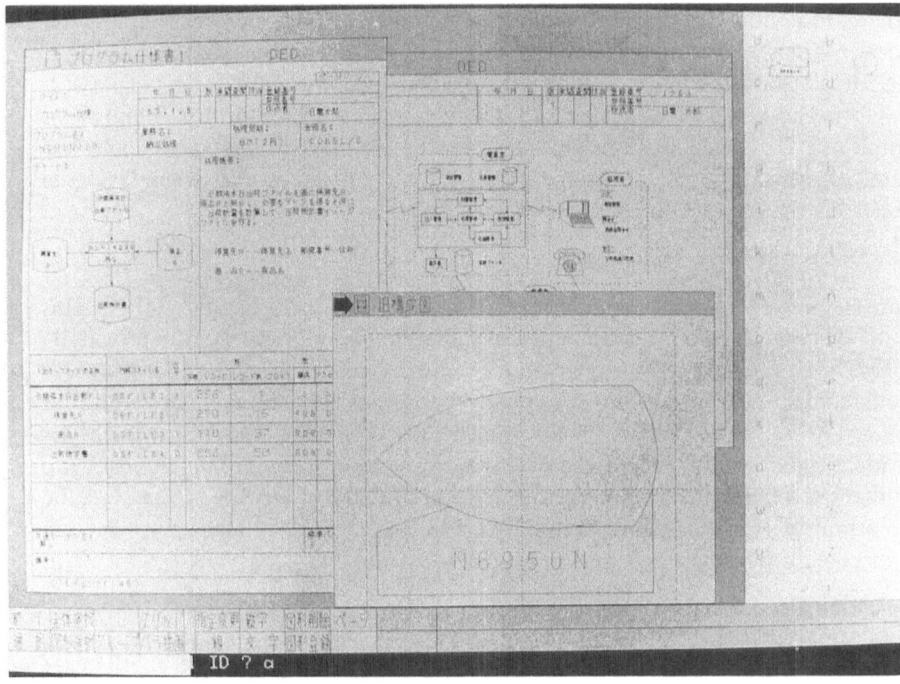

Fig. 4.27. Graphics type handling

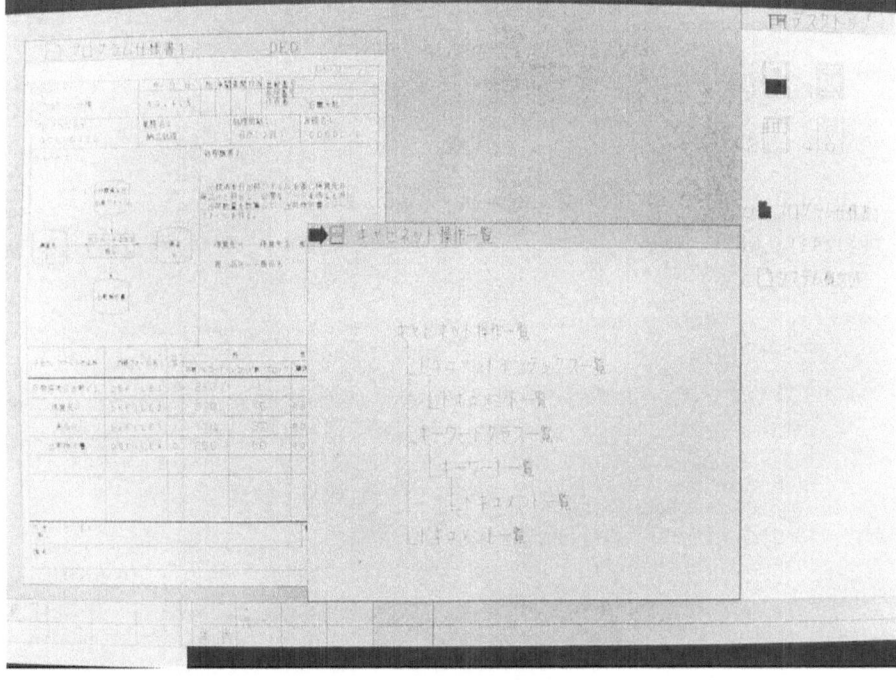

Fig. 4.28. Form document base manipulation

tenance of the holder hierarchy, and index maintenance are all performed in the
window. When a document search using the query-by-form (QBF) facility is
initiated, a separate window, automatically provided by the system, displays a
blank form sheet into which search specifications are entered. Figure 4.29 shows an
example of a QBF specification. This session example has been taken from another
preliminary version of the prototype FORMDOQ. Therefore, the screen layout is
slightly different from other session examples.

Form Document Heap Handling

Figure 4.30 shows a window associated with the heap procedure handler (HPH). This
session example has also been taken from the preliminary version of the prototype
FORMDOQ. Therefore, the screen layout is same as in Fig. 4.29, and the syntax for
form document heap procedure specification does not coincide precisely with that
discussed in Sect. 4.5.9. When a heap procedure is defined, a text-editing facility is
activated in the window. Then, the user may input and/or edit a sequence of heap
primitives specifying the heap procedure. When the heap procedure is executed, the
heap primitive sequence is interpreted by HPH, and heap handling is performed in
the specified order.

Application Processing

Figure 4.31 shows an execution of an application program in FORMDOQ
environments. This example program generates a document listing hardware

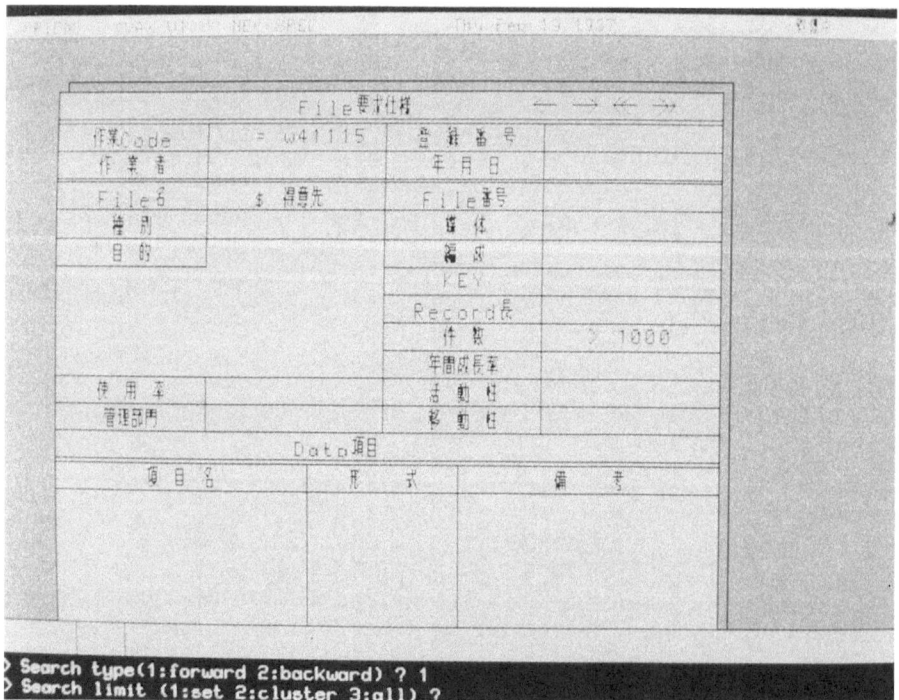

Fig. 4.29. Query-by-form

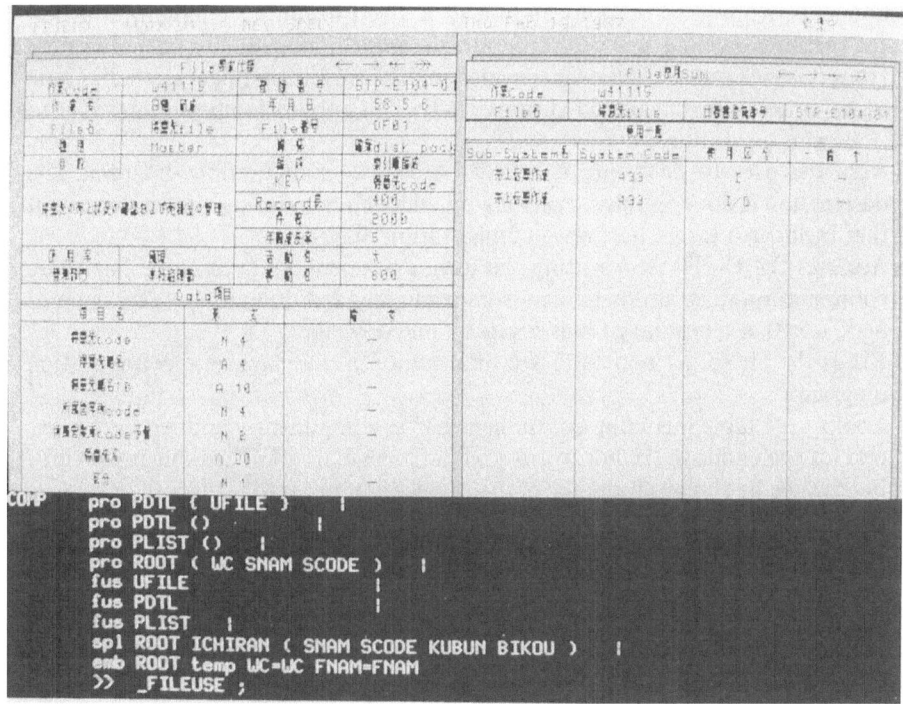

Fig. 4.30. Form document heap handling

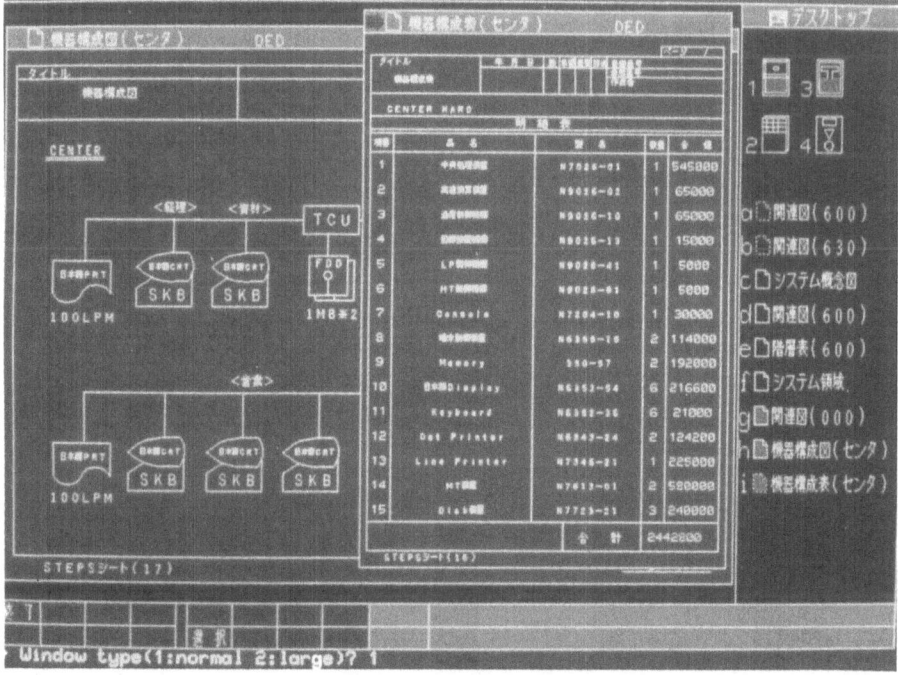

Fig. 4.31. Application processing

components, from graphics information in a given hardware configuration diagram. The generated list includes component name, component identifier, quantity, and unit price for each component specified in the hardware configuration diagram. The total price is also calculated automatically. This application program performs the following operations:

a) Asks the user to designate a source hardward configuration diagram. The designation is done simply by picking up an icon representing a form document that includes a target hardware configuration diagram.

b) Accesses the D-NT representing the form document, and reads the hardware configuration diagram as an occurrence of extended domain. As explained in Sect. 4.5.10, a temporary file is given by an API call.

c) Reads the file to get node and arc information in the hardware configuration diagram.

d) Looks up a table including component name, component identifier, unit price, etc., for each node in the hardware configuration diagram. The table is provided in advance by the programmer of the application program. Then, the program derives the contents of the target document.

e) Generates a D-NT to represent a working form document giving the hardware component list.

Here, the form schema for the document generated in (e) has to be defined with FED before execution of the application program. This example program is coded in C and based on functions of the application program interface (API) explained in Sect. 4.5.10. After the compile and link phases, the generated executable code is stored in the application program base APB. Its execution is initiated by APH and communication between the program and system modules in FORMDOQ is performed through API.

4.7 Prototype Implementation

The prototype FORMDOQ for single user environment was implemented under the UNIX operating system 4.1 BSD running on a VAX11/780. Tektronix 4112 and 4115 graphics terminals were used for workstations on a time-shared basis. The prototype FORMDOQ is composed of several programs all written in C programming language. Screen snapshots as shown in previous sections can be taken using video hard copy equipment directly connectable to the graphic terminals. High-quality hard copies of form documents can be obtained using electrostatic plotter connected to the host VAX system. Here, we discuss major implementation issues concerning the prototype development.

4.7.1 Process Structure

The process structure of the prototype FORMDOQ is shown in Fig. 4.32. Circles represent processes. Most system modules defined in the system architecture are implemented by processes in UNIX environments. Therefore, Fig. 4.32 is similar to Fig. 4.14. Major differences are as follows:

1. The graphics driver provides primitive functions to handle graphics objects on

the screen. It is not implemented as an independent process but linked with other programs that need to handle graphics objects.
2. Similar to the graphics driver, the file manager (FM) provides primitive functions to manipulate file structures implementing FSB, FDB, and GTB. Therefore, these functions are linked with three processes—FSBM, FDBM, and GTH. Access requests to FSB, FDB, and GTB from other system modules are coordinated by these three processes.
3. Similar to the graphics driver and FM, API is linked with each application program process AP.
4. FED, DED, GTH, FDBM, and HPH initiate one or more sub-processes, each of which runs to perform sub-tasks for the main process.

In 4.1 BSD UNIX environments, communications among processes are accomplished only by pipes or files, neither of which are very high speed communication media. In addition, there is a restriction on a structure composed of processes and pipes. Incorporating some of system modules into others by function call linkage as outlined in points (1) through (3) above, we have managed to construct a simple tree process structure. Moreover, this implementation scheme has brought about a reduction in the number of processes so that slow pipe communications are also diminished. In contrast to this, the decomposition in (4) was based on the consideration that tasks for FED, DED, GTH, FDBM, and HPH processes are decomposable into fairly independent sub-tasks and that these processes would

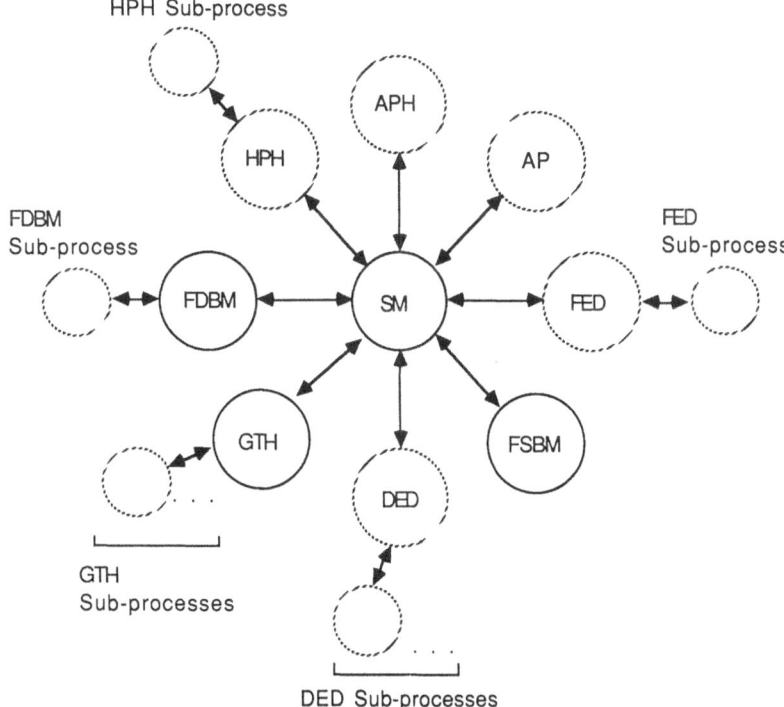

Fig. 4.32. Process structure

become unwieldy unless they were properly split into sub-processes. For example, DED calls a number of sub-processes to perform editing, dependent on domain and data structure as shown in Fig. 4.16. (The table editor (TED) is not split into a separate process.)

As indicated by rigid circle representations in Fig. 4.32, the SM, FSBM, FDBM, and GTH processes are always alive in the system. In other words, these processes are created when FORMDOQ is first started, since their tasks are critical for document handling in FORMDOQ. In contrast, the other processes represented by dotted circles in the figure are created on demand. They are started when the user directly or indirectly requests activities to be implemented by these processes, and cease when the activities are finished. As mentioned above, communications among the processes are all performed by means of message-passing through pipes. In a more recent version of UNIX such as 4.3 BSD and System V, we can use different types of interprocess communication methods to accomplish more efficient process co-operation.

4.7.2 File Management

Figures 4.33 and 4.34 give an overview of the FORMDOQ file system structure constructed in UNIX environments. In these figures, ovals and circles represent directories and files, respectively, in a UNIX file system. Figure 4.33 shows the core of information management in the prototype FORMDOQ. Several directories are defined to categorize information. Directory *.wdh* corresponds to the working document holder, and D-files including data items in working form documents are created under the directory. Directory *.wsh* implements the working form schema holder, and S-files for working form schemas are maintained. Directories *.fdb* and *.fsb* correspond to the form document base (FDB) and the form schema base (FSB), respectively. Directory *.fdb* further includes directories for managing holders in FDB, and for implementing the key word index and the link index structures. The holder list file including the directory information of all holders, and holder files listing information of all D-files and subordinate holders are managed under directory *.hol*. Files implementing the key word index and the link index are placed under directories *.kix* and *.lix*, respectively. Holders in FDB are mapped to directories in UNIX, and can be distributed through the whole UNIX file system. Therefore, structures such as that shown in Fig. 4.34 are created in the user-designated part of the UNIX file system, and D-files underlying registered form documents are stored in the structures. Holder nesting is managed according to the directory information stored in the holder list file, and is not directly correlated with directory hierarchies in UNIX. Directories *.gtb*, *.hpb*, and *.apb* correspond to the graphics type base (GTB), the heap procedure base (HPB), and the application program base (APB), respectively.

Although we mentioned in Sect. 4.3, that S-files include NT schemas, they actually store form schemas as indicated above. In other words, an S-file includes information on the external presentation incorporated into the form schema, as well as the NT schema representing the logical-level data structure. The organization of an S-file is depicted Fig. 4.35. The first section is the NT schema associated with the form schema, and the last section contains the information on external presentation.

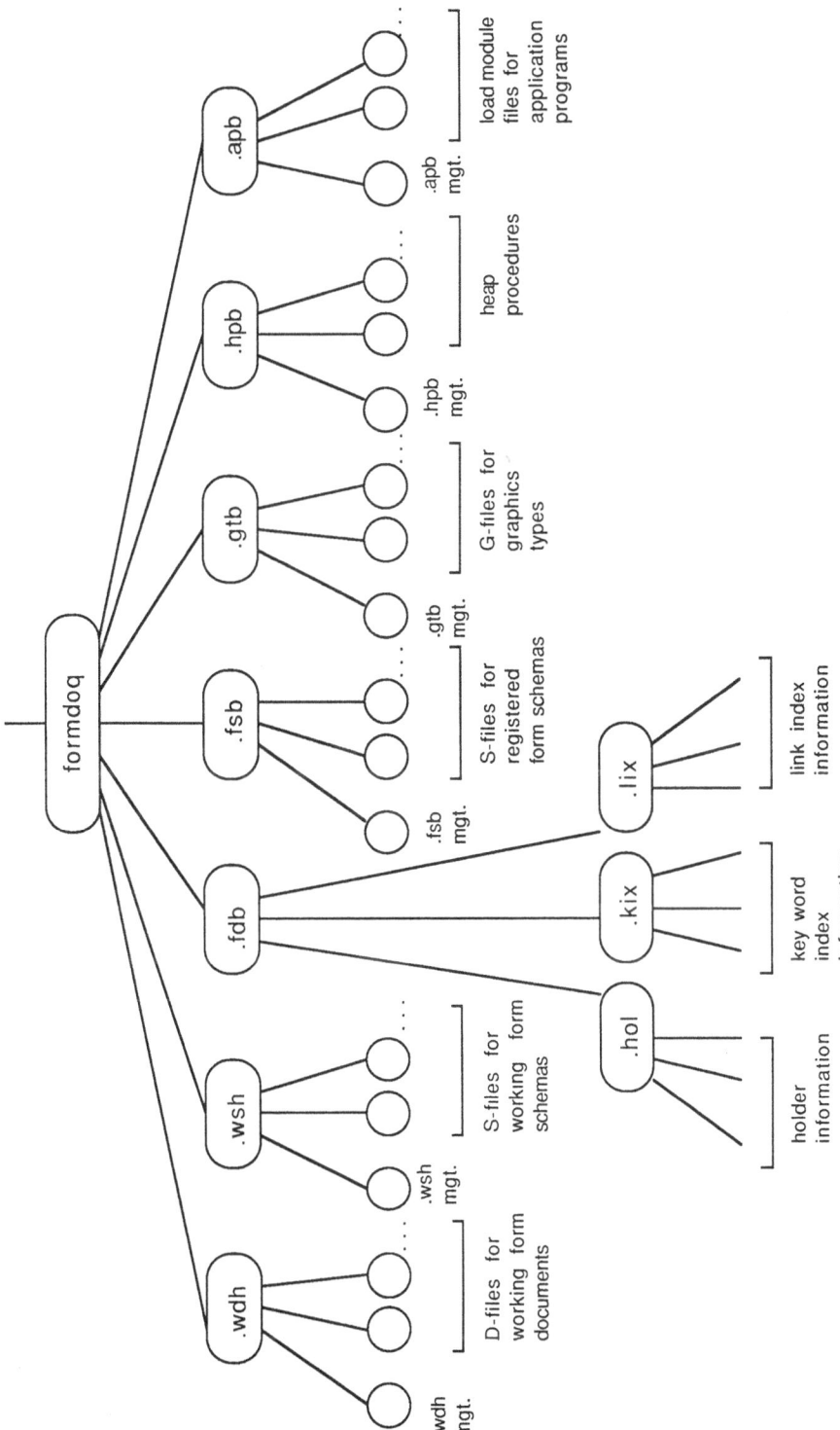

Fig. 4.33. File system structure (1) *mgt.*, management

A D-file is created for a form document, and it stores a cluster of a D-NT representing the form document at the logical level. The NT schema necessary to interpret the contents of the D-file is stored in an S-file. Therefore, a D-file includes only data occurrences of the D-NT at the logical level. Data items included in one form document are stored in a D-NT. Thus, the amount of data in a D-file usually is not so voluminous as in conventional database files. For this reason, data items in a D-file are arranged in a simple sesquential layout. Figure 4.36 illustrates the D-file organization corresponding to the D-NT shown in Fig. 4.9. As indicated in Fig. 4.36, graphics and text data items are also embedded in the sequence. At this stage, this filing scheme takes advantage of UNIX file features.

Use of a D-file from, for example, the form document editor (DED), is performed as shown in Fig. 4.37. Conventional alphanumeric data items are read into a buffer allocated in the working memory area of DED, and manipulated in the buffer. Therefore, the size of a D-file is basically restricted by the buffer size obtainable in the system. A sophisticated buffer management function has not been implemented in the prototype. Data items of extended data types, namely graphics and text data, are copied once into graphics data files and text data files by DED, and the sub-editors GED, XED, and KED work on these data files. Owing to this copy process, the global organization of D-files is invisible to the sub-editors, and coordination among editor processes is simplified. This scheme causes no performance problem in the prototype system. A similar scheme is used for D-file accesses by application programs through the application program interface (API).

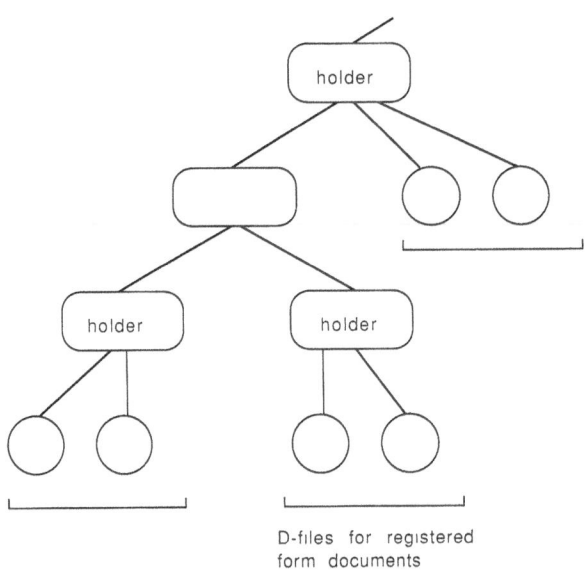

D-files for registered
form documents

Fig. 4.34. File system structure (2)

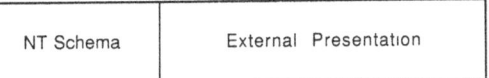

Fig. 4.35. S-file organization

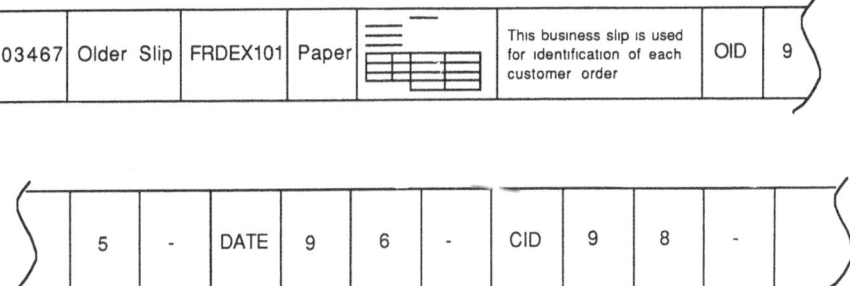

Fig. 4.36. D-file organization example

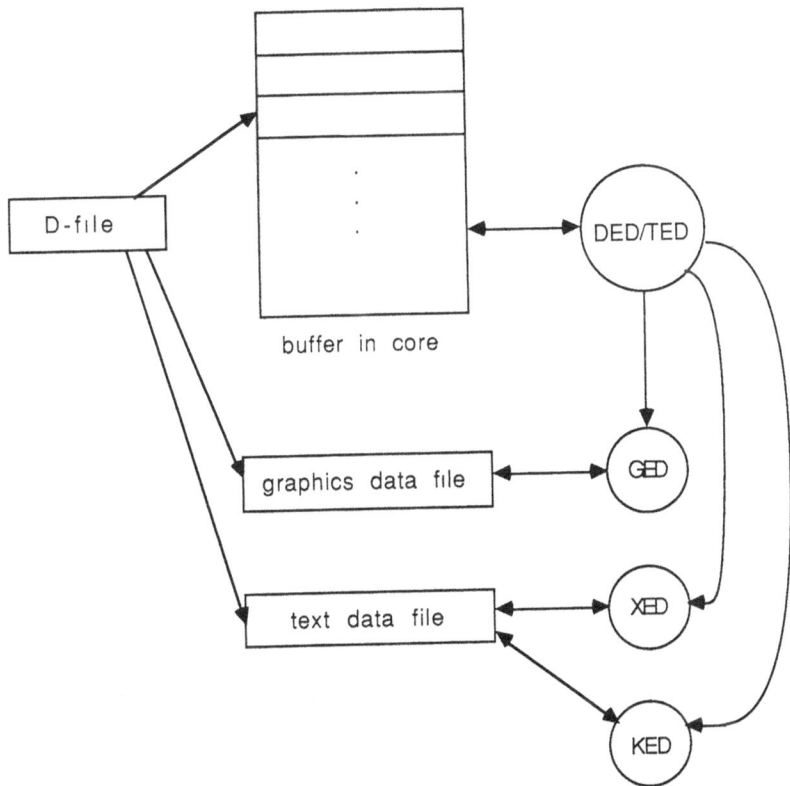

Fig. 4.37. D-file manipulation by DED

4.7.3 Form Document Heap Handling

Another important implementation issue related to file management is form
document heap handling performed by the heap procedure handler (HPH). As
explained in Sect. 4.5, a heap procedure is basically an execution of NT operations
on H-NTs logically representing form document heaps. At the internal level, H-files
are constructed to store NT occurrences of H-NTs. Since H-NTs are alive during a
heap procedure, and their structures are dynamically edited by heap procedure
primitives, NT schemas of H-NTs are maintained in the working memory area of
the HPH process. Although the size of an H-file can be much larger than that of a
D-file, its use is only for storing data temporarily. Therefore, storage schemes such
as sophisticated indexing are not appropriate for H-files. Heap handling is
implemented on the basis of a pointer-chained record structure embedded in UNIX
files.

Clusters in H-NTs are stored hierarchically by means of forward/backward and
parent/child pointers in H-files. The prototype implementation employed a small
file-handling utility package as an underlying tool to support the chained record
structure. As mentioned in Sect. 4.3, only logical pointers to data items stored in D-
files are given in H-files for graphics and text data. Because of this implementation
scheme, evaluation of graphics and text data items is performed at this logical
pointer level in heap handling. Their actual contents are not evaluated. Therefore,
for example, heap procedures involving conditional selections of data items of
extended data types cannot be handed by the prototype FORMDOQ. The
prototype implementation of heap procedures has some additional restrictions, and
functions of heap procedure primitives specified in Sect. 4.5 have not yet been
implemented completely. However, outlines of solutions to the major problems of
implementation are given below.

The implementation of each NT operation can be done for the H-files in a
straightforward manner. Sorting is useful for efficient execution of some NT
operations. For example, let us consider the NEST operation shown in Fig. 3.5. In
this case, sorting of clusters in the input NT (let it be T) by the sort key consisting of
fields F_1 and F_2 is effective to perform this operation. The heap procedure primitive
corresponding to this NEST operation can be implemented as shown in Fig. 4.38.
First, relevant clusters in an H-file for T are read, and a table for sorting is created in
the working memory area allocated to the HPH process. If the memory size
required for storing the table is too large, a file has to be used for the purpose. The
table includes field values for the sort key (namely, F_1 and F_2) and the address of
each cluster in the H-file. Then, the entries in the table are sorted. Finally, from the
sorted result, a new H-file for NEST(T) (precisely, $N[G_1, G_2\langle F_3, F_4\rangle](T)$) is
created. In this example, the NEST operation is applied to the root group. When the
NEST operation is applied to a non-root group, the above processing has to be
performed repetitively for each occurrence of the group.

Sorting is also useful in implementing heap procedure primitives such as **diff,
inter, embed, sort,** and **rmdup.** However, in practical situations, this method has two
problems. The first problem is that there are cases where the sort key includes too
many elements. For example, if the group G_1 in the above NT T has additional
components C_1, C_2, etc., all of them have to be included in the sort key to execute

NEST $N[G_1, G_2\langle F_3, F_4\rangle]$. Secondly, the sort key may include groups rather than fields. For example, components C_1, C_2, etc., may be groups. The schemes for solution of the problems in our prototype implementation are as follows:

1. In a case where some (local) functional dependencies hold in the source NT, the number of fields in the sort key can be reduced. If LFD $F_1 \to F_2$ holds in T in the above example, the sorting has to be done only for field F_1. However, it is not so easy for the system to analyze the dependencies and to determine essential key fields. The prototype FORMDOQ was designed to provide a feature allowing the user to specify explicitly the fields composing sort keys, if any, for primitives such as **nest**, **rmdup**, and **embed**. HPH can use this information, and execute the primitives more efficiently with a smaller amount of memory.

2. In the prototype implementation, if a group is included in a sort key, HPH assumes that the group is functionally determined by fields included in the sort key. In other words clusters are sorted only by field values, and group occurrences are not evaluated in the sorting.

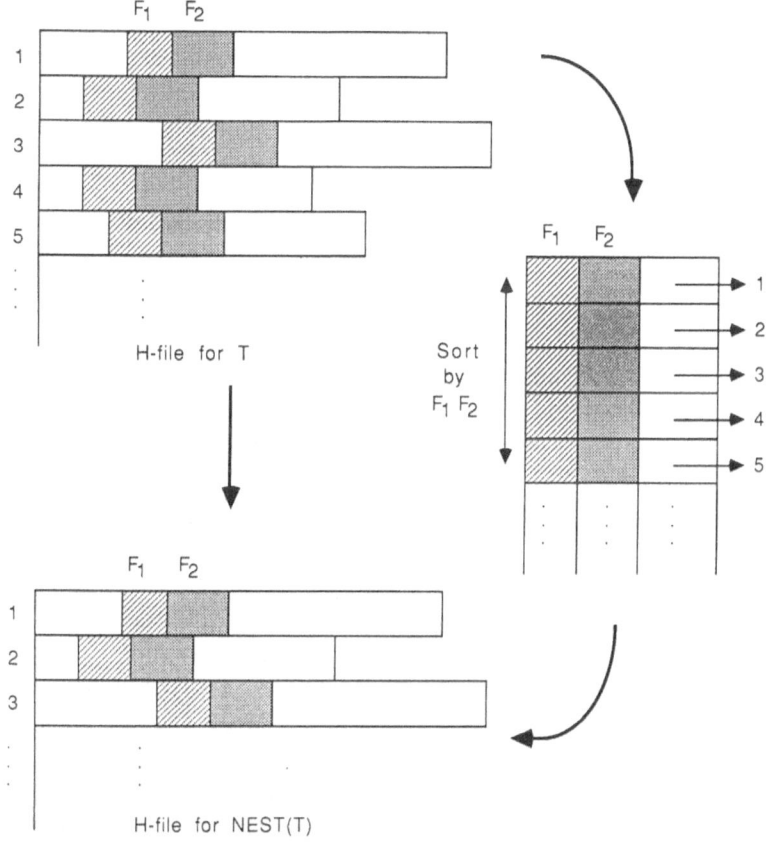

Fig. 4.38. Implementation of NEST operation

Execution of a heap procedure can be optimized in two ways. The first approach is optimization from the standpoint of reduction of the amount of data to be handled. Given a sequence of heap procedure primitives, the first approach is to find another sequence of primitives which generates the same final result as the original one but reduces the amount of data faster. For example, if primitives such as **project**, **take**, and **select** are applied at the beginning in the heap procedure, the H-file size can be reduced earlier. This optimization criterion is often used in query evaluation in the relational database system [133, 148, 157]. To apply this optimization, the study of the commutativity of NT operations is essential.

The second approach is more implementation dependent than the first one. In the prototype implementation, a new H-file is created as a result of the execution of each heap procedure primitive. The second approach tries to reduce the number of files created by performing multiple primitives at one time. For example, suppose, that in Fig. 4.38, **project** is the next primitive to be executed. Then, it would be unwise to create an H-file for NEST(T), and to execute the **project** primitive independently reading the new H-file. Rather, the new H-file should be created for PROJECT(NEST(T)) to reduce file handling. If the next primitive is again **project**, this second **project** should also be executed at the same time to create an H-file for PROJECT(PROJECT(NEST(T))). Figure 4.39 illustrates the execution of heap procedures based on this optimization. In the figure, H_1 and H_2 represent H-files for the input and output NTs, respectively, and S_i is a table created to perform sorting for H-file H_i. Fig. 4.39a shows an execution of the following sequence of heap procedure primitives:

$$\left[\left\{\begin{matrix}\text{project}\\\text{take}\\\text{add}\end{matrix}\right\}\right]* \left\{\begin{matrix}\text{nest}\\\text{diff}\\\text{inter}\\\text{embed}\\\text{rmdup}\\\text{sort}\end{matrix}\right\}$$

Here, { } means one of primitives listed in the bracket, [ ]* means $n\,(n \geq 0)$ times repetition of a primitive, and the above sequence is evaluated from right to left according to the convention in this book. If **nest, diff, inter, embed, rmdup**, or **sort** is applied to H_2 as the next step, a table S_2 is created at the same time. Figure 4.39b shows an execution of

$$\left[\left\{\begin{matrix}\text{project}\\\text{take}\\\text{add}\end{matrix}\right\}\right]* \left\{\begin{matrix}\text{select}\\\text{flat}\\\text{union}\\\text{table}\\\text{graphics}\end{matrix}\right\}$$

In this case, the sorting procedure is not included in the NT processing. Therefore, table S_1 does not exist. Table S_2 is created as in case (a).

These optimization mechanisms have not yet been implemented in the prototype. Although the simple implementation scheme mentioned above works in the prototype FORMDOQ environments, there remain many open problems on implementation of the extended relational algebra in general.

4.7.4 Graphics Manipulation

The graphics driver provides a two-dimensional graphics manipulation capability almost equivalent to that specified by ACM/SIGGRAPH CORE standard Level 4 [13]. Most of the graphics driver functions send ESC sequences to the 4112/4115 graphics terminal, to drive terminal intelligence implemented by firmware installed in the terminal. For example, the terminal has local segment memory and affords two-dimensional local manipulation of graphics segments. The terminal firmware also implements local zooming. Therefore, at any time during execution of FORMDOQ, any section of the current window can be zoomed in. Owing to the use of local graphics manipulation, even though complicated graphics objects are manipulated on the terminal in heavily loaded TSS environments, the user can get fairly quick responses from the system. As mentioned before, the multiple window mechanism of the prototype FORMDOQ was implemented almost from scratch on the basis of a primitive window-handling feature provided by the terminal firmware.

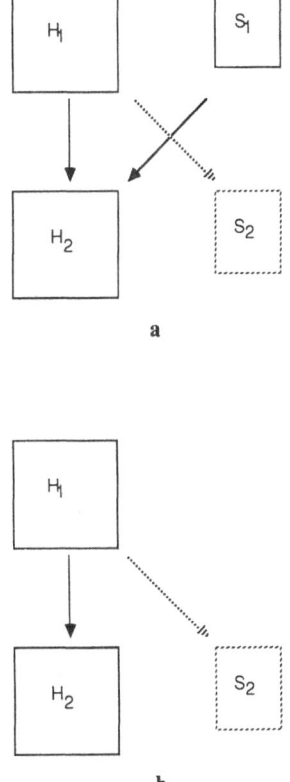

Fig. 4.39a, b. Optimization of H-file manipulation

4.8 Experimental Evaluation

The prototype FORMDOQ was used experimentally for handling system specification documents to support engineers' activities in software engineering offices. Machine support of software development based on STEPS (Standardized Technology and Engineering for Programming Support) [2, 7, 8] methodology was also included in the experimental study. STEPS was developed by NEC Corporation and provides systematically integrated standards for software development baselining, documentation, progamming style, and so on, covering the whole life cycle of software. STEPS is a form-based tool. For example, more than 40 types of standard paper form sheets are provided to satisfy requirements and system design specification. In addition, various types of graphics diagrams are used for specification, in combination with textual and tabular specifications. Evaluation of FORMDOQ from the viewpoint of STEPS support is summarized as follows:

Efficient Schema and Document Development

Owing to the capability of the form schema editor to cope with complicated form structure, we were able to define a form schema for almost every standard STEPS form sheet. Thus, we developed a library of form schemas to be used for STEPS specification in the form schema base. Consequently, software engineers could develop STEPS documents interactively on the screen just by filling in the form schemas. The form schemas look as if they were original paper form sheets, and efficient document development was attained with the form document editor. In particular, time-consuming manual drawing of diagrams was replaced by work with the powerful graphics editor. In practical software system development, it is often the case that a lot of similar but slightly different specifications are developed. Therefore, the reuse of stored specifications with modifications was essential to reduce the time needed for data input. For this reason, relevant facilities of the editor including cutting and pasting, were useful for specification development. Such editing capability also proved useful in form schema design. Since many STEPS form sheets have common sub-structures, for example, fields for specifying document title, date, author name, etc., those sub-structures could be copied from existing form schemas and reused.

Organized Specification Base

The form document base was used as a specification base in STEPS environments. Both completed and incomplete specifications could be stored in a well-organized way in the specification base. Thanks to the key word index and the link index, relevant specifications could be retrieved quickly. Conditional searches using QBF were also useful for specification retrieval. In addition, various kinds of report documents were generated from the specification base by executing form document heap procedures. Those report documents were used for analyzing specifications from various viewpoints to validate the descriptions.

Basis for Application Development

Utilizing the application program interface of FORMDOQ, a number of software engineering tools were developed to accomplish STEPS-specific data handling. As mentioned above, STEPS specifications include various types of interrelated diagrams. Although manipulation of graphics data can be performed partly in form document heap procedures, it was sometimes necessary to have application programs handle raw graphics data to comply with application requirements. From the experimental use of FORMDOQ, it has become clear that there are many applications requiring specifications stored in the form document base by the current facilities of FORMDOQ. In this respect, we have solved many problems related to modeling of external form documents. The next important topic is how to handle application requirements for data modeled in the system. Heap procedures provide solutions to some part of this problem. However, they are not enough: a more general scheme supporting the development of application procedures is required. Chapter 5 summarizes our research in this direction.

4.9 Summary

In this chapter, the design and implementation of the form document workbench FORMDOQ have been discussed. In the context of FORMDOQ, it has been demonstrated that NTs are good logical abstractions of form documents manipulated in various types of offices.

The first section (Sect. 4.1) gave an overview of FORMDOQ. In Sect. 4.2, generic functions of a form document workbench were summarized and four important requirements were posted for a form document workbench. Then, features of FORMDOQ were discussed from the viewpoints of those requirements. In Sect. 4.3, the basic system hierarchy consisting of the external, logical, and internal levels was introduced, and the major building blocks at each level were defined. In particular, form schemas and form documents were defined as building blocks at the external level, and it was shown how they are mapped into NT structures at the logical level. In Sect. 4.4, a form document manipulation model FDM was given, in order to specify system functions of FORMDOQ. FDM clarifies six phases in form document manipulation performed at the external level of FORMDOQ. In Sect. 4.5, the global system architecture of FORMDOQ was shown, and the function of each system module was clarified. In Sect. 4.6, the design of the man-machine interface of FORMDOQ was explained, and the explanation was reinforced by session samples from the prototype FORMDOQ. In Sect. 4.7, the major implementation issues concerning the development of the prototype FORMDOQ were discussed. The prototype FORMDOQ was implemented on UNIX system. In Sect. 4.8, the prototype FORMDOQ was evaluated, based on its experimental use for software specification handling in software engineers' offices.

5 Form-Based Application Generation

5.1 Overview

In this chapter, an architecture for form-based application generation is presented. The architecture is named *FORMAG*, and features the use of NTs as cononical representations of objects including databases, interactive screens, and output reports. Since database manipulation, screen-based interactive sessions, and report generation are major components of most conventional application systems, FORMAG can provide a sound basis for their modeling and generation.

As mentioned in Chap. 2, the approach described here is related to our previous research on application generation in the context of XDB [158]. The uniqueness of the approach was that application generation was based on a structured application system model. However, in that study, the relational data model was used for modeling database manipulation and report generation, and an informal model was provided to represent the interactive session. In the approach presented in this chapter, application data processing such as database manipulation and interactive data entry is based on NTs. Therefore, the entire data manipulation in the target application system can be specified in a uniform way. Moreover, various new constructs such as the form procedure, NT procedure, and NTPL are introduced for NT handling.

FORMAG includes two important elements. One is a structured model for application systems, and the other is a facility for generating target application systems specified in the model. In the next section, Sect. 5.2, the application system model is defined. Two major concepts for application procedure modeling, namely the form procedure and the NT procedure, are also defined. In Sect. 5.3, an application procedure specification language NTPL is explained. NTPL is used to specify form procedures and NT procedures in this context. However, NTPL itself could be applied to more general procedural specifications of NT manipulations. In Sect. 5.4, the conceptual design of the application generation facility in FORMAG is presented, and an outline of application generation processes is explained with a simple example. Section 5.5 gives a summary of this chapter.

5.2 Application System Model

In this section, we define an application system model in FORMAG. Application systems to be generated in FORMAG are first specified in this model. In other

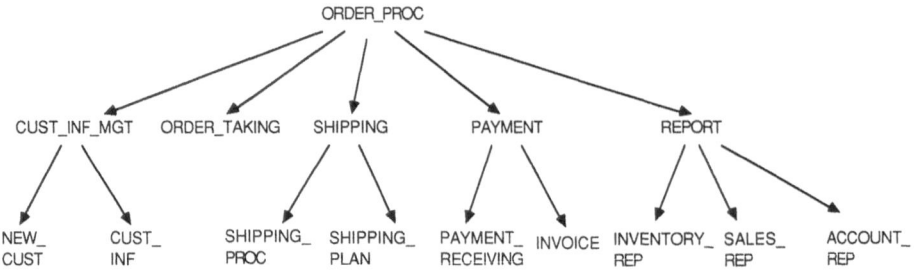

Fig. 5.1. Activity tree

words, this model determines the range of application systems able to be modeled and generated within FORMAG.

As several studies in software engineering have emphasized, an application system can be modeled from a number of viewpoints. Common viewpoints include functional hierarchy, control flow, and data flow. In our model, an application system is first specified from the viewpoint of functional hierarchy. This corresponds to the hierarchical decomposition of the target system. A tree of functional components called *activities* results from this analysis. Figure 5.1 shows an example of such a tree. Upper level activities correspond to more abstract functions and lower level activities correspond to more primitive functions. In the decomposition here, leaf activities are to be represented as networks of *steps*. Typical data manipulations involved in steps are data entry, database browsing, query, database update, and report generation. A more precise definition of the model follows.

5.2.1 Activity Tree and Activity Diagram

An *application system AP* is modeled as the following tuple:

$$AP = (T = (A, de), D, tf, DB).$$

Here, T is a functional hierarchy called an *activity tree*, and is denoted by $T = (A, de)$, where A is a set of functional modules called *activities* and $de: A \rightarrow 2^A$ is an *activity decomposition function*, meeting the *tree condition* defined below. An activity $A_i \in A$ is called a *unit activity* if $de(A_i) = \emptyset$. D is a set of *activity diagrams*, and $tf: U \rightarrow D$, where $U \subseteq A$ is the set of unit activities, is a function associating an activity diagram with each unit activity. DB is a database of application system AP and is composed of a set of NTs.

Tree condition. Suppose (A, de) is given; then a *decomposition graph* can be created by representing each activity $A_i \in A$ by a node $n(A_i)$ and drawing a directed arc from $n(A_i)$ to $n(A_j)$ if $A_j \in de(A_i)$. If the decomposition graph forms a tree, (A, de) meets the tree condition.

Using the above formalization, we can represent the functional structure of an application system as an activity tree and associate a collection of primitive procedure modules with each unit activity. The control flow among the primitive procedure modules is represented in an activity diagram. The application database is modeled as a set of NTs. In Chap. 4, NTs were used mainly for modeling paper form documents. The modeling of a database by NTs is rather straightforward. For simplicity, an NT can be regarded as an abstract object representing a file. Therefore, the database structure can be viewed as an unnormalized relational database structure.

Figure. 5.1 shows an example of a decomposition graph forming an activity tree. Here,

$$A = \{ORDER\_PROC, CUST\_INF\_MGT, \dots, SALES\_REP,$$
$$\quad ACCOUNT\_REP\}$$
$$de(ORDER\_PROC) = \{CUST\_INF\_MGT, ORDER\_TAKING,$$
$$\quad SHIPPING, PAYMENT, REPORT\}$$
$$de(CUST\_INF\_MGT) = \{NEW\_CUST, CUST\_INF\}$$
$$de(ORDER\_TAKING) = \varnothing, \text{ etc.}$$

Note that a unit activity is represented by a leaf node in the decomposition graph. Here, we further define an activity diagram associated with a unit activity. An activity diagram $D_i \in D$ is defined as the following tuple:

$$D_i = (S_i, L_i, C_i, s_{i0}, df_i),$$

where S_i is a set of primitive procedure modules called *steps*, L_i is a set of *links*, C_i is a set of *transition conditions*, s_{i0} is an element of S_i called a *start step*, and df_i is the following function associating two steps and a condition with a link:

$$df_i : L_i \to S_i \times S_i \times C_i.$$

An activity diagram is represented in a graph, in which nodes, directed arcs, and arc labels correspond to steps, links, and conditions, respectively. Each step $s_{ij} \in S_i$ corresponds to a job step in the terminology of conventional data processing, though data manipulation in a step is more well-structured and well-defined than that in a job step. Transition conditions to be associated with links by df_i are assertions. The assertions are formulated on data stored in the database and data inputted and derived in steps. Transition conditions are specified in a language named NTPL, to be explained in Sect. 5.3. When the activity diagram D_i is activated, the start step s_{i0} is first executed. After the execution of step s_{ij}, the transition condition associated with every outward link connecting with s_{ij} is evaluated. Suppose the condition c_{ik} associated with link l_{ik} such that $df_i(l_{ik}) = (s_{ij}, s_{im}, c_{ik})$ is satisfied. Then the control is transferred to s_{im}, and s_{im} is executed. There is a special condition: DEFAULT. Only if none of the other transition conditions are satisfied is the condition DEFAULT qualified. In this context, we assume the control transfer among steps is single thread and deterministic. In other words, we do not allow cases where more than two conditions are satisfied after the execution of a single step s_{ij}. If no conditions are met, the execution of steps in D_i is terminated and D_i is inactivated. In FORMAG, the execution of a unit activity forms a transaction, and is a unit of commitment, rollback, and recovery.

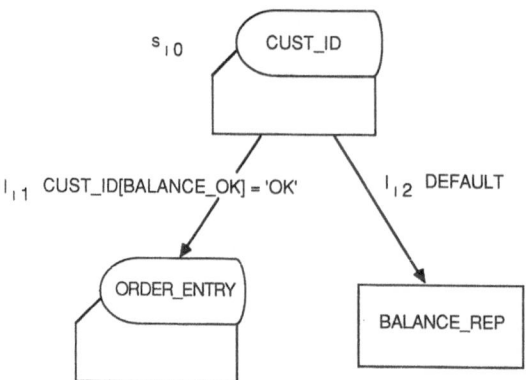

Fig. 5.2. Activity diagram

Figure 5.2 shows an example of an activity diagram. Here,

$S_i = \{\text{CUST\_ID, BALANCE\_REP, ORDER\_ENTRY}\}$
$l_i = \{l_{i1}, l_{i2}\}$
$C_i = \{\text{CUST\_ID[BALANCE\_OK]} = \text{`OK', DEFAULT}\}$
$s_{i0} = \text{CUST\_ID}$
$df_i(l_{i1}) = (\text{CUST\_ID, ORDER\_ENTRY, CUST\_ID[BALANCE\_OK]} = \text{`OK'})$
$df_i(l_{i2}) = (\text{CUST\_ID, BALANCE\_REP, DEFAULT}).$

This activity diagram specifies data-processing flow within a unit activity ORDER_TAKING, shown in Fig. 5.1. It has three steps. CUST_ID (Customer Identification) is a start step and is executed first. As explained later, the step CUST_ID is a data entry process on the display screen, and the transition condition CUST_ID[BALANCE_OK] = 'OK' is satisfied when the value 'OK' has been assigned to the field BALANCE_OK on the screen. If this transition condition is satisfied, the ORDER_ENTRY step is executed. Otherwise, the BALANCE_REP (Customer Balance Report) step is executed after the CUST_ID step.

5.2.2 Step

So far, we have not presented specific details of the data manipulation performed in each step. In the context of FORMAG, application systems are developed around database manipulation and interactive man-machine dialog based on forms. The types of steps can be classified into the following three classes:
a) Form procedure
b) NT procedure
c) User application program
   Actually, in Fig. 5.2, CUST_ID and ORDER_ENTRY are form procedure steps and represented by terminal symbols, and BALANCE_REP is an NT procedure step and represented by a rectangular symbol. We now further define each of these types of steps.

5.2.2.1 Form Procedure

Form procedures are intended to model interactive sessions performed on the screen. A form procedure is basically a process to fill in a form sheet displayed on the screen, in order to develop a form document. However, several data-processing actions triggered by the interactive data input can be incorporated into a form procedure, to model user-system interactions. For example, automatic computation of the sum, the looking up of a table in the database, and update of the database, can be embedded into a form procedure. This distinguishes a form procedure from the simple filling in of a form sheet. As we have seen in Chap. 4, NTs are good abstract models of form documents. Accordingly, a *form procedure FP* is modeled as follows:

$$FP = (FS, SS),$$

where *FS* is a form schema describing a structure of the template displayed on the screen and *SS* is a *semantic schema*. Form schema *FS* is a combination of an NT schema *NS* specifying the logical data structure and the external presentation *EP* on the screen as explained in Sect. 4.3. A semantic schema *SS* models several triggered actions embedded into the form procedure. *SS* is defined as

$$SS = (V, D, P),$$

where *V* is a set of *validations*, *D* is a set of *derivations*, and *P* is a set of *post-processings*. Fields in *NS* are classified into mutually disjointed subsets, namely *input fields IF* and *derived fields DF*. These differ from each other as follows:

Input fields. Data items for input fields are interactively entered by the user.

Derived fields. Data items for derived fields are automatically retrieved and/or calculated from data items in other fields of *NS*, fields defined in other form procedures, and the database.

Validations are assertions for validating inputted data for input fields. They can specify the following integrity constraints on the inputted data:
a) Valid value range
b) Semantic consistency with other field values
c) Semantic consistency with the database
Derivations *D* give procedures for deterministically deriving data values for derived fields from other field values and/or the database based on mathematical calculations, database look-ups, and some built-in functions (e.g., the function to get today's date). Post-processings *P* specify procedures performed when the user indicates the commitment for a form-processing step. Normally, this happens after the user enters proper data values for all input fields. Post-processings *P* include updates of the database. Validations, derivations, and post-processings are also specified in NTPL. NTPL is a language based on the NT handles explained in Sect. 3.2, and is augmented with expressions for specifying control flow among a sequence of operations and for sophisticated calculation. NTPL is defined in Sect. 5.3.

A form document developed as the result of a form procedure step is preserved during the execution of the unit activity, even after the form procedure step is

```
┌─────────────────────────────────────────────────────────┐
│                 CUSTOMER IDENTIFICATION                   │
│                                                           │
│   CUSTOMER  NUMBER    ·    [CNO              ]             │
│             NAME           [CNAME            ]             │
│             ADDRESS        [CADDR            ]             │
│             CITY           [CCITY            ]             │
│             PHONE          [CPHONE           ]             │
│             CLASS     ·    [CCLASS           ]             │
│             BALANCE        [CBALANCE         ]             │
│   ─────────────────────────────────────────               │
│                                                           │
│   BALANCE CHECK OF?        [BALANCE_OK      ]             │
└─────────────────────────────────────────────────────────┘
```

Fig. 5.3. Form schema for CUST_ID

completed. Therefore, data values inputted and derived in a form procedure step can be referred to in other steps, which may be form procedures, NT procedures, or executions of user application programs.

Figure 5.3 shows an example of a simple form schema which might be used for the form-processing step CUST_ID. Fields are represented by brackets in the figure. The NT schema for this form schema is as follows:

CUST_ID⟨CNO, CNAME, CADDR, CCITY, CPHONE, CCLASS,
     CBALANCE, BALANCE_OK⟩.

Suppose we have the customer information file in the database which is modeled as a flat NT with the following NT schema:

CUSTOMER⟨CNO, CNAME, CADDR, CCITY, CPHONE, CCLASS,
     CBALANCE⟩.

Then, we can designate the field CNO of CUST_ID as an input field, and make the others derived fields for this form procedure. That is to say,

$IF = \{CNO\}$

$DF = \{CNAME, CADDR, CCITY, CPHONE, CCLASS, CBALANCE, BALANCE\_OK\}$.

The validation for the field CNO specifies the valid range of the data inputted for CNO so that it matches exactly one occurrence of the field CNO in the above NT CUSTOMER stored in the database. The derivation specifications for the derived fields except BALANCE_OK are basically queries to the NT. The inputted CNO value will be used for the search key in these queries. The derivation procedure for BALANCE_OK involves simple if-then-else logic, which is expressed as

     if CUST_ID[CCLASS] = 'A' AND
        CUST_ID[CBALANCE] < #LIM_A OR
        CUST_ID[CCLASS] = 'B' AND

CUST_ID[CBALANCE] < #LIM_B OR
CUST_ID[CCLASS] = 'C' AND
CUST_ID[CBALANCE] < #LIM_C
then (MODIFY(CUST_ID[BALANCE_OK: 'OK']))
else (MODIFY(CUST_ID[BALANCE_OK: 'NO']))

where #LIM_A, #LIM_B, and #LIM_C are actually substituted by the desired integers. This example is a simple form procedure which essentially performs database query. Database update is not involved in this procedure, and it involves no post-processing. A more sophisticated example including post-processing is given in Sect. 5.3.

5.2.2.2 NT Procedure

NT procedures are intended to model batch-oriented report generation and file handling procedures. In the application system model, there are four types of data objects. They are form documents developed in form procedures, files stored in the database, report documents, and transaction files. They are uniformly modeled as NTs in FORMAG. NT procedure specification requires definition of NTs representing report documents and transaction files involved. Data manipulation in an NT procedure is specified in a sequence of NT operations defined in Sect. 3.4, or in NTPL statements explained in Sect. 5.3.

When NT operations are used for the specification, it is basically equivalent to a heap procedure in FORMDOQ as explained in Chap. 4. Therefore, expressions similar to the heap procedure specifications explained in Sect. 4.5 can also be employed for NT procedure specifications. Of course, for practical purposes, some extensions to the operations allowed in the present heap procedures would be necessary. For example, a certain level of arithmetic calculation would be required for sophisticated report generation. Such extensions are possible based on the heap procedure specifications. In this chapter, we consider an NT procedure just as a sequence of the NT operations allowed in heap procedures, and employ their specifications for expressing NT procedures. One or more NTs result from an NT procedure as in the case of a heap procedure. They are stored in the application database, printed out on paper as report documents, or temporarily stored as transaction files. The contents of report documents and transaction files are preserved during the execution of the unit activity, and can be referred to by other steps.

For example, suppose the database includes an NT ORDER whose NT schema consists of the following two group schemas:

ORDER⟨ONO, ODATE, CNO, SDATE, PDUE, PDATE, SUB_TOTAL,
        TOTAL, PART⟩
PART⟨PNO, QTY⟩.

Then, the NT procedure step BALANCE_REP can produce a report as shown in Fig. 5.4 from the NT ORDER together with the previously mentioned NT CUSTOMER. One of possible specifications for this NT procedure is as follows:
a) Perform SELECTION S[CUSTOMER, CNO = CUST_ID[CNO]] on the

```
┌─────────────────────────────────────────────────────────────┐
│                  CUSTOMER BALANCE REPORT                       │
│                                                               │
│     CUSTOMER  NUMBER      [CNO                    ]            │
│               NAME        [CNAME                  ]            │
│               ADDRESS     [CADDR                  ]            │
│               CITY        [CCITY                  ]            │
│               PHONE       [CPHONE                 ]            │
│               CLASS       [CCLASS                 ]            │
│               BALANCE     [CBALANCE               ]            │
│                                                               │
├─────────────────────────────────────────────────────────────┤
│                                                               │
│     OVERDUE TRANSACTIONS                      Page 1          │
│                                                               │
│        ORDER          SHIPMENT    TOTAL    DUEDATE           │
│     NUMBER  DATE                                              │
│                                                               │
│     [ONO]   [ODATE]    [SDATE]   [TOTAL]   [PDUE]            │
│                                                               │
│                                                               │
│                                                               │
└─────────────────────────────────────────────────────────────┘
```

Fig. 5.4. Report generated in BALANCE_REP

NT CUSTOMER. Here, CUST_ID[CNO] refers to the CNO value inputted in the form procedure CUST_ID.

b) Perform SELECTION S[ORDER, PDUE < TODAY AND PDATE = #NOT_YET] on the NT ORDER. Here, TODAY gives today's date and #NOT_YET is a constant specifying the payment has not yet been made.

c) Perform PROJECTION P[ORDER⟨CNO, ONO, ODATE, SDATE, TOTAL, PDUE⟩] on the NT of (b).

d) Perform NATURAL_EMBED NE[CUSTOMER] on the pair of NTs resulting from (a) and (c).

NT procedure specification can also be done using NTPL statements. The NTPL statements specifying the above report generation procedure are given in Sect. 5.3.

5.2.2.3 Application Program

Most conventional business-oriented data-processing procedures can be formulated as a combination of form procedures and NT procedures. However, since there are a variety of applications, in some cases, all the user requirements for data processing cannot be met with these two classes of steps. In such cases, the user can define a step as the execution of their own program. Of course, the user is provided with primitive program modules such as interface routines to access NTs representing form documents in form procedures, database files, transaction files, and report documents. A subset of the application program interface functions explained in Sect. 4.5 can be used for this purpose.

To summarize, the basic procedures specifiable as steps constituting an application system model of FORMAG are form procedures, NT procedures, and application programs. Data objects are modeled as NTs, and each of the three types of steps is viewed as a data manipulation process to apply to the NTs. To clarify this point, NTs involved in the unit activity ORDER_TAKING are shown in Fig. 5.5.

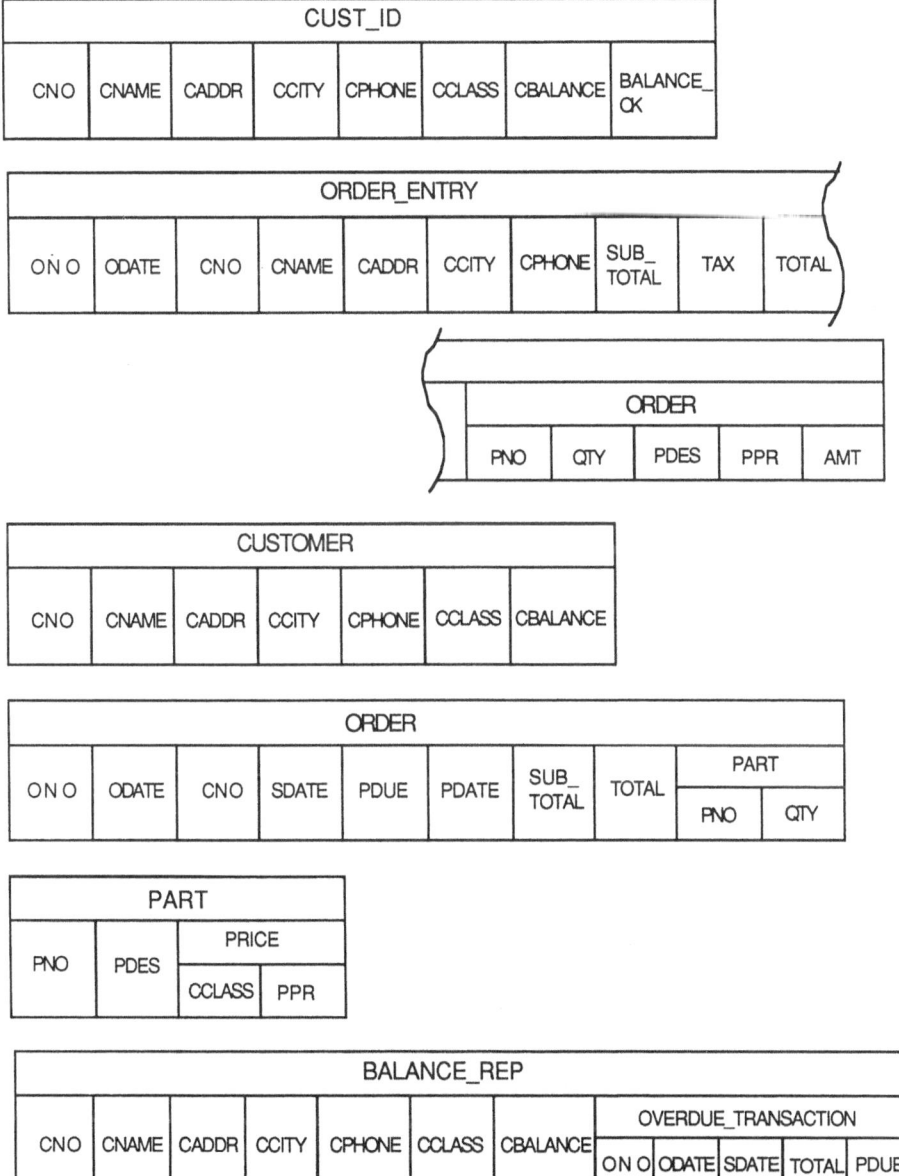

Fig. 5.5. NTs involved in ORDER_TAKING

We assume here that each NT has the same name as its root group name. The unit activity ORDER_TAKING is composed of three steps as shown in Fig. 5.2. Among them, CUST_ID and ORDER_ENTRY are form procedure steps, and BALANCE_REP is an NT procedure step. In Fig. 5.5, NTs CUST_ID and ORDER_ENTRY are associated with the two form procedure steps. At the beginning of the activation of the unit activity ORDER_TAKING, their contents are empty. When, for example, the form procedure step CUST_ID is executed, a cluster to be stored in the NT CUST_ID is appended to the NT. If the CUST_ID step were executed several times during an activation of the unit activity ORDER_TAKING, multiple clusters would be appended to the NT CUST_ID. Since Fig. 5.2 does not have a link going into the CUST_ID step, the step is actually executed only once. Other steps can refer to the data in CUST_ID while the unit activity ORDER_TAKING is activated. When ORDER_TAKING is deactivated, those NTs associated with form procedure steps are cleaned up. The NTs CUSTOMER, ORDER, and PART model files stored in the database. The last NT BALANCE_REP is associated with the NT procedure BALANCE_REP. The contents of BALANCE_REP are generated when the NT procedure is executed, and its data are printed out as a report document. The external presentations of NTs CUST_ID and ORDER_ENTRY are also given when form procedures CUST_ID and ORDER_ENTRY are defined. Similarly, the output format of NT BALANCE_REP is specified when the NT procedure is defined.

5.3 Application Procedure Specification

In this section, a language named *NTPL* (*Nested Table Processing Language*) is proposed. NTPL is used for specifying NT manipulation procedures based on the NT handles defined in Sect. 3.3. In the context of FORMAG, NTPL statements are used for specification of transition conditions, validations, derivations, and post-processings incorporated into form procedures, and also specification of NT procedures.

5.3.1 NTPL Specification

As mentioned above, NTPL is based on NT handles. In NT handles, cluster addresses are used for designating clusters in an NT. Let ca_i be the cluster address for a G_i cluster in an NT N. Then, the cluster is addressed by the expression $G_i @ ca_i$. NTPL takes over this notational convention, and the cluster is designated by $N.G_i @ ca_i$. In NTPL, the cluster address is assumed to be invariant under insertion and deletion of other clusters. Data occurrences as obtained by the GET NT handle are denoted as follows:

$$N.G_i @ ca_i[F_j] = get\, G_i @ ca_i[F_j]\ in\ N$$

$$N.G_i @ ca_i[G_j][F_k] = get\, G_i @ ca_i[G_j][F_k]\ in\ N.$$

In case a set of cluster addresses CA_i is given instead of ca_i:

$$N.G_i @ CA_i = \{N.G_i @ ca_i | ca_i \in CA_i\}$$

$$N.G_i @ CA_i[F_j] = \{N.G_i @ ca_i[F_j] | ca_i \in CA_i\}$$

$$N.G_i @ CA_i[G_j][F_k] = \{N.G_i @ ca_i[G_j][F_k] | ca_i \in CA_i\}.$$

Precisely, in NTPL, a construct referred to as a *cluster address expression* can appear instead of cluster address ca_i and cluster address set CA_i. A cluster address expression $\langle ca\_exp \rangle$ is intended to express a set of cluster addresses designating clusters of one group. In BNF, $\langle ca\_exp \rangle$ is specified as follows:

$$\langle ca\_exp \rangle ::= \langle ca\_constants \rangle | \langle ca\_variable \rangle | \langle search \rangle$$

$$| \text{'ALL('} \langle g\_spec \rangle \text{')'} | \text{'ALL'} | \langle insert \rangle | \text{'SELF'}$$

$$| \text{'TRAN('} \langle ca\_exp \rangle \text{','} \langle g\_spec \rangle \text{')'}$$

$$| \text{'('} \langle ca\_exp \rangle \text{')'} | \langle ca\_exp \rangle \langle set\_op \rangle \langle ca\_exp \rangle$$

$$\langle g\_spec \rangle ::= \langle NT\_name \rangle | \langle NT\_name \rangle \text{'.'} \langle group \rangle$$

$$\langle set\_op \rangle ::= \text{'}\cup\text{'} | \text{'}\cap\text{'} | \text{'DIFF'}$$

Here, $\langle ca\_constants \rangle$ is one or more cluster addresses, and $\langle ca\_variable \rangle$ is a variable whose value is a set of cluster addresses. The construct $\langle search \rangle$ is based on the SEARCH NT handle and defined as follows:

$$\text{SEARCH}(N.G_i, SC_i) = search\ G_i\ in\ N\ where\ SC_i.$$

Here, the selection condition SC_i is extended from that for the SEARCH NT handle. Namely, in the selection condition for $\langle search \rangle$, constructs referred to as $\langle v\_exp \rangle$ (explained later) can appear in places where $\langle value \rangle$ can appear in the original selection condition. In the case where $SC_i = \varnothing$, $\text{SEARCH}(N.G_i, \varnothing)$ can be denoted by $\text{ALL}(N.G_i)$. In particular, $N.G_i @ \text{ALL}$ is an abbreviation for $N.G_i @ \text{ALL}(N.G_i)$. The construct $\langle insert \rangle$ is based on the INSERT NT handle and defined as follows:

$$\text{INSERT}(N.G_i @ CA_j[\langle value\_list \rangle]) = insert\ G_i @ CA_j[\langle value\_list \rangle]\ in\ N.$$

Precisely, the cluster address expression $\langle ca\_exp \rangle$ may appear instead of CA_j in $\langle insert \rangle$ as follows:

$$\text{INSERT}(N.G_i @ \langle ca\_exp \rangle [\langle value\_list \rangle]).$$

In addition, constructs referred to as $\langle v\_exp \rangle$ can also appear in $\langle value\_list \rangle$. If G_i is the root of N, '$@ \langle ca\_exp \rangle$' is omitted and '$.G_i$' can also be omitted. Also, if G_i is a child of the root and N has only one root cluster, '$@ \langle ca\_exp \rangle$' can be omitted. SELF and TRAN are special functions returning cluster addresses. SELF returns the address of a cluster just under consideration. The use of SELF is explained later in an example. TRAN translates one set of cluster addresses expressed by $\langle ca\_exp \rangle$ into another, according to the hierarchical data structures embedded in the NT occurrence. Suppose CA_i is a set of G_i cluster addresses in an NT N, and G_j is another group of N. Then, let G_k be the leaf common ancestor group of G_i and G_j denoted by $lca(G_i, G_j)$ (see Sect. 3.3). $\text{TRAN}(CA_i, N.G_j)$ is the set of G_j cluster addresses ca_j such that

$$ca_i = ca_k . trailor_i$$

$$ca_j = ca_k . trailor_j,$$

where ca_i is a cluster address in CA_i, ca_k is a cluster address designating some G_k cluster in N, and $trailor_i$ and $trailor_j$ are possibly null sequences of cluster numbers concatenated by '.'.

To show BNF expressions specifying NTPL statements, constructs of the form $N.G_i @ \langle \text{ca\_exp} \rangle$ are referred to as $\langle \text{cluster} \rangle$, and constructs of the form $N.G_i @ \langle \text{ca\_exp} \rangle [F_j]$ or $N.G_i @ \langle \text{ca\_exp} \rangle [G_j][F_k]$ are referred to as $\langle \text{occurrence} \rangle$. In $\langle \text{cluster} \rangle$ and $\langle \text{occurrence} \rangle$, '.$G_i$' can be omitted if G_i is the root, and '$@ \langle \text{ca\_exp} \rangle$' can be omitted if, in addition, the root G_i has only one root cluster. Other constructs, derived from the DELETE and MODIFY NT handles, are as follows:

$$\text{DELETE}(N.G_i @ CA_i) = delete \ G_i @ CA_i \ in \ N$$

$$\text{MODIFY}(N.G_i @ CA_i[F_j:\langle \text{value}_j \rangle, \ldots])$$
$$= modify \ G_i @ CA_i[F_j:\langle \text{value}_j \rangle, \ldots] \ in \ N.$$

As in $\langle \text{cluster} \rangle$ and $\langle \text{occurrence} \rangle$, $\langle \text{ca\_exp} \rangle$ may appear instead of CA_i in these constructs. In addition, constructs referred to as $\langle \text{v\_exp} \rangle$ can also appear instead of $\langle \text{value}_j \rangle$. The constructs derived from DELETE and MODIFY are referred to as $\langle \text{delete} \rangle$ and $\langle \text{modify} \rangle$, respectively. The same abbreviations as in $\langle \text{cluster} \rangle$ and $\langle \text{occurrence} \rangle$ are also applicable to $\langle \text{delete} \rangle$ and $\langle \text{modify} \rangle$.

The complete BNF specification of NTPL is given in the Appendix B. NTPL statements are specified by the following BNF expressions:[1]

$$\langle \text{statement} \rangle ::= | \langle \text{assignment} \rangle | \langle \text{insert} \rangle | \langle \text{delete} \rangle | \langle \text{modify} \rangle$$
$$| \langle \text{if} \rangle | \langle \text{for} \rangle | \langle \text{validate} \rangle$$
$$\langle \text{assignment} \rangle ::= \langle \text{ca\_variable} \rangle \ '\leftarrow' \ \langle \text{ca\_exp} \rangle$$
$$\langle \text{if} \rangle ::= 'if' \ \langle \text{assertion} \rangle \ 'then' \ \langle \text{block} \rangle \ 'else' \ \langle \text{block} \rangle$$
$$\langle \text{for} \rangle ::= 'foreach' \ \langle \text{ca\_variable} \rangle \ 'do' \ \langle \text{block} \rangle$$
$$\langle \text{validate} \rangle ::= \text{'VALIDATE ('} \langle \text{assertion} \rangle ')'$$
$$\langle \text{block} \rangle ::= '(' \langle \text{statement\_list} \rangle ')'$$
$$\langle \text{statement\_list} \rangle ::= \langle \text{statement} \rangle | \langle \text{statement} \rangle \ \langle \text{statement\_list} \rangle$$
$$\langle \text{assertion} \rangle ::= \langle \text{v\_exp} \rangle \langle \text{comp} \rangle \langle \text{v\_exp} \rangle | '(' \langle \text{assertion} \rangle ')'$$
$$| \text{'NOT'} \ \langle \text{assertion} \rangle | \langle \text{assertion} \rangle \ \text{'AND'} \ \langle \text{assertion} \rangle$$
$$| \langle \text{assertion} \rangle \ \text{'OR'} \ \langle \text{assertion} \rangle$$
$$\langle \text{v\_exp} \rangle ::= \langle \text{occurrence} \rangle | \langle \text{value} \rangle | '\{' \langle \text{value\_list} \rangle '\}'$$
$$| '(' \langle \text{v\_exp} \rangle ')' | \langle \text{v\_exp} \rangle \langle \text{binary\_op} \rangle \langle \text{v\_exp} \rangle$$
$$| \langle \text{aggregate} \rangle \ '(' \langle \text{v\_exp} \rangle ')' | \langle \text{built\_in\_func} \rangle$$
$$\langle \text{comp} \rangle ::= \langle \text{p\_comp} \rangle | \langle \text{s\_comp} \rangle$$
$$\langle \text{p\_comp} \rangle ::= '=' | '\neq' | '<' | '>' | '\leq' | '\geq'$$
$$\langle \text{s\_comp} \rangle ::= '=' | '\neq' | '\subset' | '\not\subset' | '\subseteq' | '\not\subseteq' | '\supset' | '\not\supset' | '\supseteq' | '\not\supseteq'$$

---

[1] Constructs designated by $\langle \text{p\_comp} \rangle$, $\langle \text{s\_comp} \rangle$, $\langle \text{primitive\_op} \rangle$, $\langle \text{set\_op} \rangle$, $\langle \text{aggregate} \rangle$, and $\langle \text{built\_in\_func} \rangle$ are defined as a minimal set for the purpose here. More domain-specific extension can be done within this framework.

|'INTERSECT'|'NOT_INTERSECT'
⟨binary_op⟩:: = ⟨primitive_op⟩|⟨set_op⟩
⟨primitive_op⟩:: = '+'|'−'|'×'|'÷'
⟨set_op⟩:: = '∪'|'∩'|'DIFF'
⟨aggregate⟩:: = 'SOME'|'ANY'|'AVG'|'CNT'|'SUM'|'MAX'|'MIN'
⟨built_in_func⟩:: = 'TODAY'|'TIME'

As mentioned in Sect. 5.2, NTPL statements are used to specify validations, derivations, and post-processings for form procedures. They are also employed for the specification of transition conditions. Validation statements denoted by ⟨validate⟩ are mainly for validation specifications. Statements denoted by ⟨modify⟩ and ⟨insert⟩ are mainly for derivation and post-processing specifications. Deletion statments denoted by ⟨delete⟩ can also be included in post-processing specifications. In either case, sophisticated data handling can be expressed utilizing statements denoted by ⟨assignment⟩, ⟨if⟩, and ⟨for⟩. When a sequence of NTPL statements is given for a specification, the statements are evaluated sequentially.

5.3.2 Example

Here, we show a sample use of NTPL statements for the specification of a form procedure. The example is the form procedure ORDER_ENTRY involved in ORDER_TAKING activity. The form schema for an ORDER_ENTRY session is shown in Fig. 5.6. The underlying NT schema is included in Fig. 5.5. We can classify

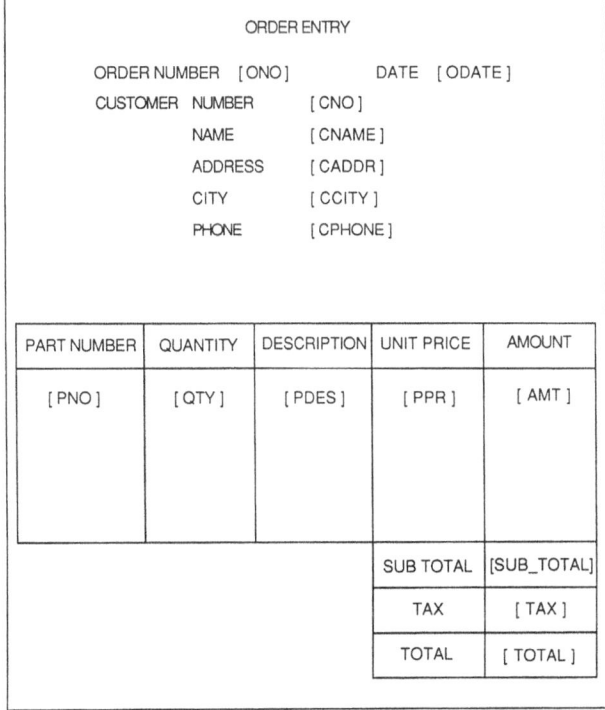

Fig. 5.6. Form schema for ORDER_ENTRY

fields embedded in the form schema into input fields *IF* and derived fields *DF* as follows:

$$IF = \{PNO, QTY\}$$

$$DF = \{ONO, ODATE, CNO, CNAME, CADDR, CCITY, CPHONE,$$
$$\qquad PDES, PPR, AMT, SUB\_TOTAL, TAX, TOTAL\}.$$

A validation to be associated with input field PNO would require that the given PNO value should appear in the part master file PART. This validation specification can be expressed by the following NTPL validation statement:

VALIDATE (ORDER_ENTRY.ORDER @ SELF[PNO]
        = SOME(PART @ ALL[PNO])).

Here, SELF is used to designate the cluster just under consideration. Note that ALL is an abbreviation for SEARCH(PART.PART, $\varnothing$).

Values for derived fields are obtained in a number of ways. An integer is incrementally assigned to the field ONO by the system. The ODATE value is derived from the built-in function TODAY. Derivations for ONO and ODATE are expressed by the following NTPL modification statements, respectively:

MODIFY(ORDER_ENTRY[ONO: MAX(ORDER @ ALL[ONO]) + 1])

MODIFY(ORDER_ENTRY[ODATE: TODAY]).

The form procedure ORDER_ENTRY is executed as the next step to CUST_ID as shown in Fig. 5.2. Since values for CNO, CNAME, CADDR, CCITY, and CPHONE have already been obtained in the CUST_ID step, they can be copied from it. For example, the derivation for CNO is specified as follows:

MODIFY(ORDER_ENTRY[CNO: CUST_ID[CNO]]).

Derivations for PDES and PPR are through look-ups to the database file PART. Values for PPR are retrieved using PNO and CCLASS values for search keys; thus:

MODIFY(ORDER_ENTRY.ORDER @ SELF
    [PPR: PART.PRICE @ SEARCH(PART.PRICE,
    PART[PNO] = ORDER_ENTRY.ORDER @ SELF[PNO] AND
    [CCLASS] = CUST_ID[CCLASS])[PPR]]).

Values for AMT, SUB_TOTAL, TAX, and TOTAL are calculated from other field values. Derivations for AMT and SUB_TOTAL are:

MODIFY(ORDER_ENTRY.ORDER @ SELF
    [AMT: ORDER_ENTRY.ORDER @ SELF[PPR]
    $\times$ ORDER_ENTRY.ORDER @ SELF[QTY]])

MODIFY(ORDER_ENTRY
    [SUB_TOTAL: SUM(ORDER_ENTRY.ORDER @ ALL[AMT])]).

In a post-processing for ORDER_ENTRY, order information has to be stored in the database file ORDER. Since NT occurrences corresponding to CUST_ID and

ORDER_ENTRY are cleared when the unit activity ORDER_TAKING is deactivated, order information is lost in this example unless it is explicitly stored in the post-processing. This task is specified in the following sequence of NTPL statements:

  item ← ALL(ORDER_ENTRY.ORDER)

  order ← INSERT(ORDER
          [ORDER_ENTRY[ONO], ORDER_ENTRY[ODATE],
           ORDER_ENTRY[CNO], , , , ORDER_ENTRY[SUB_TOTAL],

          ORDER_ENTRY[TOTAL]])

foreach item *do*
   (
   INSERT(ORDER.PART @ order
     [ORDER_ENTRY.ORDER @ item[PNO],
      ORDER_ENTRY.ORDER @ item[QTY]])
).

As mentioned in Sect. 5.2, NTPL statements can also be used to specify NT procedures. NT operation specification for the NT procedure step BALANCE_REP has been discussed in Sect. 5.2. The same NT procedure can be expressed in NTPL as follows:

  customer ← SEARCH(CUSTOMER, [CNO] = CUST_ID[CNO])

  report ← INSERT(BALANCE_REP
          [CUSTOMER @ customer[CNO],
           CUSTOMER @ customer[CNAME],
           CUSTOMER @ customer[CADDR],
           CUSTOMER @ customer[CCITY],
           CUSTOMER @ customer[CPHONE],
           CUSTOMER @ customer[CCLASS],
           CUSTOMER @ customer[CBALANCE]])

  order ← SEARCH(ORDER, [CNO] = CUSTOMER @ customer[CNO]
          AND [PDUE] < TODAY AND [PDATE] = #NOT_YET)

foreach order *do*
   (
   INSERT(BALANCE_REP.OVERDUE_TRANSACTION @ report
     [ORDER @ order[ONO], ORDER @ order[ODATE],
      ORDER @ order[SDATE], ORDER @ order[TOTAL],
      ORDER @ order[PDUE]])
).

Here, TODAY gives today's date and #NOT_YET is a constant specifying that the payment has not yet been made.

5.4 Application Generation Environments

The application generation environments of FORMAG are illustrated in Fig. 5.7. The use of facilities provided in the environments is divided into two phases, namely the *application system definition phase* and the *application system execution phase*. In the former phase, *application system descriptions* are given through interactive system-user dialog. The user is provided with several interactive modules for activity tree definition and step definition. The application system descriptions are interpreted and executed in FORMAG environments during the application system execution phase. Several types of interpreter modules are provided for the execution phase.

As the core for application development, FORMAG has a database management module which can be regarded as an NT handler. Some NTs are dynamically created in form procedures and NT procedures in the application system execution phase, while others are defined as database files (in a process conventionally referred to as the data definition phase) during the application system definition. In this chapter, we have focused on the specification of data manipulations of a target application system, assuming that file design and data definition for the application system database have already been done. Here, we present a scenario in which the data manipulations are specified and executed in the FORMAG environments.

5.4.1 Activity Tree

Application development is performed in a top-down fashion. First, an activity tree is designed to determine the functional hierarchy of the target system. For example, the activity tree shown in Fig. 5.1 is defined with the *activity tree definition module*. No specification language is used for defining the activity tree. Instead, the definition is performed step-by-step through a number of interactive sessions. In these sessions, a set of commands can be used to specify the tree nodes. The definition is completed through the command specification and the input of supplementary information, if required. *Activity tree descriptions* are generated as the result of the application system definition phase.

In the execution phase, the activity tree is mapped to a set of hierarchical menus. The *activity tree handler* prepares the menus from the activity tree descriptions. The hierarchical menu screens are utilized to traverse the activity tree and to execute data-processing operations formulated as unit activities in the tree. Figure 5.8 shows the main menu of the example ORDER_PROC system. This menu corresponds to the root activity in the activity tree shown in Fig. 5.1. When unit activities such as ORDER_TAKING and SHIPPING_PROC are selected, they are activated and the steps defined in them are executed according to the flow specified in the activity diagrams. When other activities are selected from the main menu, a sub-menu is displayed on the screen.

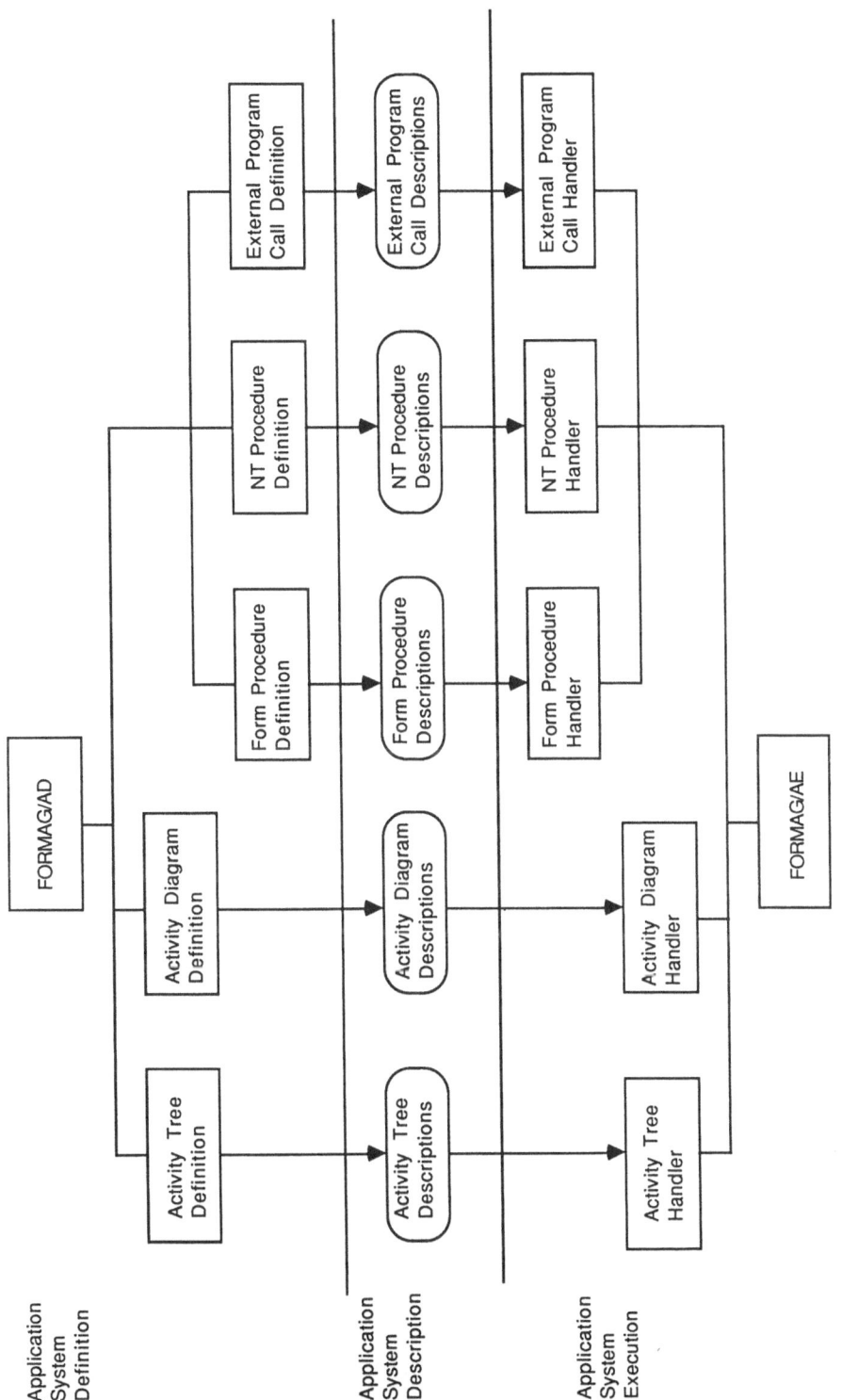

Fig. 5.7. FORMAG application system generation environments

```
┌─────────────────────────────────────────┐
│          Main Menu for ORDER_PROC         │
├─────────────────────────────────────────┤
│                                           │
│       1  CUST_INF_MGT                     │
│       2  ORDER_TAKING                     │
│       3  SHIPPING                         │
│       4  PAYMENT                          │
│       5  REPORT                           │
│                                           │
│                                           │
│                                           │
│                                           │
├─────────────────────────────────────────┤
│                                           │
└─────────────────────────────────────────┘
```

Fig. 5.8. Main menu for ORDER_PROC

5.4.2 Activity Diagram

The activity diagram determines the control flow within a unit activity. With the use of the *activity diagram definition module*, the user can interactively define the control flow structure. When the control structure is complicated, a visual aid with which the user can directly edit the activity diagrams becomes indispensable for performing the definition. Transition conditions tagged with links in activity diagrams are specified in NTPL. Constructs referred to as ⟨assertion⟩ in the BNF expressions given before are used for the transition condition specifications. *Activity diagram descriptions* are created as the result of the application system generation phase.

   The activity diagram descriptions are interpreted by the *activity diagram handler* to control the execution sequence of steps within an activity in the application system execution phase. Suppose the activity diagram shown in Fig. 5.2 is defined for the unit activity ORDER_TAKING. If ORDER_TAKING is selected from the main menu shown in Fig. 5.8, then the step CUST_ID is first executed. Then, the transition condition CUST_ID[BALANCE_OK] = 'OK' is evaluated, and either ORDER_ENTRY or BALANCE_REP is executed as explained in Sect. 5.2.

5.4.3 Step

As mentioned in Sect. 5.2, three types of procedures are allowed for steps. In our example of the activity diagram shown in Fig. 5.2, CUST_ID and ORDER_ENTRY are form procedures, and BALANCE_REP is an NT procedure.

5.4.3.1 Form Procedure

Form procedures are interactively defined with the *form procedure definition module*. To define a form procedure, the user first designs the form schema on the screen. The process is as in the form schema design phase in FORMDOQ. After designing the form schema, the user classifies fields embedded in the form schema into input fields and derived fields. For input fields, the user gives validation specifications, and for derived fields, derivation specifications. Both validations and derivations are specified in NTPL statements as explained in Sect. 5.3. In addition, the designer can give post-processing specifications, which are also expressed in NTPL statements. *Form procedure descriptions* are created as the result of the application system definition phase.

Execution of a form procedure is performed under the *form procedure handler*. In the application system execution phase, data values for derived fields are obtained in a data-driven way. In other words, they are derived as soon as their source data become available. Data stored in the database are retrieved by interpreting the NTPL statements expressed in the derivation specification. Post-processings of the form procedure, which usually include updates of the database, are temporarily performed at the end of the step execution, and committed at the end of the unit activity execution.

In the form procedure ORDER_ENTRY explained in Sect. 5.3, values for derived fields ONO, ODATE, CNO, CNAME, CADDR, CCITY, and CPHONE are derivable at the beginning. Therefore, their values appear when the form schema shown in Fig. 5.6 is displayed on the screen. When the user puts in a valid value for PNO, corresponding values for PDES and PPR are automatically retrieved. If an invalid part number for PNO is entered, an error message is displayed and a prompt to input a correct value appears. Next, when the user puts in a value for QTY, values for AMT, SUB_TOTAL, TAX and TOTAL are calculated immediately. Upon the addition of other part entries, SUB_TOTAL, TAX, and TOTAL values are automatically updated. When the user commits the interactive session of the form procedure, NTPL statements for the post-processing are interpreted, and order information is stored in the database.

5.4.3.2 NT Procedure

NT procedures are specified by sequences of NT operations like heap procedures in FORMDOQ, or in NTPL statements. Definitions of NT procedures are performed under the *NT procedure definition module*. At this time, NTs representing report documents and transaction files are defined if necessary. Output formats are also specified for report document NTs. *NT procedure descriptions* are created as the result of the application system definition phase. In the application system execution phase, the *NT procedure handler* performs NT manipulations interpreting the descriptions.

5.4.3.3 Application Program

In principle, any programs can be executed in steps in FORMAG environments to meet a variety of application system requirements. They can be the user's own coded programs or some system programs such as editors or utility programs. Typically, such application programs manipulate NTs in the database. As mentioned in Sect. 5.2, FORMAG provides primitive program modules such as interface routines to access NTs managed by the NT handler. Registration of application programs into FORMAG environments is performed under the *external program call definition module.* The execution is controlled by the *external program call handler.* When a step (say APX) is defined and execution of some user application program is associated with APX, its last return value can be referred to in NTPL statements by calling a special function RETURN(APX).[2]

5.5 Summary

In this chapter, an architecture for NT-based application generation, named FORMAG, has been proposed. Database manipulation, screen-based interactive sessions, and report generation are major components of most conventional application systems. FORMAG features the use of NTs as abstract data models for these application system components.

In the first section, Sect. 5.1, FORMAG was introduced. Section 5.2 described an application system model in FORMAG, and explained how NTs are used to model database manipulation, form-oriented interactive sessions, and report generation. In Sect. 5.3, an NT processing language NTPL was proposed. NTPL is based on the NT handles explained in Sect. 3.3, and was employed here to specify NT manipulations in FORMAG. In Sect. 5.4, the conceptual design of application generation environments for FORMAG was presented, and their application development scenario was explained.

The architecture proposed in this chapter is planned as a sub-system of a form system such as FORMDOQ. It is expected to provide the user with automated facilities for developing applications without coding lengthy application programs.

---

[2] The BNF specification of NTPL given in the Appendix B does not include this extension.

6 Conclusion

The main focus of this book has been placed on a thesis that data modeling based an unnormalized relational data model provides a sound basis for form handling in computer-based information systems. A data model named NTD has been proposed as a formal basis for our study, and its capability has been investigated through the development of a form document workbench FORMDOQ. A form-based architecture for application generation named FORMAG has also been proposed on the theoretical basis of NTD.

The contents was composed of six chapters. Chapter 1 was the Introduction, and gave an overview of the topics discussed here.

In Chap. 2, we surveyed previous work related to the contents of this book. Form handling has been one of the central issues in recent research on office automation, and it has been the subject of many reports by researchers in computer science, including ourselves. Through the survey, the contributions of our present study to this field were highlighted.

Chapters 3, 4, and 5 contained the main topics in the book. Chapter 3 was devoted to the study of our data model NTD as a typical instance of the unnormalized relational data model. NTs were defined, and a number of important concepts were introduced. To complete the definition of the data model, data manipulations in NTD were formalized by developing NT handles and NT operations. Dependencies and normalization in NTD were also considered. Important theoretical properties of the NT operations were studied using dependency concepts. The data manipulation capability of the NT operations was also considered.

In Chap. 4, we discussed the design and implementation of a form system FORMDOQ based on NTD. In FORMDOQ, a special emphasis is placed on a number of graphics-based interactive facilities for developing and managing documents based on forms. For this reason, we referred to FORMDOQ as a form document workbench. FORMDOQ uses NTD as a canonical model of form documents. The management of forms in terms of such an unnormalized relational data model is an unique point of FORMDOQ. Its logical design and form handling scheme were intensively discussed. A prototype FORMDOQ was implemented under the UNIX operating system. The major implementation issues were also discussed, and a number of session examples were shown to illustrate actual system functions. An experimental evaluation of the prototype was presented to complete the discussion.

In Chap. 5, we presented another use of the unnormalized relational data model. There, an architecture named FORMAG was proposed for form-based application system generation. Database manipulation, screen-based interactive sessions, and report generation are major components of most business-oriented application systems. FORMAG features the use of NTs as abstract data models for these application components. A structured application system model was first defined, and scenarios for developing application systems based on the model were presented. A procedural NT processing language NTPL was also proposed based on the NT handles.

Throughout the book, form handling based on the unnormalized relational data model has been discussed from both theoretical and practical viewpoints. From the systematic study, we conclude that the unnormalized relational data model has great significance as a basis for form handling.

References

1. Abiteboul S, Bidoit N (1984) Non first normal form relations to represent hierarchically organized data. Proceedings of 2nd ACM SIGACT/SIGMOD Symposium on Principles of Database Systems, Mar 1984, pp 191–200
2. ACOS software engineering – STEPS/C system development standards, NEC Corporation
3. Adiba M, Collet C (1988) Management of complex objects as dynamic forms. Proceedings of 14th International Conference on Very Large Data Bases, Los Angeles, Aug 1988, pp 134–147
4. Alford MW (1980) Software requirements engineering methodology (SREM) at the age of four. Proceedings of IEEE COMPSAC 80, Oct 1980, pp 866–874
5. Arisawa H, Moriya K, Miura T (1983) Operations and the properties on non-first-normal-form relational databases. Proceedings of 9th International Conference on Very Large Data Bases, Florence, Italy, Oct 1983, pp 197–204
6. Astrahan MM, Blasgen MW, Chamberlin DD, Eswaran KP, Gray JN, Griffiths PP, King WF, Lorie RA, McJones PR, Mehl JW, Putzolu GR, Traiger IL, Wade BW, Watson V (1976) System R: relational approach to database management. ACM Transactions on Database Systems, June 1976, 1(2): 97–137
7. Azuma M, Mizuno Y (1981) STEPS: integrated software standards and its productivity impact. Proceedings of IEEE COMPCON Fall 81, Washington DC, pp 83–95
8. Azuma M, Kitagawa H, Misaki S (1984) Integrating and standardizing requirement engineering for business systems – an experimental study. Proceedings of IEEE COMPSAC 84, Chicago, Nov 1984, pp 96–108
9. Azuma M, Tabata T, Oki Y, Kamiya S (1983) SPD: a humanized documentation technology. Proceedings of IEEE COMPSAC 83, Chicago, Nov 1983
10. Azuma M, Takahashi M, Kamiya S, Minomura K (1981) Interactive software development tool: ISDT. Proceedings of 5th International Conference of Software Engineering, San Diego, Mar 1981, pp 153–162
11. Bancilhon F (1978) On the completeness of query languages for relational data bases. In: Winkowski J (ed) Mathematical foundations of computer science 1978. Lecture notes in computer science 64, Springer-Verlag, Berlin, pp 112–123
12. Basili VR (ed) (1980) Tutorial: models and metrics for software management and engineering. IEEE Computer Society
13. Bergeron RD, Bono PR, Foley JD (1978) Graphics programming using the core system. ACM Computing Surveys, Dec 1978, 10(4): 389–443
14. Blum BI, Houghton RC (1982) Rapid prototyping of information management systems. ACM SIGSOFT Software Engineering Notes, Dec 1982, 7(5): 35–38
15. Boehm BW (1976) Software engineering. IEEE Transactions on Computers, Dec 1976, 25 (12): 1226–1241
16. Bryan W, Chadbourne C, Siegel S (eds) (1980) Tutorial: software configuration management. IEEE Computer Society
17. Cardenas AF, Grafton WP (1982) Challenges and requirements for new application generators. Proceedings of AFIPS National Computer Conference, Houston, pp 342–349

18. Chamberlin DD, Gray JN, Traiger IL (1975) Views, authorization, and locking in a relational data base system. Proceedings of AFIPS National Computer Conference, Anaheim, May 1975, pp 425–430

19. Chamberlin DD (1976) Relational data-base management systems. ACM Computing Surveys, Mar 1976, 8(1): 43–66

20. Chamberlin DD, Astrahan MM, Eswaran KP, Griffiths PP, Lorie RA, Mehl JW, Reisner P, Wade BW (1976) SEQUEL 2: a unified approach to data definition, manipulation, and control. IBM Journal of Research and Development, Nov 1976, 20(6): 560–575

21. Cleaveland JC (1988) Building application generators. IEEE Computer, July 1988, 5(4): 25–33

22. Clemons EK (1979) Design of a prototype ANSI/SPARC three-schema data base system. Proceedings of AFIPS National Computer Conference, New York, June 1979, pp 689–696

23. Codd EF (1970) A relational model of data for large shared data banks. Communications of ACM, June 1970, 13(6): 377–387

24. Codd EF (1972a) Further normalization of the data base relational model. In: Rustin R (ed) Data base systems, Prentice-Hall, pp 33–64

25. Codd EF (1972b) Relational completeness of data base sublanguages. In: Rustin R (ed) Data base systems, Prentice-Hall, pp 65–98

26. Codd EF (1974) Recent investigation in relational data base systems. In: Rosenfeld JL (ed) Information processing 74, North-Holland, pp 1017–1021

27. Couger JD (1973) Evolution of business systems analysis techniques. ACM Computing Surveys, Sep 1973, 5(3): 167–198

28. Czejdo B, Embley DW (1984) Office form definition and processing using a relational data model. Proceedings of 2nd ACM SIGOA Conference on Office Information Systems, Toronto, Canada, June 1984, pp 123–131

29. Dadam P, Kuespert K, Andersen F, Blanken H, Erbe R, Guenauer J, Lum V, Pistor P, Walch G (1986) A DBMS prototype to support extended NF^2 relations: an integrated view on flat tables and hierarchies. Proceedings of ACM SIGMOD Conference, Washington DC, May 1986, pp 356–367

30. Date CJ (1987a) An introduction to database systems Vol I, 4th edn. Addison-Wesley

31. Date CJ (1987b) A guide to the SQL standard. Addison-Wesley

32. Dayal U (1979) Schema-mapping problems in database systems. PhD dissertation, Harvard University

33. deJong SP, Zloof MM (1975) Application design within the system for business automation (SBA). IBM Research Report, RC5366, May 1975

34. Deshpande A, Van Gucht D (1988) An implementation for nested relational databases. Proceedings of 14th International Conference on Very Large Data Bases, Los Angeles, Aug 1988, pp 76–87

35. Ellis CA, Bernal M (1982) OfficeTalk-D: an experimental office information system. Proceedings of 1st ACM SIGOA Conference on Office Information Systems, Philadelphia, June 1982, pp 131–140

36. Ellis CA, Nutt GJ (1980) Office information systems and computer science. ACM Computing Surveys, Mar 1980, 12(1): 27–60

37. Embley DW (1982) A forms programming system. Proceedings of 15th Hawaii International Conference on System Sciences, Hawaii, Jan 1982, pp 142–151

38. Fagin R (1977) Multivalued dependencies and a new normal form for relational databases. ACM Transactions on Database Systems, Sep 1977, 2(3): 262–278

39. Ferrans JC (1982) SEDL – a language for specifying integrity constraints on office forms. Proceedings of 1st ACM SIGOA Conference on Office Information Systems, Philadelphia, June 1982, pp 123–130

40. Fischer PC, Van Gucht D (1985) Determining when a structure is a nested relation. Proceedings of 11th International Conference on Very Large Data Bases, Stockholm, Sweden, Aug 1985, pp 171–180

41. Fischer PC, Thomas SJ (1983) Operators for non-first-normal-form relations. Proceed-

ings of IEEE COMPSAC 83, Chicago, Nov 1983, pp 464–475

42. Fischer PC, Van Gucht D (1984) Weak multivalued dependencies. Proceedings of 3rd ACM SIGACT/SIGMOD Symposium on Principles of Database Systems, pp 266–274

43. Fischer PC, Van Gucht D, Thomas SJ (1984) Some principles and uses of nested relational structures. Technical Report CS-84-20, Department of Computer Science, Vanderbilt University, Dec 1984

44. Fong A (1983) A model for automatic form-processing procedures. Proceedings of 16th Hawaii International Conference on System Sciences, Hawaii, Jan 1983, pp 558–565

45. Freeman P, Wasserman AI (eds) (1983) Tutorial: software design techniques. IEEE Computer Society, Nov 1983

46. Goodman AM (1982) Application generators at IBM. Proceedings of AFIPS National Computer Conference, Houston, pp 360–362

47. Grochow JM (1982) Application generators: an introduction. Proceedings of AFIPS National Computer Conference, Houston, pp 390–392

48. Gyssens M, Van Gucht D (1988a) The powerset algebra as a result of adding programming constructs to the nested relational algebra. Proceedings of ACM SIGMOD Conference, Chicago, June 1988, pp 225–232

49. Gyssens M, Van Gucht D (1988b) The expressiveness of query languages for nested relations. IEEE Data Engineering, Sep 1988, 11(3): 48–55

50. Hammer M, Howe WG, Kruskal VJ, Wladawsky I (1977) A very high level programming language for data processing applications. Communications of ACM, Nov 1977, 20(11): 832–840

51. Harada M, Kunii TL (1979) A design process formalization. Proceedings of IEEE COMPSAC 79, Chicago, Nov 1979, pp 367–373

52. Harada M, Kunii TL, Saito M (1978) RGT: the recursive graph theory as a theoretical basis of a system design tool DESIGN-TOOL – with an application to medical information system design. Proceedings of MEDIS 78, Osaka, Japan, Oct 1978, pp 503–507

53. Hayes PJ (1984) Executable interface definitions using form-based interface abstractions. Technical Report CS-84-110, Department of Computer Science, Carnegie-Mellon University, Mar 1984

54. Horowitz E, Kemper A, Narasimhan B (1985) A survey of application generators. IEEE Software, Jan 1985, 2(1): 40–54

55. Houben GJ, Paredaens J (1989) A graphical interface formalism: specifying nested ralational databases. In: Kunii TL (ed) Visual database systems. North-Holland, pp 257–276

56. Housel BC, Shu NC (1976) A high-level data manipulation language for hierarchical data structures. Proceedings of Conference on Data Abstraction, Definition and Structure, Salt Lake City, Mar 1976, pp 155–169

57. Jacobs BE (1982) On database logic. Journal of ACM, Apr 1982, 29(2): 310–332

58. Jaeschke G (1985a) Nonrecursive algebra for relations with relation valued attributes. Technical Report TR85-03-001, IBM Heidelberg Scientific Center, Mar 1985

59. Jaeschke G (1985b) Recursive algebra for relations with relation valued attributes. Technical Report TR85-03-002, IBM Heidelberg Scientific Center, Mar 1985

60. Jaeschke G, Schek HJ (1982) Remarks on the algebra of non first normal form relations. Proceedings of ACM SIGACT/SIGMOD Symposium on Principles of Database Systems, Los Angeles, Mar 1982, pp 124–138

61. Kambayashi Y (1987) An overview of research on nested relations in Japan. In: Scholl MH, Schek HJ (eds) Theory and applications of nested relations and complex objects. Workshop Material, INRIA, Apr 1987, pp 1–11

62. Kambayashi Y, Le Viet C, Tokuda S, Yajima S (1982) SIFT: a simple form translator for bibliographic data. Proceedings of 15th Hawaii International Conference on System Sciences, Jan 1982, pp 112–121

63. Kambayashi Y, Tanaka K, Takeda K, Yajima S (1982) Representation of relations for database output utilizing data dependencies. Proceedings of 15th Hawaii International Conference on System Sciences, Jan 1982, pp 69–78

64. Kambayashi Y, Tanaka K, Takeda K (1983) Synthesis of unnormalized relations incorporating more meaning. Information Sciences, May-June 1983, 29 (2–3): 201–247
65. Kim W (1979) Relational database systems. ACM Computing Surveys, Sep 1979, 11(3): 185–211
66. King R, Novak M (1987) Freeform: a user-adaptable form management system. Proceedings of 13th International Conference on Very Large Data Bases, Brighton, England, Sep 1987, pp 331–338
67. Kitagawa H (1980) APAD: application-adaptable database system – its archiecture and design. MS thesis, The University of Tokyo, Jan 1980
68. Kitagawa H (1987) Structured forms handling by nested table data model. PhD dissertation, The University of Tokyo, Jan 1987
69. Kitagawa H, Kunii TL (1979 and 1982) APAD: application adaptable database system – its architecture and design. Proceedings of 13th IBM Computer Science Symposium on Database Engineering, Amagi, Japan, Nov 1979; also in: Yao SB, Kunii TL (eds) Data base design techniques II. Lecture notes in computer science 133. Springer-Verlag, Berlin, 1982, pp 320–344
70. Kitagawa H, Kunii TL (1980 and 1982) Form transformer – a formalism for office form manipulation. Proceedings of 14th IBM Computer Science Symposium on Operating System Engineering, Amagi, Japan, Oct 1980; also in: Maekawa M, Belady LA (eds) Operating system engineering. Lecture notes in computer science 143. Springer-Verlag, 1982, pp 392–406
71. Kitagawa H, Kunii TL (1982) Form transformer – formal aspects of table nests manipulation. (revised version of [70]) Proceedings of 15th Hawaii International Conference on System Sciences, Hawaii, Jan 1982, pp 132–141
72. Kitagawa H, Kunii TL, Azuma M, Misaki S (1984) Formgraphics: a form-based graphics architecture providing a database workbench. IEEE Computer Graphics and Applications, June 1984, 4(6): 38–56
73. Kitagawa H, Kunii TL, Azuma M, Mizuno Y (1980) User- and administrator- friendly architecture for interactive software development. Proceedings of International Congress on Applied Systems Research and Cybernetics, Acapulco, Mexico, Dec 1980, pp 2477–2483
74. Kitagawa H, Kunii TL, Harada M, Kaihara S, Ohbo N (1980) A language for office form processing (OFP) – with application to medical forms. Proceedings of 3rd World Conference on Medical Informatics, Tokyo, Japan, Sep 1980, pp 713–718
75. Kitagawa H, Kunii TL, Ishii Y (1981) Design and implementation of a form management system APAD using ADABAS/INQ DBMS. Proceedings of IEEE COMPSAC 81, Chicago, Nov 1981, pp 324–334
76. Kitagawa H, Gotoh M, Misaki S, Azuma M (1984) Form document management system SPECDOQ – its architecture and implementation. Proceedings of 2nd ACM SIGOA Conference on Office Information Systems, Toronto, Canada, June 1984, pp 132–142
77. Kitagawa H, Misaki S, Azuma M (1982) Toward second generation requirements engineering. Proceedings of International Symposium on Current Issues of Requirements Engineering Environments, Kyoto, Japan, Sep 1982, pp 93–99
78. Klug A, Tsichritzis D (1977) Multiple view support within the ANSI/SPARC framework. Proceedings of 3rd International Conference on Very Large Data Bases, Tokyo, Japan, Oct 1977, pp 477–488
79. Kobayashi I (1984) Validating database updates. Information systems, 9(1): 1–17
80. Kobayashi I (1985) An overview of database management technology. In: Tou JT (ed) Advances in information systems science 9. Plenum Press, pp 49–219
81. Kobayashi I (1986) Losslessness and semantic correctness of database schema transformation: another look of schema equivalence. Information Systems, 11(1): 41–59
82. Kunii TL, Harada M (1980) SID: a system for interactive design. Proceedings of AFIPS National Computer Conference, Anaheim, May 1980, pp 33–40
83. Kuo HC, Li CH, Ramanathan J (1982) A form-based approach to human engineering methodologies. Proceedings of 6th International Conference on Software Engineering, Tokyo, Japan, Sep 1982, pp 254–263

84. Lano RJ (1979) A technique for software and systems design. North-Holland
85. Lee A, Woo CC, Lochovsky FH (1984) Officeaid: an integrated document management system. Proceedings of 2nd ACM SIGOA Conference on Office Information Systems, Toronto, Canada, June 1984, pp 170–180
86. Liu Y, Xia D, Yao SB (1983) Micro XDB – a data base tool for microcomputers. Proceedings of 22nd Annual Technical Symposium of the Washington DC Chapter of ACM, June 1983
87. Lum VY, Choy DM, Shu NC (1982) OPAS: an office procedure automation system. IBM Systems Journal, Mar 1982, 21(3): 327–350
88. Lum VY, Dadam P, Erbe R, Guenauer J, Pistor P, Walch G, Werner H, Woodfill J (1985) Design of an integrated DBMS to support advanced applications. Proceedings of International Conference on Foundations of Data Organization, Kyoto, Japan, May 1985, pp 21–31
89. Luo D, Yao SB (1981) Form operation by example – a language for office information processing. Proceedings of ACM SIGMOD Conference, Ann Arbor, Apr 1981, pp 212–223
90. Makinouchi A (1977) A consideration on normal form of not-necessarily-normalized relation in the relational data model. Proceedings of 3rd International Conference on Very Large Data Bases, Tokyo, Japan, Oct 1977, pp 447–453
91. Martin J (1983) Software for application development without conventional programming. Software World 14(1): 14–21
92. Misra SK, Jalics PJ (1988) Third-generation versus fourth-generation software development. IEEE Computer, July 1988, 5(4): 8–14
93. Miura T, Moriya K, Arisawa H (1986) Normalizing non first normal form relations. Proceedings of 6th Advanced Database Symposium, Aug 1986, pp 65–71
94. Miura T, Moriya K, Arisawa H (1987) On the irreducible non first normal form relations. Information Systems 12(3): 229–238
95. Munson JB, Yeh RT (1981) Report by the IEEE Software Engineering Productivity Workshop. Proceedings of IEEE COMPCON Fall 81, Washington DC, pp 353–359
96. Nutt GJ, Richii PA (1981) Quinault: An office modeling system. IEEE Computer, May 1981, 14(6): 41–57
97. Osman IM (1979) Updating defined relations. Proceedings of AFIPS National Computer Conference, New York, June 1979, pp 733–740
98. Ozsoyoglu ZM (ed) (1988) Special issue on nested relations, IEEE Data Engineering, Sep 1988, 11(3)
99. Ozsoyoglu ZM, Yuan LY (1985) A normal form for nested relations. Proceedings of 4th ACM SIGACT/SIGMOD Symposium on Principles of Database Systems, pp 251–260
100. Ozsoyoglu ZM, Yuan LY (1987) A design method for nested relational databases. Proceedings of 3rd International Conference on Data Engineering, Los Angeles, Feb 1987, pp 599–608
101. Panko RR (1984) 38 Offices: analyzing needs in individual offices. Proceedings of 2nd ACM SIGOA Conference on Office Information Systems, Toronto, Canada, June 1984, p 21
102. Paredaens J (1978) On the expressive power of the relational algebra. Information Processing Letters, Feb 1978, 7(2): 107–111
103. Paredaens J, Van Gucht D (1988) Possibility and limitations of using flat operators in nested algebra expressions. Proceedings of 7th ACM SIGACT/SIGMOD Symposium on Principles of Database Systems, Austine, March 1988, pp 29–38
104. Paul HB, Schek HJ, Scholl MH, Weikem G, Deppisch U (1987) Architecture and implementation of the Darmstadt database kernel system. Proceedings of ACM SIGMOD Conference, San Francisco, May 1987, pp 196–207
105. Peterson J (1977) Petri Nets. ACM Computing Surveys, Sep 1977, 9(3): 223–252
106. Pistor P, Anderson F (1986) Designing a generalized NF^2 model with an SQL-type language interface. Proceedings of 12th International Conference on Very Large Data Bases, Kyoto, Japan, Aug 1986, pp 278–285
107. Purvy R, Farrell J, Klose P (1983) The design of STAR's records processing: data

processing for the noncomputer professional. ACM Transactions on Office Information Systems, Jan 1983, 1(1): 3–24

108. Putnum LH (ed) (1980) Tutorial: software cost engineering and life-cycle control (getting the software numbers). IEEE Computer Society

109. Ramamoothy CV, So HH (1977) Software requirements and specifications: status and perspectives. Appendix A to Requirements Engineering Research Recommendations, Aug 1977

110. Robinson MG (1981) SELECTOR IV: an application generator – on the way to becoming an application system. In: NCC 81 personal computing digest, pp 260–267

111. Ross DT (1977) Structured Analysis (SA): a language for communicating ideas. IEEE Transactions on Software Engineering, Jan 1977, 3(1): 16–34

112. Ross DT, Schoman KE (1977) Structured analysis for requirements definition. IEEE Transactions on Software Engineering, Jan 1977, 3(1): 6–15

113. Roth MA, Korth HF (1987) The design of ¬1NF relational databases into nested normal form. Proceedings of ACM SIGMOD Conference, San Francisco, May 1987, pp 143–159

114. Roth MA, Korth HF, Silberschatz A (1984) Theory of non-first-normal-form relational databases. Technical Report TR-84-36, University of Texas, Austin

115. Roth MA, Korth HF, Silberschatz A (1988) Extended algebra and calculus for nested relational databases. ACM Transactions on Database Systems, Dec 1988, 13(4): 389–417

116. Rowe LA (1985) Fill-in-the-form programming. Proceedings of the 11th International Conference on Very Large Data Bases, Stockholm, Sweden, pp 394–404

117. Rowe LA, Shoens KA (1982) A form application development system. Proceedings of ACM SIGMOD Conference, Orlando, June 1982, pp 28–38

118. Schek HJ (1985) Towards a basic relational NF^2 algebra processor. Proceedings of International Conference on Foundations of Data Organization, Kyoto, Japan, May 1985, pp 173–182

119. Schek HJ, Pistor P (1982) Data structures for an integrated database management and information retrieval system. Proceedings of 8th International Conference on Very Large Data Bases, Mexico City, Sep 1982, pp 197–207

120. Schek HJ, Scholl MH (1986) The relational model with relation-valued attributes. Information Systems, 11(2): 137–147

121. Schek HJ, Weikum G (1986) DASDBS: concepts and architecture of a database system for advanced applications. Technical Report DVSI-1986-T1, Technical University of Darmstadt

122. Scholl MH (1986) Theoretical foundation of algebraic optimization utilizing unnormalized relations. Technical Report DVSI-1986-T3, Technical University of Darmstadt, Mar 1986

123. Scholl MH, Schek HJ (eds) (1987) Theory and applications of nested relations and complex objects, Workshop Material, INRIA, Apr 1987

124. Scholl MH, Paul HB, Schek HJ (1987) Supporting flat relations by a nested relational kernel. Proceedings of 13th International Conference on Very Large Data Bases, Brighton, England, pp 137–146

125. Schneiderman B (1983) Direct manipulation: a step beyond programming languages. IEEE Computer, Aug 1983, 16(8): 57–69

126. Seybold J (1981) Xerox's Star. The Seybold Report, Apr 1981, 10(16)

127. Shirota Y, Shirai Y, Kunii TL (1989) Sophisticated form-oriented database interface for non-programmers. In: Kunni TL (ed) Visual database systems, North-Holland, pp 127–155

128. Shu NC, Housel BC, Lum VY (1975) CONVERT – a high level translation definition language for data conversion. Communications of ACM, Oct 1975, 18(10): 557–567

129. Shu NC, Housel BC, Taylor RW, Ghosh SP, Lum VY (1977) EXPRESS: A data extraction, processing, and restructuring system. ACM Transactions on Database Systems, June 1977, 2(2): 134–174

130. Shu NC, Lum VY, Tung FC, Chang CL (1982) Specification of forms processing and

business procedures for office automation. IEEE Transactions on Software Engineering, Sep 1982, 8(5): 499–512

131. Sibley EH (ed) (1976) Special issue: data-base management systems. ACM Computing Surveys, Mar 1976, 8(1)
132. Smith DC, Irby C, Kimball R, Verplank B, Harslem E (1982) Designing the Star user interface. BYTE, Apr 1982, 7(4): 242–282
133. Smith JM, Chang PY (1975) Optimizing the performance of a relational algebra database interface. Communications of ACM, Oct 1975, 18(10): 568–579
134. Stay JP (1976) HIPO and integrated program design. IBM Systems Journal 15(2): 143–154
135. Stephens SA, Tripp LL (1978) Requirements expression and verification aid. Proceedings of 3rd International Conference on Software Engineering, Atlanta, May 1978, pp 101–108
136. Stevens WP, Myer GJ, Constantine LL (1974) Structured design. IBM Systems Journal 14(2): 115–139
137. Stonebraker M, Wong E, Kreps P, Held G (1976) The design and implementation of INGRES. ACM Transactions on Database Systems, Sep 1976, 1(3): 189–222
138. Taylor RW, Frank RL (1976) CODASYL data-base management systems. ACM Computing Surveys, Mar 1976, 8(1): 67–103
139. Teichroew D, Hershey EA (1977) PSL/PSA: a computer-aided technique for structured decomposition and analysis of information processing systems. IEEE Transactions on Software Engineering, Jan 1977, 3(1): 41–48
140. Thomas SJ, Fischer PC (1983) Nested relational structures. Technical Report CS-83-09, Department of Computer Science, Vanderbilt University
141. Thurber KJ, Freeman HA (eds) (1987) Tutorial: office automation systems. IEEE Computer Society
142. Tsichritzis DC (1982) Form management. Communications of ACM, July 1982, 25(7): 453–478
143. Tsichritzis DC (ed) (1985) Office automation. Springer-Verlag
144. Tsichritzis DC, Lochovsky FH (1976) Hierarchical data-base management: a survey. ACM Computing Surveys, Mar 1976, 8(1): 105–123
145. Tsichritzis DC, Lochovsky FH (1977) Data base management systems. Academic Press
146. Tsichritzis DC, Lochovsky FH (1982) Data models. Prentice-Hall
147. Tsuruoka K, Watabe K, Nishihara Y (1985) PALET: a flexible office form management system. Journal of Information Processing, Mar 1985, 8(4): 280–287
148. Ullman JD (1982) Principles of database systems, 2nd edn. Computer Science Press
149. Van Gucht D (1987) On the expressive power of the extended relational algebra for the unnormalized relational model. Proceedings of 6th ACM SIGACT/SIGMOD Symposium on Principles of Database Systems, San Diego, Mar 1987, pp 302–312
150. Van Gucht D, Fischer PC (1986) Some classes of multilevel relational structures. Proceedings of 5th ACM SIGACT/SIGMOD Symposium on Principles of Database Systems, pp 60–69
151. Verner J, Tate G (1988) Estimating size and effort in fourth-generation development. IEEE Computer, July 1988, 5(4): 15–22
152. Wasserman AI (1981) User software engineering and the design of interactive systems. Proceedings of 5th International Conference on Software Engineering, San Diego, Mar 1981, pp 387–393
153. Wasserman AI (ed) (1981) Tutorial: interactive development environments. IEEE Computer Society, Nov 1981
154. Wasserman AI, Stinson SK (1979) A specification method for interactive information systems. Proceedings of Conference on Specification of Reliable Software, Apr 1979
155. Wegner LM (1989) ESCHER – interactive, visual handling of complex objects. In: Kunii TL (ed) Visual database systems. North-Holland, pp 277–297
156. Yamamoto Y, Morris RV, Hartsough C, Calender ED (1982) The role of requirements analysis in the system life cycle. Proceedings of AFIPS National Computer Conference, pp 382–387

157. Yao SB (1979) Optimization of query evaluation algorithms. ACM Transactions on Database Systems, June 1979, 4(2): 133–155
158. Yao SB, Kitagawa H (1985) Structured application generation using XDB. Proceedings of AFIPS National Computer Conference, Chicago, July 1985, pp 481–491
159. Yao SB, Hevner AR, Shi Z, Luo D (1984) FORMANAGER: an office forms management system. ACM Transactions on Office Information Systems, July 1984, 2(3): 235–262
160. Yormark B (1977) The ANSI/X3/SPARC/SGDBMS architecture. In: Jardine DA (ed) The ANSI/SPARK DBMS model. North-Holland, pp 1–21
161. Zloof MM (1975) Query by example. Proceedings of AFIPS National Computer Conference, Anaheim, May 1975, pp 431–438
162. Zloof MM (1976) Query-by-example – operations on hierarchical data bases. Proceedings of AFIPS National Computer Conference, New York, June 1976, pp 845–853
163. Zloof MM (1977) Query-by-example: a data base language. IBM Systems Journal 16(4): 324–343
164. Zloof MM (1981) QBE/OBE: a language for office and business automation. IEEE Computer, May 1981, 14(5): 13–22
165. Zloof MM (1982) Office-by-example: a business language that unifies data and word processing and electronic mail. IBM Systems Journal 21(3): 272–304
166. Zloof MM, deJong SP (1977) The system for business automation (SBA): programming language. Communications of ACM, June 1977, 20(6): 385–396

Appendix A: Correspondence Between NTD and the NF² Relational Data Model

As surveyed in Chap. 2, several variations of unnormalized relational data models have been proposed up to the present. Among them, the NF² relational data model is relatively well known. This Appendix gives a quick summary which correlates basic terms and notations of NTD with those of the NF² relational data model presented in [120]. They would be helpful if readers are familiar with the NF² relational data model.

1. In NTD, the structure of an unnormalized relation is represented by the *NT schema* consisting of a set of *group schemas*. In the NF² relational model, it is formalized in terms of *descriptors* and *schemas*. The NT schema of an NT shown in Fig. 3.1 has been given in Sect. 3.2. The same structure is represented in the following expression in the NF² relational model:

$$\langle \text{PROG\_SPEC}, \{\langle \text{SPEC}\#, \varnothing \rangle, \langle \text{PNAME}, \varnothing \rangle, \ldots,$$
$$\langle \text{FILE}, \{\langle \text{FID}, \varnothing \rangle, \langle \text{FNAME}, \varnothing \rangle, \langle \text{USE}, \varnothing \rangle\}\rangle\}\rangle.$$

Here, constructs denoted by $\langle \ldots \rangle$ and $\{ \ldots \}$ are descriptors and schemas, respectively. As shown in this example, descriptors correspond to nested representations of group schemas in NTD.

2. *Fields* and *groups* in NTD are generically referred to as *attributes* in the NF² relational model.

3. *Domains* of groups, which are defined as powersets of sets, are specifically called *complex domains* in the NF² relational model.

4. *Clusters* in NTD are referred to as *tuples* in the NF² relational model.

5. *Occurrences* in NTD are referred to as *attribute values* in the NF² relational model.

6. Correspondence between NT operations and NF² relational algebra operations is shown below, though the function of each operation is not precisely equivalent to that of its counterpart because of the difference in operation design criteria.

NT Operations	NF² Relational Algebra
NEST:N	Nest:ν
FLAT:F	Unnest:μ
PROJECTION:P	Projection:π
SELECTION:S	Selection:σ
CARTESIAN_PRODUCT:CX	Cartesian product: $\times$
UNION:$\cup$	Set Union:$\cup$
DIFFERENCE:D	Set difference:$-$

Appendix B: BNF Specification of NTPL

⟨NTPL_spec⟩::=⟨statement_list⟩
⟨statement_list⟩::=⟨statement⟩|⟨statement⟩⟨statement_list⟩
⟨statement⟩::=|⟨assignment⟩|⟨insert⟩|⟨delete⟩|⟨modify⟩
        |⟨if⟩|⟨for⟩|⟨validate⟩
⟨assignment⟩::=⟨ca_variable⟩'←'⟨ca_exp⟩
⟨insert⟩::='INSERT(' ⟨cluster⟩ '['⟨value_list⟩ '])'
⟨delete⟩::='DELETE(' ⟨cluster⟩ ')'
⟨modify⟩::='MODIFY(' ⟨cluster⟩'['⟨value_assignment_list⟩'])'
⟨if⟩::='if'⟨assertion⟩ 'then' ⟨block⟩ 'else' ⟨block⟩
⟨for⟩::='foreach' ⟨ca_variable⟩ 'do' ⟨block⟩
⟨validate⟩::='VALIDATE(' ⟨assertion⟩ ')'
⟨ca_exp⟩::=⟨ca_constants⟩| ⟨ca_variable⟩| ⟨search⟩
    |'ALL('⟨g_spec⟩ ')'|'ALL'|⟨insert⟩|'SELF'
    |'TRAN(' ⟨ca_exp⟩ ',' ⟨g_spec⟩ ')'
    |'('⟨ca_exp⟩')'|⟨ca_exp⟩ ⟨set_op⟩ ⟨ca_exp⟩
⟨ca_constants⟩::=⟨ca_constant⟩|'{'⟨ca_constant_list⟩'}'
⟨ca_constant_list⟩::=⟨ca_constant⟩
    |⟨ca_constant⟩ ',' ⟨ca_constant_list⟩
⟨search⟩::='SEARCH(' ⟨g_spec⟩ ',' ⟨selection_condition⟩')'
⟨g_spec⟩::=⟨NT_name⟩|⟨NT_name⟩ '.'⟨group⟩
⟨set_op⟩::='∩'|'∪'|'DIFF'
⟨cluster⟩::=⟨g_spec⟩|⟨g_spec⟩ '@'⟨ca_exp⟩
⟨value_list⟩::=⟨v_exp⟩|⟨v_exp⟩ ',' ⟨value_list⟩
⟨value_assignment_list⟩::=⟨value_assignment⟩
    |⟨value_assignment⟩ ',' ⟨value_assignment_list⟩
⟨value_assignment⟩::=⟨field⟩ ':' ⟨v_exp⟩
⟨selection_condition⟩::=|⟨selection⟩|'('⟨selection_condition⟩ ')'
    |'NOT'⟨selection_condition⟩
    |⟨selection_condition⟩ 'AND' ⟨selection_condition⟩
    |⟨selection_condition⟩ 'OR' ⟨selection_condition⟩
⟨selection⟩::=⟨primitive_selection⟩|⟨set_selection⟩
⟨primitive_selection⟩::=⟨p_left⟩ ⟨p_comp⟩ ⟨p_right⟩
⟨set_selection⟩::=⟨reference⟩ ⟨s_comp⟩ ⟨s_right⟩
⟨reference⟩::=⟨group⟩ '[' ⟨field⟩ ']'|'['⟨field⟩ ']'
⟨p_comp⟩::='='|'≠'|'<'|'>'|'≤'|'≥'
⟨p_left⟩::=⟨p_term⟩

⟨p_right⟩∷ = ⟨p_term⟩ | ⟨v_exp⟩
⟨p_term⟩∷ = ⟨reference⟩|⟨aggregate⟩ '(' ⟨reference⟩ ')'
⟨aggregate⟩∷ = 'SOME' | 'ANY' | 'AVG' | 'CNT' | 'SUM' | 'MAX' | 'MIN'
⟨s_comp⟩∷ = '≠' | '⊂' | '⊄' | '⊆' | '⊈' | '⊃' | '⊅' | '⊇' | '⊉' |
                 'INTERSECT' | 'NOT_INTERSECT'
⟨s_right⟩∷ = ⟨reference⟩|⟨v_exp⟩
⟨v_exp⟩∷ = ⟨occurrence⟩|⟨value⟩|'{'⟨value_list⟩'}'
                 |'('⟨v_exp⟩')' | ⟨v_exp⟩ ⟨binary_op⟩ ⟨v_exp⟩
                 |⟨aggregate⟩ '('⟨v_exp⟩')' | ⟨built_in_func⟩
⟨occurrence⟩∷ = ⟨cluster⟩ '[' ⟨field⟩ ']' | ⟨cluster⟩ '[' ⟨group⟩ ']' '[' ⟨field⟩ ']'
⟨binary_op⟩∷ = ⟨primitive_op⟩|⟨set_op⟩
⟨primitive_op⟩∷ = '+' | '−' | '×' | '÷'
⟨built_in_func⟩∷ = 'TODAY' | 'TIME'
⟨assertion⟩∷ = ⟨v_exp⟩ ⟨comp⟩ ⟨v_exp⟩ | '('⟨assertion⟩')'
                 | 'NOT'⟨assertion⟩|⟨assertion⟩ 'AND' ⟨assertion⟩
                 |⟨assertion⟩ 'OR' ⟨assertion⟩
⟨comp⟩∷ = ⟨p_comp⟩ | ⟨s_comp⟩
⟨block⟩∷ = '('⟨statement_list⟩')'

List of Acronyms and Abbreviations

Acronyms

ACM	Association for Computing Machinery
ADE	Application development environments
ANSI	American National Standards Institute
APAD	Application adaptable database system
BNF	Backus Naur form
DB	Database
DBMS	Database management system
EDP	Electronic data processing
FADS	Form application development system
FOBE	Form operation by example
FORMAL	Forms oriented manipulation language
4GL	Fourth generation language
HDBL	Heidelberg database language
ICN	Information control net
NF	Normal form
1NF	First normal form
2NF	Second normal form
3NF	Third normal form
4NF	Fourth normal form
OA	Office automation
OBE	Office by example
OFP	Language for office form processing
OFS	Office form system
PND	Program network diagram
QBE	Query by example
SBA	System for business automation
SIGGRAPH	Special interest group on computer graphics
STEPS	Standardized technology and engineering for programming support
TSS	Time-sharing system

Acronyms Defined in the Book

APB	Application program base
APH	Application program handler

API	Application program interface
CNT	Canonical nested table
DED	Form document editor
D-file	File containing a D-NT occurrence
D-NT	Nested table representing a form document
FD	Functional dependency
FDB	Form document base
FDBM	Form document base manager
FDM	Form document manipulation model
FED	Form schema editor
FM	File manager
FORMAG	An architecture for form-based application generation
FORMDOQ	A form document workbench
FSB	Form schema base
FSBM	Form schema base manager
GED	Graphics editor
GFD	Global functional dependency
G-file	File containing graphics type data
GMD	Global multivalued dependency
GTB	Graphics type base
GTH	Graphics type handler
H-file	File containing an H-NT occurrence
H-NT	Nested table representing a form document heap
HPB	Heap procedure base
HPH	Heap procedure handler
KED	Kanji/kana text editor
LFD	Local functional dependency
LMD	Local multivalued dependency
MD	Multivalued dependency
NF operations	The NT operations NEST and FLAT
NFR decomposable	(see Definition 3.17)
NFR-expressiveness	(see Definition 3.16)
NNT	Normalized nested table
NT	Nested table
NT handles	Nested table handles
NT operations	Nested table operations
NTD	Nested table data model
NTPL	Nested table processing language
QBF	Query by form
S-file	File containing a nested table schema, plus information on the external presentation
SM	System manager
TED	Table editor
WNT	Well-classified nested table
XED	Text editor
XR operations	The NT operations PROJECTION, SELECTION, PRODUCT, UNION, and DIFFERENCE

Mnemonic Abbreviations Used in the Book

A	Arcs, attribute(s), or activities
af	Arc function
ag	Ancestor groups
AP	Application system
asd	Arc semantics domain
asf	Arc semantics function
atf	Arc type function
ATYPE	Arc types
c	Transition condition
C	Component(s), comments, or transition conditions
ca	Cluster address
CA	Cluster addresses
cc	Components
cdom	Cluster domain
cf, CF	Component fields
cg, CG	Child groups
cn	Cluster number
D	Derivations or activity diagram(s)
de	Activity decomposition function
DF	Derived fields
dg	Descendant groups
dom	Domain
E	Field or group
EP	External presentation
F	Field or FLAT operation
FP	Form procedure
FS	Form schema
FT	Flat nested table
G	Group
GS	Group schema
ID	Identifier
IF	Input fields
L	Links
lca	Leaf common ancestor
MS	Mapping specification
N	Nested table, NEST operation, or nodes
NN	Nested table name
NO	Nested table occurrence
NS	Nested table schema
nsd	Node semantics domain
nsf	Node semantics function
NSS	Nested table subschema
NT	Nested table
ntf	Node type function
ntype	Node type

NTYPE	Node types
O	Occurrence
P	Post-processings or permutation
Q	Permutation
R	Root or permutation
s	Step
S	Form schema section, permutation, node symbol, or steps
SC	Selection condition
SS	Semantic schema
t, u, v, w	Cluster
T	Nested table or table
U	Unit activities
V	Validations
Φ	XR operation
Ψ	Relational equivalent NT operation

Subject Index